3rd Workshop on Linked Data in Linguistics: Multilingual Knowledge Resources and Natural Language Processing 2014 (LDL-2014)

Co-located with LREC 2014

Reykjavik, Iceland
27 May 2014

Editors:

Christian Chiarcos
John Philip McCrae
Petya Osenova
Cristina Vertan

ISBN: 978-1-5108-1587-2

Printed from e-media with permission by:

Curran Associates, Inc.
57 Morehouse Lane
Red Hook, NY 12571

Some format issues inherent in the e-media version may also appear in this print version.

Printed by Curran Associates, Inc. (2015)

For permission requests, please contact the Association for Computational Linguistics at the address below.

Association for Computational Linguistics
209 N. Eighth Street
Stroudsburg, Pennsylvania 18360

Phone: 1-570-476-8006
Fax: 1-570-476-0860

acl@aclweb.org

Additional copies of this publication are available from:

Curran Associates, Inc.
57 Morehouse Lane
Red Hook, NY 12571 USA
Phone: 845-758-0400
Fax: 845-758-2634
Email: curran@proceedings.com
Web: www.proceedings.com

3rd Workshop on Linked Data in Linguistics: Multilingual Knowledge Resources and Natural Language Processing

Workshop Programme

08:30 - 09:00 – Opening and Introduction by Workshop Chair(s)

09:00 – 10:00 – Invited Talk
Piek Vossen, *The Collaborative Inter-Lingual-Index for harmonizing wordnets*

10:00 – 10:30 – Session 1: Modeling Lexical-Semantic Resources with *lemon*
Andon Tchechmedjiev, Gilles Sérasset, Jérôme Goulian and Didier Schwab, *Attaching Translations to Proper Lexical Senses in DBnary*

10:30 – 11:00 Coffee break

11:00-11:20– Session 1: Modeling Lexical-Semantic Resources with *lemon*
John Philip McCrae, Christiane Fellbaum and Philipp Cimiano, *Publishing and Linking WordNet using lemon and RDF*

11:20-11:40– Session 1: Modeling Lexical-Semantic Resources with *lemon*
Andrey Kutuzov and Maxim Ionov, *Releasing genre keywords of Russian movie descriptions as Linguistic Linked Open Data: an experience report*

11:40-12:00– Session 2: Metadata
Matej Durco and Menzo Windhouwer, *From CLARIN Component Metadata to Linked Open Data*

12:00-12:20– Session 2: Metadata
Gary Lefman, David Lewis and Felix Sasaki, *A Brief Survey of Multimedia Annotation Localisation on the Web of Linked Data*

12:20-12:50– Session 2: Metadata
Daniel Jettka, Karim Kuropka, Cristina Vertan and Heike Zinsmeister, *Towards a Linked Open Data Representation of a Grammar Terms Index*

12:50-13:00 – Poster slam – Data Challenge

13:00 – 14:00 Lunch break

14:00 – 15:00 – Invited Talk
Gerard de Mello, *From Linked Data to Tightly Integrated Data*

15:00 – 15:30 – Section 3: Crosslinguistic Studies
Christian Chiarcos and Maria Sukhareva, *Linking Etymological Databases. A case study in Germanic*

15:30 – 16:00 – Section 3: Crosslinguistic Studies
Fahad Khan, Federico Boschetti and Francesca Frontini, *Using lemon to Model Lexical Semantic Shift in Diachronic Lexical Resources*

16:00 – 16:30 Coffee break

16:30 – 17:00 – Section 3: Crosslinguistic Studies
Steven Moran and Michael Cysouw, *Typology with graphs and matrices*

17:00 – 17:30 – Section 3: Crosslinguistic Studies
Robert Forkel, *The Cross-Linguistic Linked Data project*

17:30 – 18:30 – Poster Session – Data Challenge
Gilles Sérasset and Andon Tchechmedjiev, *Dbnary: Wiktionary as Linked Data for 12 Language Editions with Enhanced Translation Relations*

Maud Ehrmann, Francesco Cecconi, Daniele Vannella, John Philip McCrae, Philipp Cimiano and Roberto Navigli, *A Multilingual Semantic Network as Linked Data: lemon-BabelNet*

Gabriela Vulcu, Raul Lario Monje, Mario Munoz, Paul Buitelaar and Carlos A. Iglesias, *Linked-Data based Domain-Specific Sentiment Lexicons*

Tomáš Kliegr, Vaclav Zeman and Milan Dojchinovski, *Linked Hypernyms Dataset - Generation framework and Use Cases*

Ismail El Maarouf, Jane Bradbury and Patrick Hanks, *PDEV-lemon: a Linked Data implementation of the Pattern Dictionary of English Verbs based on the Lemon model*

18:30 – 19:00 – Discussions and Closing

Editors

Christian Chiarcos	Goethe-University Frankfurt am Main, Germany
John Philip McCrae	University of Bielefeld, Germany
Petya Osenova	Bulgarian Academy of Sciences, Sofia, Bulgaria
Cristina Vertan	University of Hamburg, Germany

Workshop Organizers/Organizing Committee

Christian Chiarcos	Goethe-University Frankfurt am Main, Germany
John Philip McCrae	University of Bielefeld, Germany
Kiril Simov	Bulgarian Academy of Sciences, Sofia, Bulgaria
Antonio Branco	University of Lisbon, Portugal
Nicoletta Calzolari	ILC-CNR, Italy
Petya Osenova	University of Sofia, Bulgaria
Milena Slavcheva	JRC-Brussels, Belgium
Cristina Vertan	University of Hamburg, Germany

Workshop Programme Committee

Eneko Agirre	University of the Basque Country, Spain
Guadalupe Aguado	Universidad Politécnica de Madrid, Spain
Peter Bouda	Interdisciplinary Centre for Social and Language Documentation, Portugal
Steve Cassidy	Macquarie University, Australia
Damir Cavar	Eastern Michigan University, USA
Walter Daelemans	University of Antwerp, Belgium
Ernesto William De Luca	University of Applied Sciences Potsdam, Germany
Gerard de Melo	University of California at Berkeley, USA
Dongpo Deng	Institute of Information Sciences, Academia Sinica, Taiwan
Alexis Dimitriadis	Universiteit Utrecht, The Netherlands
Jeff Good	University at Buffalo, USA
Asunción Gómez Pérez	Universidad Politécnica de Madrid, Spain
Jorge Gracia	Universidad Politécnica de Madrid, Spain
Walther v. Hahn	University of Hamburg, Germany
Eva Hajicova	Charles University Prague, Czech Republic
Harald Hammarström	Radboud Universiteit Nijmegen, The Netherlands
Yoshihiko Hayashi	Osaka University, Japan
Sebastian Hellmann	Universität Leipzig, Germany
Dominic Jones	Trinity College Dublin, Ireland
Lutz Maicher	Universität Leipzig, Germany

Pablo Mendes	Open Knowledge Foundation Deutschland, Germany
Steven Moran	Universität Zürich, Switzerland/Ludwig Maximilian University, Germany
Sebastian Nordhoff	Max Planck Institute for Evolutionary Anthropology, Leipzig, Germany
Maciej Piasecki	Wroclaw University of Technology, Poland
Adam Przepiorkowski	IPAN, Polish Academy of Sciences, Poland
Laurent Romary	INRIA, France
Felix Sasaki	Deutsches Forschungszentrum für Künstliche Intelligenz, Germany

Table of contents

Linked Data in Linguistics 2014. Introduction and Overview

Christian Chiarcos[1], **John McCrae**[2], **Petya Osenova**[3], **Cristina Vertan**[4]
[1] Goethe-Universität Frankfurt am Main, Germany, chiarcos@uni-frankfurt.de
[2] Universität Bielefeld, Germany, jmcrae@cit-ec.uni-bielefeld.de
[3] University of Sofia, Bulgaria, petya@bultreebank.org
[4] Universität Hamburg, Germany,cristina.vertan@uni-hamburg.de

Abstract

The Linked Data in Linguistics (LDL) workshop series brings together researchers from various fields of linguistics, natural language processing, and information technology to present and discuss principles, case studies, and best practices for representing, publishing and linking linguistic data collections. A major outcome of our work is the Linguistic Linked Open Data (LLOD) cloud, an LOD (sub-)cloud of linguistic resources, which covers various linguistic data bases, lexicons, corpora, terminology and metadata repositories. As a general introduction into the topic, we describe the concept of Linked Data, its application in linguistics and the development of the Linguistic Linked Open Data (LLOD) cloud since LDL-2013. We present the contributions of LDL-2014, the associated data challenge and its results and present the newly compiled LLOD cloud diagram.
The third instantiation of this series, collocated with the 9th Language Resources and Evaluation Conference (LREC-2014), May 27th, 2014, in Reykjavik, Iceland, is specifically dedicated to the study of Multilingual Knowledge Resources and Natural Language Processing, although contributions with respect to any application of Linked Data to linguistically and/or NLP-relevant resources are welcome, as well.

Keywords: Linked Data in Linguistics (LDL), Linguistic Linked Open Data (LLOD) cloud

1. Background and Motivation

After half a century of computational linguistics (Dostert, 1955), quantitative typology (Greenberg, 1960), empirical, corpus-based study of language (Francis and Kucera, 1964), and computational lexicography (Morris, 1969), researchers in computational linguistics, natural language processing (NLP) or information technology, as well as in Digital Humanities, are confronted with an immense wealth of linguistic resources, that are not only growing in number, but also in their heterogeneity. Accordingly, the limited interoperability between linguistic resources has been recognized as a major obstacle for data use and re-use within and across discipline boundaries, and represents one of the prime motivations for adopting Linked Data to our field.
Interoperability involves two aspects (Ide and Pustejovsky, 2010):

(a) How to access a resource? (Structural interoperability) Resources use comparable formalisms to represent and to access data (formats, protocols, query languages, etc.), so that they can be accessed in a uniform way and that their information can be integrated with each other.

(b) How to interpret information from a resource? (Conceptual interoperability) Resources share a common vocabulary, so that information from one resource can be resolved against information from another resource, e.g., grammatical descriptions can be linked to a terminology repository.

With the rise of the Semantic Web, new representation formalisms and novel technologies have become available, and different communities are becoming increasingly aware of the potential of these developments with respect to the challenges posited by the heterogeneity and multitude of linguistic resources available today. Many of these approaches follow the **Linked (Open) Data paradigm** (Berners-Lee, 2006), and this line of research, and its application to resources relevant for linguistics and/or NLP represent the focus of our work.

1.1. Linked Data

The Linked Open Data paradigm postulates four rules for the publication and representation of Web resources: (1) Referred entities should be designated by using URIs, (2) these URIs should be resolvable over HTTP, (3) data should be represented by means of W3C standards (such as RDF), (4) and a resource should include links to other resources. These rules facilitate information integration, and thus, interoperability, in that they require that entities can be addressed in a globally unambiguous way (1), that they can be accessed (2) and interpreted (3), and that entities that are associated on a conceptual level are also physically associated with each other (4).
In the definition of Linked Data, the **Resource Description Framework (RDF)** receives special attention. RDF was designed to provide metadata about resources that are available either offline (e.g., books in a library) or online (e.g., eBooks in a store). RDF provides a generic data model based on labeled directed graphs, which can be serialized in different formats. Information is expressed in terms of *triples* - consisting of a *property* (relation, i.e., a labeled edge) that connects a *subject* (a resource, i.e., a labeled node) with its *object* (another resource, or a literal, e.g., a string). RDF resources (nodes)[1] are repre-

[1]The term 'resource' is ambiguous: *Linguistic* resources are structured collections of data which can be represented, for example, in RDF. In RDF, however, 'resource' is the conventional name of a node in the graph, because, historically, these nodes were meant to represent objects that are described by metadata. We use the terms 'node' or 'concept' whenever *RDF* resources

sented by *Uniform Resource Identifiers (URIs)*. They are thus globally unambiguous in the web of data. This allows resources hosted at different locations to refer to each other, and thereby to create a network of data collections whose elements are densely interwoven.

Several data base implementations for RDF data are available, and these can be accessed using **SPARQL** (Prud'Hommeaux and Seaborne, 2008), a standardized query language for RDF data. SPARQL uses a triple notation like RDF, only that properties and RDF resources can be replaced by variables. SPARQL is inspired by SQL, variables can be introduced in a separate `SELECT` block, and constraints on these variables are expressed as triples in the `WHERE` block. SPARQL does not only support querying against individual RDF data bases that are accessible over HTTP ('SPARQL end points'), but also, it allows us to combine information from multiple repositories (federation). RDF can thus not only be used to *establish* a network, or cloud, of data collections, but also, to *query* this network directly.

Beyond its original field of application, RDF evolved into a generic format for knowledge representation. It was readily adopted by disciplines as different as biomedicine and bibliography, and eventually it became one of the building stones of the **Semantic Web**. Due to its application across discipline boundaries, RDF is maintained by a large and active community of users and developers, and it comes with a rich infrastructure of APIs, tools, databases, query languages, and multiple sub-languages that have been developed to define data structures that are more specialized than the graphs represented by RDF. These sub-languages can be used to create *reserved vocabularies* and *structural constraints* for RDF data. For example, the Web Ontology Language (OWL) defines the datatypes necessary for the representation of ontologies as an extension of RDF, i.e., *classes* (concepts), *instances* (individuals) and *properties* (relations).

The concept of Linked Data is closely coupled with the idea of **openness** (otherwise, the linking is only partially reproducible), and in 2010, the original definition of Linked Open Data has been extended with a 5 star rating system for data on the Web.[2] The first star is achieved by publishing data on the Web (in any format) under an open license, and the second, third and fourth star require machine-readable data, a non-proprietary format, and using standards like RDF, respectively. The fifth star is achieved by linking the data to other people's data to provide context. If (linguistic) resources are published in accordance with these rules, it is possible to follow links between existing resources to find other, related data and exploit network effects.

1.2. Linked Data for Linguistics and NLP

Publishing Linked Data allows resources to be globally and uniquely identified such that they can be retrieved through standard Web protocols. Moreover, resources can be easily linked to one another in a uniform fashion and thus become structurally interoperable. Chiarcos et al. (2013a) identified five main benefits of Linked Data for Linguistics and NLP:

(1) Conceptual Interoperability Semantic Web technologies allow to provide, to maintain and to share centralized, but freely accessible terminology repositories. Reference to such terminology repositories facilitates conceptual interoperability as different concepts used in the annotation are backed up by externally provided definitions, and these common definitions may be employed for comparison or information integration across heterogeneous resources.

(2) Linking through URIs URIs provide globally unambiguous identifiers, and if resources are accessible over HTTP, it is possible to create resolvable references to URIs. Different resources developed by independent research groups can be connected into a cloud of resources.

(3) Information Integration at Query Runtime (Federation) Along with HTTP-accessible repositories and resolvable URIs, it is possible to combine information from physically separated repositories in a single query at runtime: Resources can be uniquely identified and easily referenced from any other resource on the Web through URIs. Similar to hyperlinks in the HTML web, the web of data created by these links allows to navigate along these connections, and thereby to freely integrate information from different resources in the cloud.

(4) Dynamic Import When linguistic resources are interlinked by references to resolvable URIs instead of system-defined IDs (or static copies of parts from another resource), we always provide access to the most recent version of a resource. For community-maintained terminology repositories like the ISO TC37/SC4 Data Category Registry (Wright, 2004; Windhouwer and Wright, 2012, ISOcat), for example, new categories, definitions or examples can be introduced occasionally, and this information is available immediately to anyone whose resources refer to ISOcat URIs. In order to preserve link consistency among Linguistic Linked Open Data resources, however, it is strongly advised to apply a proper versioning system such that backward-compatibility can be preserved: Adding concepts or examples is unproblematic, but when concepts are deleted or redefined, a new version should be provided.

(5) Ecosystem RDF as a data exchange framework is maintained by an interdisciplinary, large and active community, and it comes with a developed infrastructure that provides APIs, database implementations, technical support and validators for various RDF-based languages, e.g., reasoners for OWL. For developers of linguistic resources, this ecosystem can provide technological support or off-the-shelf implementations for common problems, e.g., the development of a database that is capable of support flexible, graph-based data structures as necessary for multi-layer corpora (Ide and Suderman, 2007).

(6) Distributed Development To these, Chiarcos et al. (2013b) add that the distributed approach of the Linked Data paradigm facilitates the distributed development of a web of resources and collaboration between researchers

are meant in ambiguous cases.

[2] `http://www.w3.org/DesignIssues/LinkedData.html`, paragraph 'Is your Linked Open Data 5 Star?'

that provide and use this data and that employ a shared set of technologies. One consequence is the emergence of interdisciplinary efforts to create large and interconnected sets of resources in linguistics and beyond. The LDL workshop series provides a forum to discuss and to facilitate such on-going developments, in particular, the emerging Linguistic Linked Open Data cloud.

2. Linguistic Linked Open Data

Recent years have seen not only a number of approaches to provide linguistic data as Linked Data, but also the emergence of larger initiatives that aim at interconnecting these resources. The **Open Linguistics Working Group (OWLG)**[3] is an interdisciplinary network open to any individual interested in linguistic resources and/or the publication of these under an open license. The OWLG is a working group of the Open Knowledge Foundation (OKFN),[4] a community-based non-profit organization promoting open knowledge (i.e., data and content that is free to use, re-use and to be distributed without restriction). In this context, the Open Linguistics Working Group (OWLG) of the Open Knowledge Foundation (OKFN) has spearheaded the creation of new data and the republishing of existing linguistic resources as part of an emerging Linked Open Data (sub-) cloud of linguistic resources.

This Linguistic Linked Open Data (LLOD) cloud is a result of a coordinated effort of the OWLG, its members and collaborating initiatives, most noteably the W3C Ontology-Lexica Community Group (OntoLex, see below) specializes in lexical-semantic resources. As the OWLG organizes the LDL workshop series also as a vehicle to facilitate, to promote and to support this process, we would like to take the chance to unveil a revised cloud diagram on the occasion of LDL-2014.

2.1. The LLOD Cloud

In our current, informal understanding, **Linguistic Data** is pragmatically defined as any kind of resource considered relevant for linguistic research or Natural Language Processing tasks. Our assessment of relevance follows the classification of resources provided by data providers or the community, as reflected, for example, in tags assigned to resources at `datahub.io`, the meta data repository from which the LLOD cloud is currently being built. During diagram compilation, resources associated with the OWLG, or with tags like 'LLOD', 'linguistics', etc. are gathered, stored in a JSON document, categorized according to manually defined classification rules, and plotted and reformatted using a GraphML editor.[5]

Among these data sets, we encourage the use of **open** licenses and limit the diagram to such data sets. As defined by the Open Definition, "openness" refers to "[any] piece of content or data [that] is open if anyone is free to use, reuse, and redistribute it – subject only, at most, to the requirement to attribute and share-alike."[6]

Linguistic **Linked** Open Data, then, comprises resources that are provided under an open license and published in conformance with the Linked Data principles as stated above. Typically, these do not represent resources which are RDF-native, but resources that have been transformed into Linked Data.

This also has an impact on the types of linguistic resources considered here, in particular the concept of **corpora**: In empirical linguistics and NLP, *collections of primary data* represent the elementary foundation of research and development. Yet, while it is possible to represent primary data such as plain text in RDF, this is not necessarily the most efficient way of doing so – also given the fact that specialized XML-based standards such as the Text Encoding Iniative[7] are well-established and widely used. However, RDF provides highly flexible data structures that can be employed to represent linguistic annotations of arbitrary complexity. As understood *here*, a 'corpus' is thus always a linguistically analyzed resource: Along with classical representations where both annotations *and* primary data are modeled in RDF (e.g., in the seminal study of (Burchardt et al., 2008)), but also hybrid data sets where only annotations are provided as Linked Data, but the primary data is stored in a conventional format (e.g., (Cassidy, 2010)). At the moment, corpora in the LLOD cloud seem to be relatively rare (see 'CORPUS' resources in Fig. 1), but this only reflects the fact that several corpora had to be excluded from the diagram because they were not linked yet with other LLOD data sets such as lexical resources or repositories of annotation terminology.

Beyond representing linguistic analyses for collections of examples, text fragments, or entire discourses, the Linked Data paradigm particularly facilitates the management of **information about language and language resources** ('METADATA' in Fig. 1). These include linguistic databases (collections of features and inventories of individual languages, e.g., from linguistic typology), repositories of linguistic terminology (e.g., grammatical categories or language identifiers), and metadata about language resources (incl. bibliographical data). While bibliographical data and terminology management represent classical Linked Data applications, our *databases* are a specifically linguistic resource: Databases of features of individual languages are a particularly heterogeneous group of linguistic resources; they contain complex and manifold types of information, e.g., feature structures that represent typologically relevant phenomena, along with examples for their illustration and annotations (glosses) and translations applied to these examples (structurally comparable to corpus data), or word lists (structurally comparable to lexical-semantic resources). RDF as a generic representation formalism is thus particularly appealing for this class of resources.

The third major group of resources in the diagram are **lexical-semantic resources** ('LEXICON', 1), i.e., resources focusing on the general meaning of words and the structure of semantic concepts. These represent by far the most established type of linguistic resources in the LD context: They have been of inherent interest to the Semantic Web

[3] `http://linguistics.okfn.org`

[4] `http://okfn.org/`

[5] The extraction scripts can be found under `https://github.com/jmccrae/llod-cloud.py`.

[6] `http://opendefinition.org`

[7] `http://www.tei-c.org`

community, and hence a long tradition in this regard, going back to earliest attempts to integrate WordNet into the SW world (Gangemi et al., 2003). In the diagram, we distinguish two types of lexical-semantic resources, i.e., *lexical resources* in a strict sense (which provide specifically linguistic information, e.g., grammatical features, as found, e.g., in a dictionary, or in a WordNet), and and *general knowledge bases* (such as classical thesauri or semantic repositories such as YAGO and DBpedia) whose origins lay outside of the stricter boundaries of linguistics or NLP. While the latter do not provide us with grammatical information, they formalize semantic knowledge, and in this respect, they are of immanent relevance for Natural Language Processing tasks such as Named Entity Recognition or Anaphora Resolution.

2.2. Recent Developments

Since the publication of the last LLOD cloud diagram at LDL-2013, Sep 2013 in Italy, Pisa, we have continued to gather and to convert data sets, to refine our classification of language resources and encouraged others to contribute, e.g., by organizing LDL-2014 and the associated data challenge (see below).

These efforts have met with success such that the number of candidate resources for the cloud has increased substantially, from 65 resources in September 2013 to 107 in April 2014. We thus enforced the constraints imposed on resources in the cloud diagram. As of April 2014, we limit datasets in the cloud diagram to those with links to other LLOD data sets. Applying these stricter filters, we arrive at 68 resources in the new diagram. For generating the diagram, we rely on the metadata as provided by Datahub.io, so only datasets are considered whose links with other LLOD data sets are explicitly documented there. During diagram generation, we test whether the URLs given for the data are responding. At the moment, we do not, however, validate the information provided there, but a stricter validation routine is envisioned.

Among others, novel data sets include resources prepared for LDL-2014 and the data challenge, but also resources that have not been covered by earlier diagram instantiations because they lacked the necessary tags to recognize them as being linguistically relevant. An example for the latter is the Greek WordNet (RDF edition released in early 2013),[8] but also several thesauri and multilingual vocabularies. This partially explains the growth of the cloud particular with respect to lexical resources.

At the same time, the growing number of linked lexical resources also reflects the activities of the W3C Ontology-Lexica Community Group (OntoLex). The OntoLex group is not only closely collaborating with the OWLG, but both also have a considerable overlap in terms of their members, and as for LDL-2013, several LDL-2014 organizers are active in both groups. While the OWLG is interested in open linguistic resources in general, the OntoLex group takes a specific focus on lexical resources, culminating in the proposal of a common model for machine-readable lexicons in RDF, the *lemon* model (McCrae et al., 2012). By now, already 41% of lexical resources (7 out of 17) in the diagram (lemonWordNet, PDEVlemon, Parole/Simple, lemonUby, lemonBabelNet, germlex, DBnary) employ *lemon* or *lemon*-derived vocabularies, so that we see a considerable degree of convergence in this field. The resulting degree of interoperability and visibility arising from the use of shared vocabularies is certainly one of the most concrete achievements of the community activities we aimed to initiate with forming the OWLG, preparing the LLOD diagram and conducting workshops at linguistic, NLP and IT conferences.

2.3. Organizing LDL-2014

The LDL workshop series and LDL-2014 are organized by the Open Linguistics Working Group to bring together researchers from various fields of linguistics, NLP, and IT to present and discuss principles, case studies, and best practices for representing, publishing and linking linguistic data collections, and aims to facilitate the exchange of technologies, ideas and resources across discipline boundaries, that (to a certain extend) find a material manifestation in the emerging LLOD cloud.

LDL-2014, collocated with the 9th International Conference on Language Resources and Evaluation (LREC-2014), May 2014, Reykjavik, Iceland, is the third workshop on Linked Data in Linguistics following LDL-2012 (March 2012 in Frankfurt am Main, Germany), LDL-2013 (Sep 2013 in Pisa, Italy), as well as more specialized events such as the workshops on Multilingual Linked Open Data for Enterprises (MLODE-2012: Sep 2012 in Leipzig, Germany), and Natural Language Processing and Linked Open Data (NLP&LOD-2013: Sep 2013 in Hissar, Bulgaria), and the theme session on Linked Data in Linguistic Typology (at the 10th Biennial Conference of the Association for Linguistic Typology, ALT-2013, Aug 2013 in Leipzig, Germany), as well as presentations, panels and informal meetings at various conferences.

LDL-2014 is organized in the context of two closely related community efforts, the *Open Linguistics Working Group* (OWLG), and the *W3C Ontology-Lexica Community Group* (OntoLex), and supported by two recently started EU projects, *LIDER*, and *QTLeap*.

The **Open Linguistics Working Group** was founded in October 2010, and since its formation, it has grown steadily. One of our primary goals is to attain openness in linguistics through:

1. Promoting the idea of open linguistic resources,
2. Developing the means for the representation of open data, and
3. Encouraging the exchange of ideas across different disciplines.

The OWLG represents an open forum for interested individuals to address these and related issues. At the time of writing, the group consists of about 130 people from 20 different countries. Our group is relatively small, but continuously growing and sufficiently heterogeneous. It includes people from library science, typology, historical linguistics, cognitive science, computational linguistics, and

[8] `http://datahub.io/de/dataset/greek-wordnet`, cf. `http://okfn.gr/2013/01/983/`.

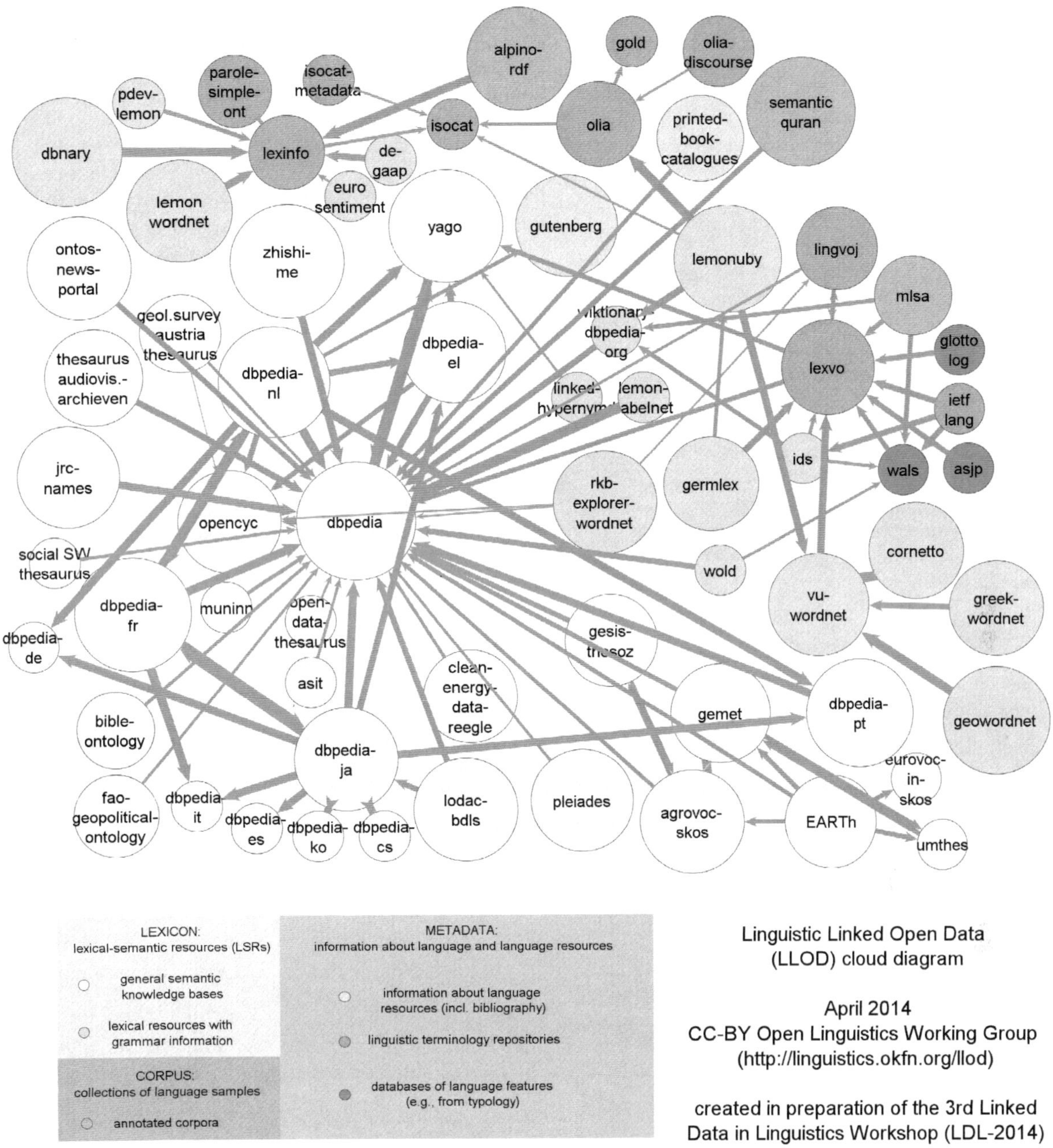

Figure 1: Linguistic Linked Open Data cloud as of April 2014.

information technology; the ground for fruitful interdisciplinary discussions has been laid out. One concrete result emerging out of collaborations between a large number of OWLG members is the LLOD cloud as already sketched above.

The emergence of the LLOD cloud out of a set of isolated resources was accompanied and facilitated by a series of **workshops and publications** organized by the OWLG as sketched above. Plans to create a LLOD cloud were first publicly announced at LDL-2012, and subsequently, a first instance of the LLOD materialized as a result of the MLODE-2012 workshop, its accompanying hackathon and the data postproceedings that will appear as a special issue of the Semantic Web Journal (SWJ). The Second and Third Workshop on Linked Data in Linguistics continued this series of workshops. In order to further contribute to the integration of the field, their organizers involved members of both the OWLG and the W3C Ontology-Lexica Community Group.

The **Ontology-Lexica Community (OntoLex) Group**[9]

[9] `http://www.w3.org/community/ontolex`

was founded in September 2011 as a W3C Community and Business Group. It aims to produce specifications for a lexicon-ontology model that can be used to provide rich linguistic grounding for domain ontologies. Rich linguistic grounding include the representation of morphological, syntactic properties of lexical entries as well as the syntax-semantics interface, i.e., the meaning of these lexical entries with respect to the ontology in question. An important issue herein will be to clarify how extant lexical and language resources can be leveraged and reused for this purpose. As a byproduct of this work on specifying a lexicon-ontology model, it is hoped that such a model can become the basis for a web of lexical linked data: a network of lexical and terminological resources that are linked according to the Linked Data Principles forming a large network of lexico-syntactic knowledge.

The OntoLex W3C Community Group has been working on realizing a proposal for a standard ontology lexicon model, currently discussed under the the designation *lemon*. By now, the core specification of the model is almost complete, the group started to develop additional modules for specific tasks and use cases, and some of these are presented at LDL-2014.

As mentioned above, LDL-2014 is supported by two recently started EU Projects. The project **Linked Data as an Enabler of Cross-Media and Multilingual Content Analytics for Enterprises Across Europe** (LIDER) aims to provide an ecosystem for the establishment of linguistic linked open data, as well as media resources metadata, for a free and open exploitation of such resources in multilingual, cross-media content analytics across Europe. The project **Quality Translation with Deep Language Engineering Approaches** (QTLeap) explores novel ways for attaining machine translation of higher quality that are opened by a new generation of increasingly sophisticated semantic datasets (including Linked Open Data) and by recent advances in deep language processing.

To accomodate the importance of multilinguality and semantically-oriented NLP that we encounter in the community as well as these initiatives, LDL-2014 takes a focus on Multilingual Knowledge Resources and Natural Language Processing, although contributions on Linked Data emphasising other aspects of linguistics or NLP were explicitly encouraged.

3. LDL-2014: The 3rd Workshop on Linked Data in Linguistics

For the 3rd edition of the workshop on Linked Data in Linguistics, we invited contributions discussing the application of the Linked Open Data paradigm to linguistic data in various fields of linguistics, natural language processing, knowledge management and information technology in order to to present and discuss *principles*, *case studies*, and *best practices* for representing, publishing and linking mono- and multilingual linguistic and knowledge data collections, including corpora, grammars, dictionaries, wordnets, translation memories, domain specific ontologies etc.

In this regard, the Linked Data paradigm might provide an important step towards making linguistic data: i) easily and uniformly queryable, ii) interoperable and iii) sharable over the Web using open standards such as the HTTP protocol and the RDF data model. The adaptation of some processes and best practices to **multilingual linguistic resources and knowledge bases** acquires special relevance in this context. Some processes may need to be modified to accommodate the publication of resources that contain information in several languages. Also the linking process between linguistic resources in different languages poses important research questions, as well as the development and application of freely available knowledge bases and crowdsourcing to compensate the lack of publicly accessible language resources for various languages.

Further, LDL-2014 provides a forum for researchers on natural language processing and semantic web technologies to present case studies and best practices on the exploitation of linguistic resources exposed on the Web for **Natural Language Processing** applications, or other content-centered applications such as content analytics, knowledge extraction, etc. The availability of massive linked open knowledge resources raises the question how such data can be suitably employed to facilitate different NLP tasks and research questions. Following the tradition of earlier LDL workshops, we encouraged contributions to the Linguistic Linked Open Data (LLOD) cloud and research on this basis. In particular, this pertains to contributions that demonstrate an added value resulting from the combination of linked datasets and ontologies as a source for semantic information with linguistic resources published according to as linked data principles. Another important question to be addressed in the workshop is how Natural Language Processing techniques can be employed to further facilitate the growth and enrichment of linguistic resources on the Web.

The call for papers emphasized the following topics:

1. **Use cases** for creating or publishing linked linguistic data collections
2. **Modelling** linguistic data and metadata with OWL and/or RDF
3. **Ontologies** for linguistic data and metadata collections as well as for cross-lingual retrieval
4. Description of **data sets** following Linked Data principles
5. **Applications of such data**, other ontologies or linked data from any subdiscipline of linguistics
6. **NLP&LLOD**: Application and applicability of (Linguistic) Linked Open Data in NLP / NLP contributions to (Linguistic) Linked Open Data
7. Challenges of **multilinguality** and **collaboratively constructed open resources** for knowledge extraction, machine translation and other NLP tasks.
8. **Legal and social aspects** of (L)LOD
9. **Best practices** for the publication and linking of multilingual knowledge resources

Along with regular workshop submissions, we invited contributions to the associated data challenge (see below) for data sets together with data set descriptions. In total, we received 19 submissions in response to our calls, including 5 data set descriptions for the associated data challenge. Regular submissions were reviewed by at least 3 members of the program committee. On this basis, we accepted 6 submissions as full papers and 4 as short papers.

The 10 accepted papers address a wide range of problems in the area of NLP and (Linguistic) Linked Open Data, pertaining to modeling, representation, analysis and publishing of various data or metadata.

Taken together, the contributions cover a vast and heterogeneous field, they involve different types of linguistic resources, such as machine-readable lexicons, etymological and diachronic databases, web, movies, and grammar terminology, but also address issues of localization and multilinguality. Our tentative classification, that we apply both to the proceedings and the remainder of this section, is a compromise between a classification on grounds of resource types and prospective applications:

A particularly popular branch of research is concerned with **modeling lexical-semantic resources** using RDF-based vocabularies and lexicon-to-ontology mappings, most noteably *lemon*. This group of submissions partially overlaps with a surprisingly large number of papers concerned with the modeling of multilingual resources in more academic fields of linguistics, namely **cross-linguistic studies** in linguistic typology and comparative linguistics. A third group of papers involves different conceptions of **metadata**, i.e., terminology for linguistic categories and language resources, but also annotations to multimedial content. Finally, we sketch the contributions to the data set challenge, all of which were concerned with lexical-semantic resources.

3.1. Modelling Lexical-Semantic Resources with *lemon*

In their paper **Attaching translations to proper lexical senses in DBnary**, Andon Tchechmedjiev, Gilles Sérasset, Jérôme Goulian and Didier Schwab present the current status of the DBnary project: DBnary aims at extracting linked open data from Wiktionaries in various languages, for which the authors present a similarity technique for disambiguation of linked translations.

John Philip McCrae, Christiane Fellbaum and Philipp Cimiano describe their approach on **Publishing and linking WordNet using *lemon* and RDF** where they propose a strategy for publishing the Princeton WordNet as linked data through an open model. The advantage of this approach is that it provides linking also to the resources which have been already integrated into WordNet.

The paper **Releasing genre keywords of Russian movie descriptions as Linked Open Data: An experience report** by Andrey Kutuzov and Maxim Ionov describes efforts on publishing genre-classified movie keywords as LOD using the *lemon* model. The resource is also linked to Russian component of the Wiktionary RDF dump created by the DBpedia team.[10]

[10] http://dbpedia.org/Wiktionary

3.2. Cross-linguistic Studies: Applications in Comparative Linguistics and Typology

Although most of the following papers also involve lexical resources, they are special in their domain of application, i.e., the study of cross-linguistic and/or diachronic relationships in linguistics.

In **Linking etymological databases. A case study in Germanic**, Christian Chiarcos and Maria Sukhareva describe the modeling of etymological dictionaries of various Germanic languages in a machine-readable way as Linguistic Linked Open Data. The authors adopted *lemon*, and identified several problematic aspects in its application to this kind of data. The work is challenging, since it handles different language stages, but the current model represents a solid basis to discuss possible adjustments of both *lemon* and the authors' approach in order to develop a *lemon*-conformant representation that meets the requirements of diachronic data.

More focusing on semantic shift than etymological (phonological) continuity, but operating in a similar setting, Fahad Khan, Federico Boschetti and Francesca Frontini describe an approach on **Using *lemon* to model lexical semantic shift in diachronic lexical resources**. They propose *lemonDIA*, an ontology-based extension of the *lemon* model for representing lexical semantic change in temporal context that formalizes notions of perdurance and temporal anchoring of lexical senses.

Coming from the slightly different angle of cross-linguistic language comparison in linguistic typology, the paper **Typology with graphs and matrices** by Steven Moran and Michael Cysouw describes how to extract information from LLOD representations of different typological data sets, and how to transform and operate with the extracted information in order to determine associations between syntactic and phonological features.

Robert Forkel introduces **The Cross-Linguistic Linked Data project**, an ongoing initiative and its infrastructure aiming towards establishing a platform for interoperability among various language resources assembled in typological research. The important role of Linguistic Linked Open Data has long been recognized as publishing strategy for typological datasets (Chiarcos et al., 2012), but here, a unified publication platform is described which may have a considerable effect on the typological publicating practice.

3.3. Metadata

As used here, metadata refers to information provided *about* another resource, including language resources, linguistic terminology and multimedia contents.

From CLARIN Component Metadata to Linked Open Data by Matej Durco and Menzo Windhouwer describes the conversion from CMDI resource descriptions to LOD. As a result, the RDF metadata can be accessed with standard query languages using SPARQL endpoints.

In **Towards a Linked Open Data Rrepresentation of a grammar terms index**, Daniel Jettka, Karim Kuropka, Cristina Vertan and Heike Zinsmeister introduce onoing work on creating a Linked Open Data representation of German grammatical terminology, an effort which nicely complements established efforts to create repositories for linguistic terminology used in language documentation, NLP and the development of machine-readable lexicons. Given the great amount of language-specific terminology, the proposed strategy is also applicable to other languages and their linking may eventually improve the multilingual coverage of linguistic terminology repositories.

A different kind of metadata is subject to **A brief survey of multimedia annotation localization on the web of Linked Data** by Gary Lefman, David Lewis and Felix Sasaki. The authors focus on the localization of multimedia ontologies and Linked Data frameworks for Flickr data. In this respect, Linguistic Linked Open Data may serve as a mediator between multimedia annotation in social media and the Web of Linked Data.

3.4. Data Challenge

The workshop was associated with an open challenge for the creation of datasets for linguistics according to linked data principles. Unlike the preceding Monnet challenge[11] that was organized by the W3C OntoLex community at MLODE-2012, the LDL-2014 was not restricted to the application of the *lemon* format. Nevertheless, all submissions were, indeed, lexical-semantic resources.

This challenge required submissions of new or substantially updated linked datasets and was evaluated by reviewers on technical grounds. The following criteria were applied:

1. *Availability*, i.e. (a) whether the resource uses Linked Data and RDF, (b) whether it is hosted on a publicly accessible server and is available both during the period of the evaluation and beyond, and (c) whether it uses an open license.

2. *Quality*, i.e. (a) whether the resource represents useful linguistically or NLP-relevant information, (b) whether it reuses relevant standards and models, and (c) wheter it contains complex, non-trivial information (e.g., multiple levels of annotation, manually validated analyses).

3. *Linking*, i.e., (a) wheter the resource contains links to external resources, and (b) whether it reuses existing properties and categories.

4. *Impact/usefulness* of the resource, i.e., (a) whether it is relevant and likely to be reused by many researchers in NLP and beyond, and (b) whether it uses linked data to improve the quality of and access to the resource.

5. *Originality*, i.e., (a) whether the data set represents a type of resource or a community currently underrepresented in (L)LOD cloud activities, or (b) whether the approach facilitates novel and unforeseen applications or use cases (as described by the authors) enabled through Linked Data technology.

This year there were five accepted submissions to the challenge. Every challenge committee member provided a ranking of these resources, and the average rank was taken as decisive criterion. In this process, we chose two joint winners and one highly commended paper.

The winners were **DBnary: Wiktionary as Linked Data for 12 Language Editions with Enhanced Translation Relations** by Gilles Sérraset and Andon Tchechmedjiev and **Linked-data based domain-specific sentiment lexicons** by Gabriela Vulcu, Raul Lario Monje, Mario Munoz, Paul Buitelaar and Carlos A. Iglesias, describing the EuroSentiment lexicon. An outstanding characteristic of the DBnary data is its high degree of maturity (quality, usefulness, linking, availability). The EuroSentiment dataset is specifically praised for its originality and quality, as it represents the *only* manually corrected sentiment lexicon currently available as Linguistic Linked Open Data.

Sérraset and Tchechmedjiev describe the extraction of multilingual data from Wiktionary based on 12 language editions of Wiktionary, and as such represents a large and important lexical resource that should have application in many linguistic areas. **Vulcu et al.** describe the creation of a lexicon for the EuroSentiment project, which tackles the important field of sentiment analysis through the use of sophisticated linguistic processing. The resource described extends the *lemon* model with the MARL vocabulary to provide a lexicon that is unique in the field of sentiment analysis due to its linguistic sophistication.

Beyond this, we highly commend the work presented in **A multilingual semantic network as linked data: Lemon-BabelNet** by Maud Ehrmann, Francesco Cecconi, Daniele Vannelle, John P. McCrae, Philipp Cimiano and Roberto Navigli, which describes the expression of BabelNet using the *lemon* vocabulary. BabelNet is one of the largest lexical resources created to date and its linked data version at over 1 billion triples will be one of the largest resources in the LLOD cloud. As such, the clear usefulness of the resource as a target for linking and also the use of the widely-used *lemon* model make this conversion a highly valuable resource for the community as noted by the reviewers.

Finally, we will note that our two runner-up participants **PDEV-LEMON: A linked data implementation of the pattern dictionary of English verbs based on the *lemon* model** by Ismail El Maarouf, Jane Bradbury and Patrick Hanks, and **Linked Hypernyms Dataset - Generation Framework and Use Cases** by Tomáš Kliegr, Vaclav Zeman and Milan Dojchinovski were also well received as resources that continue to grow the linguistic linked open data cloud and are likely to find applications for a number of works in linguistics and natural language processing.

3.5. Invited Talks

In addition to regular papers and dataset descriptions, LDL-2014 features two invited speakers, Piek Vossen, VU Amsterdam, and Gerard de Melo, Tsinghua University.

Piek Th.J.M. Vossen is a Professor of computational lexicology at the Vrije Universiteit Amsterdam, The Netherlands. He graduated from the University of Amsterdam in Dutch and general linguistics, where he obtained a PhD in computational lexicology in 1995, and is probably most well-known for being founder and president of the Global WordNet Association.

In his talk, he will describe and elaborate on the application of **The Collaborative Inter-Lingual-Index for harmonizing WordNets**. The Inter-Lingual-Index, originally

[11] `http://sabre2012.infai.org/mlode/monnet-challenge`

developed in the context of EuroWordNet, provides a set of common reference points through which WordNets can be linked with each other across different languages and thereby establishes a semantic layer for the interpretation of text in a multilingual setting. Although devised before the advent of modern Linked Data technology, the applications developed on this basis are inspiring for applications of Linguistic Linked Open Data and we are therefore very happy to welcome Piek for discussions and exchange of ideas.

Gerard de Melo is an Assistant Professor at Tsinghua University, where he is heading the Web Mining and Language Technology group. Previously, he was a post-doctoral researcher at the the ICSI AI group of the UC Berkeley, and a doctoral candidate at the Max Planck Institute for Informatics.

In his talk, Gerard de Melo will describe the transition **From Linked Data to Tightly Integrated Data**. He argues that the true potential of Linked Data can only be appreciated when extensive cross-linkage and integration leads to an even higher degree of interconnectedness. Gerard compares different approaches on integration into unified, coherent knowledge bases and develops ideas on how to address some remaining challenges that are currently impeding a more widespread adoption of Linked Data.

Acknowledgements

We thank the organizers of the 9th International Conference on Language Resource and Evaluation (LREC-2014) for hosting and supporting LDL-2014, in particular for joining us in promoting Linked Open Data in our field by establishing it as a main topic of the main conference.

The LDL workshop series and LDL-2014 are organized by the Open Linguistics Working Group (OWLG) of the Open Knowledge Foundation. LDL-2014 is supported by two EU projects, LIDER (Linked Data as an Enabler of Cross-Media and Multilingual Content Analytics for Enterprises Across Europe), as well as QTLeap (Quality Translation with Deep Language Engineering Approaches).

We thank the OWLG and its members for active contributions to the LLOD cloud, to the workshop and beyond. In particular, we have to thank our contributors, our co-organizers, the committee and the organizers of the data challenge for their invaluable work and engagement.

4. References

Berners-Lee, T. (2006). Design issues: Linked data. URL `http://www.w3.org/DesignIssues/LinkedData.html` (July 31, 2012).

Burchardt, A., Padó, S., Spohr, D., Frank, A., and Heid, U. (2008). Formalising multi-layer corpora in OWL/DL – lexicon modelling, querying and consistency control. In *3rd International Joint Conference on NLP (IJCNLP 2008)*, Hyderabad, India.

Cassidy, S. (2010). An RDF realisation of LAF in the DADA Annotation Server. In *5th Joint ISO-ACL/SIGSEM Workshop on Interoperable Semantic Annotation (ISA-5)*, Hong Kong, January.

Chiarcos, C., Nordhoff, S., and Hellmann, S., editors. (2012). *Linked Data in Linguistics. Representing and Connecting Language Data and Language Metadata.* Springer, Heidelberg.

Chiarcos, C., McCrae, J., Cimiano, P., and Fellbaum, C. (2013a). Towards open data for linguistics: Linguistic linked data. In Oltramari, A., Lu-Qin, Vossen, P., and Hovy, E., editors, *New Trends of Research in Ontologies and Lexical Resources*. Springer, Heidelberg.

Chiarcos, C., Cimiano, P., Declerck, T., and McCrae, J. (2013b). Linguistic linked open data (llod). introduction and overview. In Chiarcos, C., Cimiano, P., Declerck, T., and McCrae, J., editors, *Proceedings of the 2nd Workshop on Linked Data in Linguistics (LDL-2013): Representing and linking lexicons, terminologies and other language data*, pages i–xi, Pisa, Italy, Sep.

Dostert, L. (1955). The Georgetown-IBM experiment. In Locke, W. and Booth, A., editors, *Machine Translation of Languages*, pages 124–135. John Wiley & Sons, New York.

Francis, W. N. and Kucera, H. (1964). Brown Corpus manual. Technical report, Brown University, Providence, Rhode Island. revised edition 1979.

Gangemi, A., Navigli, R., and Velardi, P. (2003). The OntoWordNet project: Extension and axiomatization of conceptual relations in WordNet. In Meersman, R. and Tari, Z., editors, *Proceedings of On the Move to Meaningful Internet Systems (OTM2003)*, pages 820–838, Catania, Italy, November.

Greenberg, J. (1960). A quantitative approach to the morphological typology of languages. *International Journal of American Linguistics*, 26:178–194.

Ide, N. and Pustejovsky, J. (2010). What does interoperability mean, anyway? Toward an operational definition of interoperability. In *Second International Conference on Global Interoperability for Language Resources (ICGL 2010)*, Hong Kong, China.

Ide, N. and Suderman, K. (2007). GrAF: A graph-based format for linguistic annotations. In *1st Linguistic Annotation Workshop (LAW 2007)*, pages 1–8, Prague, Czech Republic.

McCrae, J., Montiel-Ponsoda, E., and Cimiano, P. (2012). Integrating WordNet and Wiktionary with lemon. In Chiarcos, C., Nordhoff, S., and Hellmann, S., editors, *Linked Data in Linguistics. Representing and Connecting Language Data and Language Metadata*, pages 25–34, Heidelberg. Springer.

Morris, W., editor. (1969). *The American Heritage Dictionary of the English Language*. Houghton Mifflin, New York.

Prud'Hommeaux, E. and Seaborne, A. (2008). SPARQL query language for RDF. *W3C working draft*, 4(January).

Windhouwer, M. and Wright, S. (2012). Linking to linguistic data categories in ISOcat. In Chiarcos, C., Nordhoff, S., and Hellmann, S., editors, *Linked Data in Linguistics*, pages 99–107. Springer, Heidelberg.

Wright, S. (2004). A global data category registry for interoperable language resources. In *Proceedings of the Fourth Language Resources and Evaluation Conference (LREC 2004)*, pages 123–126, Lisboa, Portugal, May.

Data Challenge Organizers

Christian Chiarcos (Goethe-Universität Frankfurt am Main, Germany)
Philipp Cimiano (Universität Bielefeld, Germany)
John McCrae (Universität Bielefeld, Germany)

Data Challenge Committee

Christian Chiarcos (Goethe-Universität Frankfurt am Main, Germany)
Philipp Cimiano (Universität Bielefeld, Germany)
Thierry Declerck (Deutsches Forschungszentrum für Künstliche Intelligenz, Germany)
Jorge Gracia (Universidad Politécnica de Madrid, Spain)
Sebastian Nordhoff (Max Planck Institute for Evolutionary Anthropology, Leipzig, Germany)
John McCrae (Universität Bielefeld, Germany)
Steven Moran (Universität Zürich, Switzerland/Ludwig Maximilian University, Germany)
Petya Osenova (University of Sofia, Bulgaria)

Invited Talks

The Collaborative Inter-Lingual-Index for harmonizing wordnets

Piek Vossen, Vrije Universiteit Amsterdam, The Netherlands
p.t.j.m.vossen@vu.nl

Abstract
The EuroWordNet project proposed an Inter-Lingual-Index (ILI) to link independently developed wordnets. The ILI was initially filled with the English WordNet. Since then many wordnets have been developed following this model but no work has been done on the ILI since.

At the last Global Wordnet Conference in Tartu (2014), we decided to take up the initial ideas from EuroWordNet and establish a ILI platform that will result in a fund of concepts and meanings that is not just dependent on English.

This concept repository will be published as Linked Open Data with a collaborative social platform to add new concepts and link synsets from different wordnets. In this way, we can match synsets across wordnets even if there is no English equivalent. Modifications and changes are reported back to the community and feedback is given on 'semantic impact' of changes.

The ILI supports a harmonization process for wordnets. It will allow us to flesh out differences in lexicalizations across languages. As proposed in EuroWordNet, the conceptual index can also be formalized by linking ontologies to these concepts, such as SUMO, DOLCE or DBPedia. The project seeks to establish a semantic layer for interpretation of text across languages. In a number of projects, we develop deep-reading technologies to extract information from texts across different languages. Such projects directly benefit from ILI.

As an example, we explain how we were able to do semantic-role-labelling in Dutch using the SemLink mappings for English that were transferred to the Dutch wordnet.

Biography: Piek Th. J. M. Vossen is a Professor of computational lexicology at the Vrije Universiteit Amsterdam, The Netherlands. He graduated from the University of Amsterdam in dutch and general linguistics, where he obtained a PhD in computational lexicology in 1995, and is probably most well-known for being founder and president of the Global WordNet Association. For more information please visit http://vossen.info/

From Linked Data to Tightly Integrated Data

Gerard de Mello, Tsinghua University, Beijing, China

gdm@demelo.org

Abstract:
The ideas behind the Web of Linked Data have great allure. Apart from the prospect of large amounts of freely available data, we are also promised nearly effortless interoperability. Common data formats and protocols have indeed made it easier than ever to obtain and work with information from different sources simultaneously, opening up new opportunities in linguistics, library science, and many other areas.

In this talk, however, I argue that the true potential of Linked Data can only be appreciated when extensive cross-linkage and integration engenders an even higher degree of interconnectedness. This can take the form of shared identifiers, e.g. those based on Wikipedia and WordNet, which can be used to describe numerous forms of linguistic and commonsense knowledge. An alternative is to rely on sameAs and similarity links, which can automatically be discovered using scalable approaches like the LINDA algorithm but need to be interpreted with great care, as we have observed in experimental studies. A closer level of linkage is achieved when resources are also connected at the taxonomic level, as exemplified by the MENTA approach to taxonomic data integration. Such integration means that one can buy into ecosystems already carrying a range of valuable pre-existing assets. Even more tightly integrated resources like Lexvo.org combine triples from multiple sources into unified, coherent knowledge bases.

Finally, I also comment on how to address some remaining challenges that are still impeding a more widespread adoption of Linked Data on the Web. In the long run, I believe that such steps will lead us to significantly more tightly integrated Linked Data.

Biography: Gerard de Melo is an Assistant Professor at Tsinghua University, where he is heading the Web Mining and Language Technology group. Previously, he was a post-doctoral researcher at UC Berkeley working in the ICSI AI group, and a doctoral candidate at the Max Planck Institute for Informatics. He has published over 30 research papers on Web Mining and Natural Language Processing, winning Best Paper Awards at conferences like CIKM and ICGL. For more information, please visit http://gerard.demelo.org/.

Section 1:
Modelling Lexical – Semantic Resources with *lemon*

Attaching Translations to Proper Lexical Senses in DBnary

Andon Tchechmedjiev, Gilles Sérasset, Jérôme Goulian, Didier Schwab

LIG-GETALP, Univ Grenoble Alpes
BP 53 – 38051 Grenoble cedex 9
firstname.lastname@imag.fr

Abstract

The DBnary project aims at providing high quality Lexical Linked Data extracted from different Wiktionary language editions. Data from 10 different languages is currently extracted for a total of over 3.16M translation links that connect lexical entries from the 10 extracted languages, to entries in more than one thousand languages. In Wiktionary, glosses are often associated with translations to help users understand to what sense they refer to, wether through a textual definition or a target sense number. In this article we aim at the extraction of as much of this information as possible and then the disambiguation of the corresponding translations for all languages available. We use an adaptation of various textual and semantic similarity techniques based on partial or fuzzy gloss overlaps to disambiguate the translation relations (to account for the lack of normalization, e.g. lemmatization and PoS tagging) and then extract some of the sense number information present to build a gold standard so as to evaluate our disambiguation as well as tune and optimize the parameters of the similarity measures. We obtain F1 score of the order of 80% (on par with similar work on English only), across the three languages where we could generate a gold standard (French, Portuguese, Finnish) and show that most of the disambiguation errors are due to inconsistencies in Wiktionary itself that cannot be detected during the generation of DBnary (shifted sense numbers, inconsistent glosses, etc.).

Keywords: Wiktionary, Linked Open Data, Multilingual Resources

1. Introduction

Wiktionary is a lexical-semantic resource built collaboratively under the patronage of the Wikimedia Foundation (which also hosts the well known Wikipedia initiative). It is currently the biggest collaborative resource for lexical data. Wiktionary pages usually describe lexical entries by giving their part of speech, a set of definitions, examples, lexico-semantic relations and many translations in more than a thousand target languages.

The DBnary project (Sérasset, 2012) aims at providing high quality Lexical Linked Data extracted from different Wiktionary language editions. It currently extracts data from 10 editions and gathers 3.16M translation links relating lexical entries from the 10 extracted languages to entries in more than a thousand languages. These numbers are steadily growing as the DBnary dataset is extracted as soon as Wikimedia releases new dumps of the data (around once every 10-15 days for each language edition).

The sources of these translation links are *lexical entries*. The purpose of this work is to attach these translations to the correct *word sense* and hence to increase the value and quality of the DBnary dataset. Comparable efforts have been carried out (mainly on the UBY dataset), but are limited to English and German. In this paper we worked on 10 language editions. Among them, we were faced with the various habits of the different Wiktionary communities. For example different languages editions exhibit different linguistic properties. After detailing related works, we present the structure of the DBnary dataset. Then, after showing how we built an endogenous golden standard used to evaluate this work, we detail the methods used to achieve our purpose. Finally we evaluate our method and discuss the results.

2. Related Work

2.1. Extracting Data from Wiktionary Language Editions.

Since its inception in 2002, Wiktionary has steadily increased in size (both with collaborative work and with automatic insertions of available lexical data). Interest in Wiktionary as a source for lexical data for NLP applications has quickly risen. Studies like (Zesch et al., 2008b) or (Navarro et al., 2009) show the richness and power of this resource.
Since then, efforts have mostly been focussed on the systematic extraction of Wiktionary data. Many of them, as resources for a specific project and thus merely snapshots of Wiktionary at a fixed point in time. As all Wiktionary language editions evolve regularly (and independently) in the way their data is represented, such efforts are not suitable to provide a sustainable access to Wiktionary data.
Some efforts, however are maintained and allow access over time. One of the most mature project is the *JWKTL* API (Zesch et al., 2008a) giving access to the English, German and Russian language editions. It is used in the UBY project (Gurevych et al., 2012) which provides an LMF based version of these editions.
We should also mention the wikokit project (Krizhanovsky, 2010) that provides access to the English and Russian editions and that was used by *JWKTL*.
(Hellmann et al., 2013) presents another attempt under the umbrella of the DBpedia project (Lehmann et al., 2014), whose purpose is specifically to provide the Wiktionary data as Lexical Linked Open Data. The main reason this approach is interesting is the collaborative nature extraction template creation process (following the culture of the DBpedia project). Currently English, French, Russian and German Wiktionary editions are supported.
This paper is part of the DBnary project (Sérasset, 2012) that has a similar purpose to that of (Hellmann et al., 2013).

Our goal is to provide LEMON (McCrae et al., 2012) based lexical databases that are structured like traditional lexica. Indeed, we extract data from Wiktionary, but we currently restrict ourselves to the "native" data of each language edition, e.g. the French data is extracted from the French language edition and we disregard French data contained in other editions. To the best of our knowledge DBnary is currently the most advanced extractor for Wiktionary with an active support of 10 languages. It is also the only initiative giving access to the whole extracted data history.

2.2. Disambiguation of the Source of Translations.

As far as attaching translations to the proper word sense (translation disambiguation) is concerned, the most similar work to ours is that of (Meyer and Gurevych, 2012b). Their intent matches our own, however their efforts only deal with the German and English editions. In their work, the gold standard was manually created and was significantly smaller than the endogenous gold standard we extracted from the resource itself. They use a backoff strategy (to the most frequent sense) when the heuristic based on similarity measures and the resource's structure fails. The other heuristics used with their similarity measure also imply a finer analysis of definitions and glosses so as to distinguish between linguistic labels (domain, register, title, etc.).
Herein, we achieve similar scores on the languages we were able to evaluate with an endogenous gold standard, even though we only used string and token similarity measures in the context of languages with less common features (e.g. the agglutinative aspect of the Finnish language).

2.3. Similarity measures

Our method is based on the application of gloss overlap measures and their extension with ideas taken from Hybrid textual similarity measures that match sentences both at the character and at the token level. In the work mentioned above (Meyer and Gurevych, 2012b), a feature-based similarity is used (gloss overlap), while in some of their prior work (Meyer and Gurevych, 2010), they use a textual similarity measure based on vector-spaces generated from corpora (Explicit Semantic Analysis).
We propose a simple similarity measure where we replace the exact word match of the overlap calculation with an approximate string distance measure and place ourselves in the general framework of the Tversky (Tversky, 1977) index (can be seen as a generalization of Lesk, the Dice coefficient , the Jaccard and Tatimono indexes, etc.)
The idea of "soft-cardinality" proposed by (Jimenez et al., 2010; Jimenez et al., 2012) is very similar in the sense that it exploits the Tversky index as a base and conjugates it with a textual similarity measure. That is, instead of incrementing the overlap count by 0 or 1, incrementing it by the value returned by the text similarity measure between the current pair of words being considered in the overlap calculation.
Their text similarity measure is based on an an empirical q-gram model (character-grams that correspond to substrings) combined with point-wise mutual information weighting. However in our work, generating a language model for 10 languages would require considerable effort and with future additions of more languages, become a daunting task.
In the textual similarity tasks in SemEval, using approximate string matching for overlap calculation is not new and has been exploited by several system, including in 2013 a soft cardinality system by (Jimenez et al., 2013) or other systems such as that of (Wu et al., 2013) who use longest common sub-strings and greedy string tiling .
As such, we chose to use a simple string distance measure for the approximate string match calculations. However, there are many such measure and it is necessary to select the right one for the task as will be detailed in Section 5. Moreover, there are existing so called "Level 2" or "Hybrid" similarity measures that already combine token overlap with token distance measures. Thus, we will need to evaluate our proposed method with some of the existing methods so as to evaluate their viability. The various measures and a detailed performance comparison in a name matching task are presented by (Cohen et al., 2003).

3. The DBnary Dataset

DBnary is a Lexical Linked Open Dataset extracted from 10 Wiktionary language editions (English, Finnish, French, German, Greek, Italian, Japanese, Portuguese, Russian and Turkish). It is available on-line at `http://kaiko.getalp.org/about-DBnary`. DBnary currently contains 35+M triples. This number is steadily growing as the dataset evolves in parallel with the original Wiktionary data. Indeed, the dataset is automatically updated as soon as Wikimedia releases new Wiktionary dumps, i.e. every 10-15 days per language edition.
DBnary is structured according the LEMON ontology for lexical linked data (McCrae et al., 2012). Table 1 shows the number of Lexical Elements, as defined in the LEMON ontologies, for the different extracted languages.
The elements in DBnary that couldn't be represented with LEMON, were defined as a custom ontology built on top of existing LEMON classes and relations, most notably lexico-semantic relation and what we call `Vocables`, the top level entries in Wiktionary that correspond to Wiktionary pages for specific words, and that can contain several `lemon:LexicalEntrys` categorised in two levels:

1. Homonymous distinction of words of different etymological origins (e.g. `river [water stream]` v.s. `river [one who rives or split]`)
2. For each etymological origin, the different lexico-grammatical categories (PoS) (e.g. `cut#V [I cut myself]` v.s. `cut#Noun [I want my cut of the winning]`)

3.1. Translation relations

The DBnary dataset represents translation relations in an ad-hoc manner: the LEMON model does not have a vocabulary for such information. A `Translation` is a RDF resource that gathers all extracted information pertaining to a translation relation. For instance, one of the translations of the lexical entry *frog* is represented as follows[1]:

```
eng:__tr_fra_1_frog__Noun__1
```

[1]The Turtle syntax is used throughout the paper for RDF data.

Language	Entries	LexicalSense	Translations	Glosses	Text	Sense Num	Text+Sense Num.
English	544,338	438,669	1,317,545	1,288,667	1,288,667	515	515
Finnish	49,620	58,172	121,278	120,728	120,329	115,949	115,550
French	291,365	379,224	504,061	136,319	135,612	28,821	28,114
German	205,977	100,433	388,630	388,553	3,101	385,452	0
Modern Greek	242,349	108,283	56,638	8,368	8,368	12	12
Italian	33,705	47,102	62,546	0	0	0	0
Japanese	24,804	28,763	85,606	22,322	20,686	4,148	2,512
Portuguese	45,109	81,023	267,048	74,901	72,339	71,734	69,172
Russian	129,555	106,374	360,016	151,100	150,985	115	0
Turkish	64,678	91,071	66,290	53,348	585	52,901	138

Table 1: Number of elements in the current DBnary dataset, detailing the number of entries and word senses, along with the number of translations. The table also details the number of Glosses attach to translations, among which the amount of textual glosses, of glosses giving the sense identifier and, finally, the number of glosses that contain both a textual description and a word sense identifier.

```
a          dbnary:Translation ;
dbnary:gloss "amphibian"@en ;
dbnary:isTranslationOf
           eng:frog__Noun__1 ;
dbnary:targetLanguage
           lexvo:fra ;
dbnary:usage "f" ;
dbnary:writtenForm "grenouille"@fr .
```

The properties of this resource point to the source `LexicalEntry`, the language of the target (represented as a `lexvo.org` entity (de Melo and Weikum, 2008)), the target written form and optionally, a gloss and usage notes. Usage notes give information about the target of the translation (e.g. the gender or a transcription of the target).
The gloss gives disambiguation information about the source of the translation. In the example given, it states that the given translation is valid for the word sense of *frog* that may be described by the hint "*amphibian*". Some of these glosses are textual and summarize or reprise the definition or part thereof for one or more specific sense to which the translation specifically applies to.
As an example, the English `LexicalEntry` *frog* contains 8 word senses, defined as follows:

1. A small tailless amphibian of the order Anura that typically hops
2. The part of a violin bow (or that of other similar string instruments such as the viola, cello and contrabass) located at the end held by the player, to which the horsehair is attached
3. (Cockney rhyming slang) Road. Shorter, more common form of frog and toad
4. The depression in the upper face of a pressed or handmade clay brick
5. An organ on the bottom of a horse's hoof that assists in the circulation of blood
6. The part of a railway switch or turnout where the running-rails cross (from the resemblance to the frog in a horse's hoof)
7. An oblong cloak button, covered with netted thread, and fastening into a loop instead of a button hole.
8. The loop of the scabbard of a bayonet or sword.

Translations of this entry are divided in 4 groups corresponding to: "*amphibian*", "*end of a string instrument's bow*", "*organ in a horse's foot*" and "*part of a railway*".
Additionally among the glosses, some may contain sense numbers, indicated by users in an ad-hoc way (may or may not be present, and if they are no standard format is systematically followed or enforced). Furthermore, the presence of disambiguation information is very irregular and varies greatly between languages, both in terms of wiki structure and representation.
In the current state of the Wiktionary extraction process, we extract translation and when possible the associated glosses. However up to now, we have not exploited the information contained in the glosses to enrich and disambiguate the source senses of translation relations.
As mentioned above, the information contained in translation glosses and their format is very variable across languages, both quantitatively and qualitatively.
Indeed, as shown in Table 1 some language like Italian, contain no gloss altogether, others, like English attaches textual glosses to translations almost systematically, but with no sense numbers. Others still, like German hardly contain textual glosses but give sense numbers to translations. In other cases, such as for Finnish, French and Portuguese, many translations have an attached (textual) gloss with associated sense numbers.
In order to evaluate our method we use mixed glosses that both contain a textual hint and a sense number, so as to create a endogenous gold standard.

3.1.1. Creation of a gold standard

False positives and variability are often present among available translation glosses that do contain textual information or sense numbers due the variety of structures employed in Wiktionary as well as artefacts resulting from the extraction process. Before we can proceed further we need to filter this information so as to keep only the relevant parts. However, no other preprocessing is performed.
More concretely two steps must be followed if we are to successfully extract the information we need :

- Remove empty glosses, or glosses containing irrelevant textual content that often correspond to TO DO notes in various forms (e.g. *translations to be checked*)

- Extract sense numbers from the glosses when available using language dependent templates (e.g. "*textual gloss (1)*" or "*1. textual gloss*")

When enough glosses contained both a textual hint and sense numbers, we removed the sense numbers[2] from the gloss and used them to create a gold standard in the trec_eval format. Only three of the ten language met the requirements as for many of the 10 languages there are no numbered glosses or no translation glosses altogether.
After successfully extracting as much information as possible from translation glosses, we disambiguatthe translation. While, the steps above are indeed language specific, our process is designed to be as generic and computationally efficient as possible. Indeed, we are required to periodically perform the disambiguation, whenever a new version of DBnary is extracted from the latest Wiktionary dumps.

4. Attaching Translations to Word Senses

4.1. Formalization of translation disambiguation

Let T be the set of all translation relations, L the set of all `LexicalEntry` in a given language edition of DBnary. Let $T_i \in T : Gloss(T_i)$ be a function that returns the gloss of any translation $T_i \in T$ and let $Source(T_i) = L_{T_i}$ be a function that returns a reference to the source `LexicalEntry`, L_{T_i} of a translation T_i. Let $Senses(L_i) = S_{L_i}$ be the set of all the senses associated with `LexicalEntry` L_i. Let $S^k_{L_i}$ be the k-th sense contained in S_{L_i} and let $Def(S^k_{L_i})$ be a function that returns the textual definition of a sense $S^k_{L_i}$. Finally let $Sim(A, B)$ be a function that returns a semantic similarity or relatedness score between A and B, where A, B are a pair of textual definitions or textual glosses.
Then, we can express the disambiguation process as:

$$\forall T_i \in T, S = Senses(Source(T_i)) :$$

$$Source^*(T_i) \leftarrow \underset{S^k \in S}{\operatorname{argmax}}\{Score(Gloss(T_i), Def(S^k))\}$$

This corresponds exactly to a standard semantic similarity maximisation and yields one disambiguated source sense per translation. However in many cases a translation corresponds to one or more senses. The solution adopted by (Meyer and Gurevych, 2012a) is to use a threshold k for their gloss overlap, however in our case, we want to be able to plug-in several different measures so as to find the most suitable one, thus, fixed and arbitrary value for k is not an option. Thus, we need to add one more constraint: that the values returned by our similarity function need to be normalized between 0 and 1.
Here, instead of taking a threshold k, we set a window δ around the best score in which the senses are accepted as a disambiguation of a given translation. We hypothesise that a relative threshold dependant on the maximal score will set a precedent and be more representative of the possible range of values. Of course, setting a fixed threshold has the effect of not assigning any senses if all the scores are low, thus increasing precision at the cost of lowering recall. While in a general setting, it is better to remove answers that are more likely to be mistakes, as detecting errors *a posteriori* is difficult. However in the context of the experiment, we prefer to keep such low or null scores as we will then be able to pin-point errors more precisely with the help of the gold standard for the sake of our analysis.
We can express this formally by modifying the $argmax$ function as such:

$$\forall T_i \in T, S = Senses(Source(T_i)) :$$

$$M_S = \max_{S_k \in S}(Score((Gloss(T_i), Def(S^k))),$$

$$\underset{S_i \in S}{\overset{\delta}{\operatorname{argmax}}}\{Score(Gloss(T_i), Def(S^k))\} =$$

$$\{S^k \in S | M_S > Score((Gloss(T_i), Def(S^k)) > M_S - \delta\}$$

4.2. Similarity Measure

In order to disambiguate the translation, we need to be able to compute some form of semantic similarity measure. Given that the only information available in the translations is the gloss that summarises the definition of the corresponding sense, we need a measure to capture the similarity by comparing the translation glosses and the sense definitions. The Lesk (Lesk, 1986) measure is a standard semantic similarity measure well suited for such tasks, as it computes a similarity based on the number of exact overlapping words between definitions. The Lesk similarity however, has several important issues that need to be addressed when its use is mandated:

- If the sizes of the glosses are not the same, the Lesk measure will always favor longer definitions.
- The size and the appropriateness of the words contained in the definitions is important, as one key word to the meaning of the definition missing (or the presence of a synonym for that matter) can lead to an incorrectly low similarity.
- The Lesk overlap is not in itself normalized, and the normalization process requires some though depending of the distinct problems at hand.

The issues of normalization and of the unequal length of definitions are actually related, as one way of compensating for unequal lengths is to divide by the length of the shortest definition, which also normalizes the score. Moreover, there is a striking similarity between Lesk and other overlap coefficients: the Dice Coefficient or the Jaccard or Tatimono indices. In fact, all of these measures are special forms of the Tversky index (Tversky, 1977).
The Tversky index can be defined as follows. Let $s_1 \in Senses(L_1)$ and $s_2 \in Senses(L_2)$ be the senses of two lexical entries L_1 and L_2. Let $d_i = Def(s_i)$ be the definition of s_i, represented as a set of words. The similarity between the senses $Score(s_1, s_2)$ can be expressed as

$$Score(s_1, s_2) = \frac{|d_1 \cap d_2|}{|d_1 \cap d_2| + \alpha|d_1 - d_2| + \beta|d_2 - d_1|}$$

The measure can further be generalized following (Pirrò and Euzenat, 2010) by replacing the cardinality function

[2]Translation are ban be valid for several source senses

by any function F. Depending on the values of α and β, the Tversky index takes the particular form of other similar indexes. For ($\alpha = \beta = 0.5$) for example it is equivalent to the dice coefficient, and for ($\alpha = \beta = 1$) to the Tatimono index. More generally, the values of α and β express how much emphasis one wants to attribute to the commonality or differences of one or the other set.

The Tversky index in itself is not a metric in the mathematical sense, as it is neither symmetric nor respects the triangular inequality, however, a symmetric variant has been proposed by (Jimenez et al., 2010) for such cases where the symmetry property is important or required. However there are no indications that the space of overlap-based semantic similarity is actually a metric space where those properties are beneficial. We actually obtained better results with the non-symmetric variant.

We motivate our choice of the Tversky index firstly because translation glosses are systematically composed of few words, whereas sense definitions are longer: the weights of the Tversky index allow for a good normalization in such situations. Furthermore, we are dealing with many languages so that building statistical similarity measures would require considerable efforts especially for lesser resourced languages. An overlap-based measure is a good choice for this situation.

4.2.1. Multilingual Setting & Partial overlaps

When working on a single language such as English or French, we have at our disposal tools such as a lemmatizer or a stemmer that may help to retrieve a canonical representation of the terms. Thus, we can hope to maximize the overlap and reduce the usual sparsity of glosses or sense definitions. For agglutinative languages like German or Finnish, highly inflective language (for example in the Bangla language, common stems are often composed of a single character, which makes stemming difficult to exploit) or languages with no clear segmentation, the preprocessing steps are paramount in order to make overlap based measures viable. If one is working on a single language, even if stemmers and lemmatizers do not exist, it is possible to build such a tool.

However, in the context of this work we are currently dealing with 10 languages (and potentially in the future with all the languages present in Wiktionary) and thus, in order to propose a truly general method, we cannot expect as a prerequisite, the presence of such tools.

How then, can we manage to compute overlaps effectively? When computing Lesk, if two words overlap, the score is increased by 1. Otherwise the overlap value does not change. What if we had a way to count meaningful partial overlaps between words? Instead of adding 1, we could add a value between 0 and 1 that represents a partial overlap.

The simplest approach is to use a form of partial string matching to compute these partial overlaps: a seemingly trivial approach that can however, greatly improve the result (Jimenez et al., 2012).

As mentioned in the Related Work section, there are many approximate string matching measures as reviewed by (Cohen et al., 2003). We integrate these measures in the Tversky index by setting the F function that replaces the set cardinality function appropriately (a simplified version of soft cardinality):

$$A \text{ , a set} : F(A) = \Big(\sum_{A_i, A_j \in A} sim(A_i, A_j)\Big)^{-1}$$

In our case, sim will be an string distance measure.

4.2.2. Longest Common Substring Constraints

With this similarity measure, we are mainly interested in capturing word that have common stems, without the need for a stemmer: for example, we do not want to consider the overlap of prefixes or suffices, as they do not carry the main semantic information of the word. If two words only match by a common suffix that happens to be used very often in that particular language, we will have a non-zero overlap, but we will have captured no sematic information whatsoever. Thus, in this work we put a lower-bound of three characters on the longest common subsequence.

5. Experiments

We extracted a gold standards from the sense numbered textual glosses of translations (when we could). Then we strip all sense number information from the glosses, so we can disambiguate those same translation and then evaluate the results on the previously generated gold standard.

We first describe how we generated the gold standard and the tools and measures used for the evaluation. We then proceed onto the empirical selection of the best parameters for our Tversky index as well as the most appropriate string distance measure to use for the fuzzy or soft cardinality. Then, we compare the results of the optimal Tversky index with other Level 2 similarity measures.

5.1. Evaluation

Let us first describe the gold standard generation process, then proceed on to describing how we represented the gold standard in Trec_eval format, a scorer program from the query answering Trec_Eval campaign. Let us then finish with the description of the evaluation measures we use.

5.2. Gold Standard

Only certain languages meet the requirements for the generation of a gold standard. To be more specific, we could only use languages where:

1. There are textual glosses (for the overlap measures)
2. There are numbers in said glosses indicating the right sense number
3. The above are available in a sufficient quantity (at least a few thousand)

Four languages could potentially meet the criteria (see the last column of Table 1): French, Portuguese, Finnish and Japanese.Due to the fact that the data available for Japanese was much smaller in size, we generated gold standards only for French, Portuguese and Finnish.

5.2.1. Trec_eval, scoring as a query answering task

A query answering task is more generally a multiple-labelling problem, which is exactly equivalent to what we are producing when we use the threshold δ. Here, we can consider that each translation number is the query identifier and that each sense URI is a document identifier. We answer the "translation" queries by providing one or more senses and an associated weight.

Thus, we can generate the gold standard and the results in the Trec_eval format, the very complete scorer for an information retrieval evaluation campaign of the same name.

5.2.2. Measures

We will use the standard set-matching metrics used in Information Retrival and Word Sense Disambiguation, namely Recall, Precision and F_1 score. Where, $P = \frac{|\{Relevant\} \cap \{Disambiguated\}|}{|\{Disambiguated\}|}$, $R = \frac{|\{Relevant\} \cap \{Disambiguated\}|}{|\{Relevant\}|}$, and $F1 = \frac{2 \cdot P \cdot R}{P+R}$, the harmonic mean of R and P. However, for the first step consisting in the estimation of the optimal parameters, we will only provide the $F1score$, as we are interested in maximising both recall and precision in an equal fashion.

5.3. Similarity Measure Tuning

There are parameters to set in our Tversky index: the first step is to find the most suitable string distance measure.

5.3.1. Optimal String Distance Metric

The δ parameter influences performance independently of the similarity measure, so we can first operate with $\delta = 0$, which restricts us to a single disambiguation per translation. Furthermore, the weights of the Tvsersky index are applied downstream from the string edit distance, and thus do not influence the relative performance of the different string distance metrics combined to our Tversky index. In simple terms, the ratio of the Tverski indices computed on different measures is constant, independently of α and β. Thus for this first experiment, we will set $\alpha = \beta = 0.5$, in other words the index becomes the Dice coefficient.

As for the selection of the string similarity measures to compare, we take the best performing measures from (Cohen et al., 2003), namely Jaro-Winkler, Monge-Elkan, Scaled Levenshtein Distance, to which we also add the longest common substring for reference. As a baseline measure, we will use the Tversky index with a standard overlap cardinality.

We give the following short notations for the measures: Tversky Index – Ts; Jaro-Winkler – JW; Monge-Elkan – ME; Scaled Levenshtein – Ls; Longest Common Substring – Lcss; F – Fuzzy. For example standard Tversky index with classical cardinality shall be referred to as "Ti", while the fuzzy cardinality version with a Monge-Elkan string distance shall be referred to as "FTiME".

Table 2 presents the results for each string similarity measure and each of the languages (Fr, Fi, Pt).

As we can see, for all language, the best string similarity measure is clearly the scaled Levenstein measure as it systematically exhibits a score higher from +1% to +1.96%.

	French	Portuguese	Finnish
	F1	F1	F1
FTiJW	0.7853	0.8079	0.9479
FTiLcss	0.7778	0.7697	0.9495
FTiLs	**0.7861**	**0.8176**	**0.9536**
FTiME	0.7684	0.7683	0.9495
Ti	0.7088	0.7171	0.8806

Table 2: Results comparing the performance in terms of F_1 score for French, Finnish and Portuguese (highest in bold).

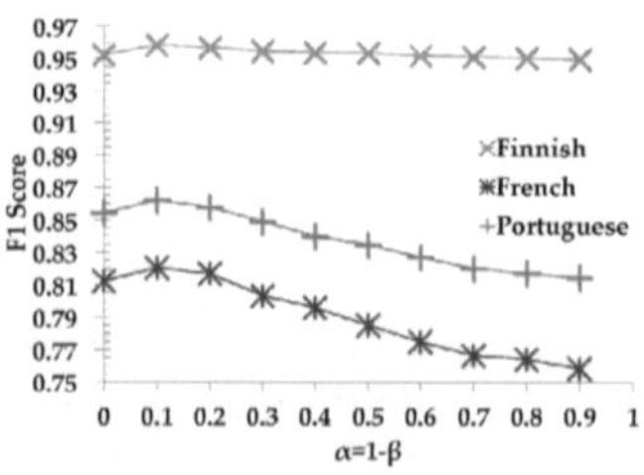

Figure 1: F1 score for Finnish, French and Portuguese depending on the value of α and β.

5.3.2. Optimal α, β selection

Now that we have found the optimal string distance measure, we can look for the optimal ratio of α and β. We keep both values complementary, that is $\alpha = 1 - \beta$ so as to obtain balanced score (i.e. 0 to 1 range)

Given that translation glosses are short (often a single word), it is likely that the optimum is around $\alpha = 1 - \beta = 0.1$. What interests us is that the single word or few words in the translation gloss matches any of the definition words. If we give equal importance to α and $beta$, then the overlap score will be very small even if it indicates an exact match. A smaller $alpha$ will ensure that if all the words of the translation match, the score will be closer to 1.

We chose, here, to evaluate the values of α and β in steps of 0.1. Figure 1 graphically shows the F_1 score for each pair of values of $alpha$ and $beta$ for all three languages. We can indeed confirm our hypothesis as the optimal value in all three cases is indeed $\alpha = 1 - \beta = 0.1$ with a difference between $+0.15\%$ to $+0.43\%$ with the second best scores.

5.3.3. Optimal δ selection

Now that we have fixed the best values of α and β, we can search for the best value for δ. We make delta vary in steps of 0.05 between 0 and 0.3. The choice of the upper bound is based on the hypothesis that the optimal value is somewhere closer to 0, as a too large threshold essentially means that that most or all senses will be considered as disambiguation of the translation, as if, we had disambiguated nothing.

The δ heuristic affects the results of the disambiguation whether the measure is Tversky index or another Level 2 Textual similarity. Thus, in this experiment, we will also include Level 2 version of the three string distance measures that we used in the first experiment.

Figure 2 graphically presents the $F1$ scores for each value of $delta$ and each language. The first apparent trend is that

	P	R	F1	MFS F1	Random
Portuguese	0.8572	0.8814	0.8651	0.2397	0.3103
Finnish	0.9642	0.9777	0.9687	0.7218	0.7962
French	0.8267	0.8313	0.8263	0.3542	0.3767

Table 3: Final results with optimal measure and parameter values. Precision, Recall, F1 score for all three languages compared against the MFS and Random Baselines.

Level 2 measures systemically perform much worse (by up to 30%) than our own similarity measure. Depending on the language different values of *delta* are optimal, even though it is difficult to see a great difference. For French $\delta = 0.10$, for Finnish $\delta = 0.15$ and for Portuguese $\delta = 0.10$. In all three previous experiments, it became apparent, that the same string similarity measure, the same values for alpha and beta as well as the same value for delta were optimal, which leads us to believe that their optimality will be conserved across all languages. However, especially for the string similarity measure, it is reasonable to believe that for languages such a Chinese or Japanese that lack segmentation, the optimal choice for the string distance measure may be entirely different.

5.4. Final Disambigation Results

Now that we estimated the optimal parameters, we can present the final results based on them in Table 3). We use the chance of random selection as well as the most frequent sense selection as baselines for this comparison.

The first thing one can notice is that there is a stark difference between the scores of Finnish, and the rest. Indeed, first of all, the random baseline and most frequent sense baselines are an indication that the French and Portuguese DBNaries are highly polysemous, while Finnish contains a very large amount of monosemous entries, which artificially inflates the value of the score.

Interestingly he random baseline is higher (up to 6.6%) than the most frequent sense baseline, which indicates that the first sense if often not the right sense to select to match the translation. This could be explained by the fact that translations in other language can often lead to different target words for every source sense and thus selecting the first sense will be correct of a most a small proportion of the translation relations leaving from the source word.

We can see that for all three languages we achieve a good performance compared to what is presented in the literature, most notably in the fact that most of the errors, can easily be identified as such just by looking at whether they produced any overlap.

5.5. Error analysis

We did not perform a full fledged and systematic error analysis, but rather an informal manual sampling so as to have an idea of what the error can be and if there are ways to correct them by adapting the measures or the methodology. We looked at some of the errors and manually categorized them:

1. No overlap between the gloss and sense definitions (Random choice by our algorithm), this happens when the translation gloss is a paraphrase of the sense definition or simply a metaphor for it.

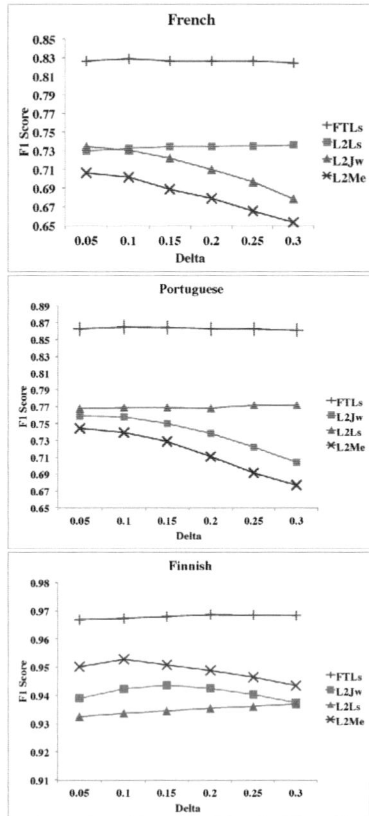

Figure 2: Graphical representation of the F1 score against delta for our measure and other Level 2 Measures.

2. The overlap is with the domain category label or the example glosses, which we do not currently extract. This is a particular case of the first type of error.

3. New senses have been introduced in Wiktionary and shifted sense numbers, which were not subsequently updated in the resource. Such errors cannot be detected during the extraction process.

We can in fact easily find all the errors due to the lack of overlap and correct the errors of type 2 by enriching the extraction process of DBnary. Thus we can single out errors that are due to inconsistencies in the resource and thus potentially use the disambiguation results to indicate to users where errors are located an need to be updated.

6. Conclusion

With our method, we were able to find an optimal similarity measure for translation disambiguation in DBnary. Similar results across three languages suggests that it is a general optimality that can be applied to all the languages currently present in DBnary, although for Asian Languages that have no segmentation, it is likely not the case.

Then, we compared the results and concluded that our method is viable for the task of disambiguating glossed translation relations, especially considering the low random baselines and first sense baselines compared to the top score of our method.

For translation relations without glosses, the disambiguation process is more complex and is part of the Future Work that we plan on carrying out.

7. References

William W. Cohen, Pradeep Ravikumar, and Stephen E. Fienberg. 2003. A comparison of string distance metrics for name-matching tasks. In *Proceedings of IJCAI-03 Workshop on Information Integration*, pages 73–78, August.

Gerard de Melo and Gerhard Weikum. 2008. Language as a Foundation of the {Semantic Web}. In Christian Bizer and Anupam Joshi, editors, *Proceedings of the Poster and Demonstration Session at the 7th International Semantic Web Conference (ISWC)*, volume 401 of *CEUR WS*, Karlsruhe, Germany. CEUR.

Iryna Gurevych, Judith Eckle-Kohler, Silvana Hartmann, Michael Matuschek, Christian M Meyer, and Christian Wirth. 2012. Uby: A large-scale unified lexical-semantic resource based on LMF. In *Proceedings of the 13th Conference of the European Chapter of the Association for Computational Linguistics*, pages 580–590. Association for Computational Linguistics.

Sebastian Hellmann, Jonas Brekle, and Sören Auer. 2013. Leveraging the Crowdsourcing of Lexical Resources for Bootstrapping a Linguistic Data Cloud. *Semantic Technology*, pages 191—-206.

Sergio Jimenez, Fabio Gonzalez, and Alexander Gelbukh. 2010. Text comparison using soft cardinality. In *Proceedings of the 17th International Conference on String Processing and Information Retrieval*, pages 297–302, Los Cabos, Mexico, October. Springer-Verlag.

Sergio Jimenez, Claudia Becerra, and Alexander Gelbukh. 2012. Soft Cardinality: A Parameterized Similarity Function for Text Comparison. In **SEM 2012: The First Joint Conference on Lexical and Computational Semantics – Volume 2: Proceedings of the Sixth International Workshop on Semantic Evaluation (SemEval 2012)*, June.

Sergio Jimenez, Claudia Becerra, and Alexander Gelbukh. 2013. SOFTCARDINALITY: Hierarchical Text Overlap for Student Response Analysis. *Atlanta, Georgia, ...*

A A Krizhanovsky. 2010. Transformation of Wiktionary entry structure into tables and relations in a relational database schema. *arXiv preprint arXiv:1011.1368*.

Jens Lehmann, Robert Isele, Max Jakob, Anja Jentzsch, Dimitris Kontokostas, Pablo N Mendes, Sebastian Hellmann, Mohamed Morsey, Patrick van Kleef, Sören Auer, and Christian Bizer. 2014. DBpedia - A Large-scale, Multilingual Knowledge Base Extracted from Wikipedia. *Semantic Web Journal*.

Michael Lesk. 1986. Automatic Sense Disambiguation Using Machine Readable Dictionaries: How to Tell a Pine Cone from an Ice Cream Cone. In *Proceedings of the 5th annual international conference on Systems documentation*, SIGDOC '86, pages 24–26, New York, NY, USA. ACM.

John McCrae, Guadalupe Aguado-de Cea, Paul Buitelaar, Philipp Cimiano, Thierry Declerck, Asunción Gómez-Pérez, Jorge Gracia, Laura Hollink, Elena Montiel-Ponsoda, Dennis Spohr, and Tobias Wunner. 2012. Interchanging lexical resources on the Semantic Web. *Language Resources and Evaluation*, 46(4):701–719, May.

Christian M. Meyer and Iryna Gurevych. 2010. Worth its weight in gold or yet another resource – a comparative study of wiktionary, openthesaurus and germanet. In Alexander Gelbukh, editor, *Proceedings of the 11th International Conference on Intelligent Text Processing and Computational Linguistics*, volume 6008 of *Lecture Notes in Computer Science*, pages 38–49. Berlin/Heidelberg: Springer, March.

Christian M Meyer and Iryna Gurevych. 2012a. *Electronic Lexicography*, chapter Wiktionary: A new rival for expert-built lexicons? Exploring the possibilities of collaborative lexicography, page (to appear). Oxford University Press.

Christian M Meyer and Iryna Gurevych. 2012b. To Exhibit is not to Loiter: A Multilingual, Sense-Disambiguated Wiktionary for Measuring Verb Similarity. In *Proceedings of COLING 2012*, pages 1763–1780, Mumbai, India. The COLING 2012 Organizing Committee.

Emmanuel Navarro, Franck Sajous, Bruno Gaume, Laurent Prévot, ShuKai Hsieh, Tzu Yi Kuo, Pierre Magistry, and Chu Ren Huang. 2009. Wiktionary and NLP: Improving synonymy networks. In Iryna Gurevych and Torsten Zesch, editors, *Proceedings of the 2009 Workshop on The People's Web Meets NLP: Collaboratively Constructed Semantic Resources (People's Web)*, pages 19–27, Suntec, Singapore, August. Association for Computational Linguistics.

Giuseppe Pirrò and Jérôme Euzenat. 2010. A Semantic Similarity Framework Exploiting Multiple Parts-of Speech. In Robert Meersman, Tharam S Dillon, and Pilar Herrero, editors, *OTM Conferences (2)*, volume 6427 of *Lecture Notes in Computer Science*, pages 1118–1125. Springer.

Gilles Sérasset. 2012. Dbnary: Wiktionary as a Lemon Based RDF Multilingual Lexical Resource. *Semantic Web Journal - Special issue on Multilingual Linked Open Data*.

Amos Tversky. 1977. Features of Similarity. *Psychological Review*, 84(2):327–352.

Stephen Wu, Dongqing Zhu, Ben Carterette, and H Liu. 2013. MayoClinicNLP–CORE: Semantic representations for textual similarity. *Atlanta, Georgia, USA*.

Torsten Zesch, Christof Müller, and Iryna Gurevych. 2008a. Extracting Lexical Semantic Knowledge from Wikipedia and Wiktionary. In *Proceedings of the Conference on Language Resources and Evaluation (LREC)*.

Torsten Zesch, Christof Müller, and Iryna Gurevych. 2008b. Using Wiktionary for Computing Semantic Relatedness. In *Proceedings of the Twenty-Third AAAI Conference on Artificial Intelligence, AAAI*, Chicago, Illinois, USA.

Gap in pagination due to unavailable paper.

Pages 13-17

Releasing genre keywords of Russian movie descriptions as Linguistic Linked Open Data: an experience report

Andrey Kutuzov, Maxim Ionov

Mail.ru Group
{andrey.kutuzov,m.ionov}@corp.mail.ru

Abstract

This paper describes a lexical database derived from a larger dataset of movie semantic properties. The larger dataset is a collection of RDF triples from most popular Russian movie delivery sites (mostly Schema.org predicates). The movies in these triples were classified according to their respective genre, and then keywords which are characteristic to descriptions of such movies, were extracted using log-likelihood approach. The set of such keywords (about 8000 lemmas) with various keyness attributes is published as Linguistic Linked Open Data, with the help of Lemon model. Additionally, lemmas were linked to Russian DBPedia Wiktionary.

Keywords: Semantic Web, Microdata, genre detection, lexical keyness, linked data

1. Introduction

Today World Wide Web quickly adopts the ideas of Semantic Web (Berners-Lee, 2004). Internet corporations endorse implementing and using semantic markup standards like RDF and Microdata. More and more sites start deploying semantic markup on their pages and link them with others. Among them are media content providers, social networks, e-shops, Q&A services, dictionaries, etc.

At the same time language scientists try to exploit the immense opportunities of Semantic Web for linguistic research (cf. (Chiarcos et al., 2012)). One of obvious applications is creating and publishing linked open data related to linguistics.

The present paper aims to describe the creation of such a dataset, namely a lexical base of keywords for Russian-language descriptions of movies in various genres. The lexicon is published as linked open data and can be used for various tasks in the field of lexical studies or automatic genre detection.

The descriptions themselves were extracted from semantic markup in the form of Microdata[1] in Russian video hosting services.

The structure of the paper is as follows. Section 2. explains the nature of our data, how and when it was received, and under what standards it is stored. In section 3. we explain how we processed movie descriptions and the method of extracting keywords for each genre. Section 4. deals with the issue of linking our dataset to Russian Wiktionary. In the section 5. we conclude and propose future work.

[1]http://www.whatwg.org/specs/web-apps/current-work/multipage/microdata.html

2. Semantic markup deployment in Russian video sites

24% of web pages in Russian Internet segment carry semantic markup in some form[2]. One important type of semantic markup adopters are video content delivery sites. Generally these resources provide user with the possibility to watch video content on-line without downloading it.

Such sites are quite popular among Russian users. Nearly 10% of daily 40 million queries processed by Mail.ru search engine are of this type: a user seeking some particular movie or short clip to watch.

Close to 50% of top Russian video content delivery sites deployed semantic markup. Accordingly, both major Russian commercial search engines (Yandex and Mail.ru) routinely use semantic metadata from these sites to better 'understand' their content.

We studied the copy of Russian Internet made by Mail.ru crawler. Among others, it regularly downloads the content of several most popular sites distributing video content and employing semantic markup. Popularity is judged by the frequency of the site appearing in search results and its click rank. Altogether this makes for approximately 90 million URLs (the exact number increases with each crawling session). All possible semantic-markup is extracted from the pages of these sites and used as structured data to construct better snippets (including movie description, its duration, actors' and producer name, etc).

Data extracted from the user-generated content sites (like http://youtube.com), as well as from newscasts (http://newstube.ru) were filtered out, as they mostly do not deliver full-length movies. The remaining set includes 18 sites dealing with movies and TV series. All of them are Russian-based and deliver content mainly in Russian. In total the set consists of about 1.5 million web pages with semantic markup.

[2]Yandex estimation, http://tech.yandex.ru/events/yagosti/wsd-msk-dec-2013/talks/1517/

Standards used for this semantic markup differ. But most informative of all is Microdata with Schema.org vocabulary. Many pages come with one and the same information deployed in several standards. However, almost always Microdata which uses <http://schema.org/Movie> class, would provide the most extensive metadata about the movie in question. Sites show movies' metadata to end users in HTML text, at the same time allowing for automatic semantics retrieval by software agents.

Page can contain semantic markup describing lots of various objects, but as stated above, in our project we extract properties of the entities belonging to type <http://schema.org/Movie> only.

In our case, the extraction itself was performed with the help of Apache any23 (Anything to Triples) library[3]. It became the tool of choice because it is open source and allows comparatively easy incorporation into large search engine workflow based on Apache Hadoop framework. Any23 takes a web page as an input and produces as an output a set of valid RDF triples in a range of serialization formats.

In total this data set contains nearly 1.13 million entities belonging to the type <http://schema.org/Movie>. As expected, a lot of them are duplicates. Counting unique titles only, we get about 130 000 separate movies. About 70% of entities come from kinopoisk.ru, 10% from kinoestet.ru, 7% from ivi.ru, and 4% from ovideo.ru. kinomatrix.com and baskino.com together contribute to 2% of the entities, other sites are even less.

It should be noted that several popular Russian video content delivery resources still ignore semantic markup. However, general tendency for sites of this kind is to gradually adopt semantic markup. Webmasters are mostly eager to contact with representatives of search engines and discuss possible improvements in the implementation of semantic technologies. The collection of movie genre keywords described below is derived from this large dataset (crawled in January 2014)[4]. Particularly, we used objects of <http://schema.org/Movie/description> predicates. We describe the process in full in the next section.

3. Genre-related lexical distribution as Linguistic Linked data

Our aim was to extract and publish a database of words characteristic of descriptions for different movie genres. Such collection can be later used for automatic genre detection (importance of word frequencies for this task was shown in (Lee and Myaeng, 2002)).

To do this, we created a corpus of such descriptions from the set described in the previous section. To each description we assigned a genre tag according to the value of <http://schema.org/Movie/genre> predicate of the corresponding entity (movie). If the entity possessed several genres, we produced corresponding number of descriptions each with its own genre tag. Note that we did not check agreement between different sites in assigning genres to movies: if identical descriptions were tagged differently, we also produced separate descriptions with corresponding tags. After removing duplicates and noise (empty or senseless descriptions), we had about 230 thousand descriptions. They were lemmatized using Freeling library (Padró and Stanilovsky, 2012) and stop-words were removed with the help of corresponding NLTK list (Bird et al., 2009).

This collection possessed 84 different unique genres most of which occurred not more than 20 or 30 times. Trying to employ this "genre long tail" to get keywords seemed useless. Thus, we chose 20 most frequent genres, which together comprise 198375 (86%) of our descriptions. The genres we omit are mostly exotic ones like "movie about movie" and "vampires". Notable exceptions are adult movies (2300 descriptions), biographic movies (1806 descriptions) and movies about animals (1500 descriptions). For now they fall out from top 20 genres, however in the future we plan to integrate them into our data set as well. The table 1 gives the list of selected genres (their English translations, to be more precise) with corresponding number of descriptions.

Table 1: Extracted genres and number of descriptions tagged with them

Genre	Number of descriptions
drama	41859
comedy	25698
thriller	16351
criminal	15050
action	12833
cartoon	12716
adventure	9601
children	9137
horror	8231
science fiction	7478
series	7272
romantic	6444
fantasy	4378
family	4374
military	3057
documentary	3032
educational	3008
historical	2640
Soviet	2613
anime	2603

It should be noted that we excluded descriptions for 'short film' genre ("короткометражка" in Russian), 3103 in total. The reason was that 'short film' is hardly a movie genre per se, it is more of a movie format. Thus, we instead added to our list the set of descriptions for "anime" genre. It was the next candidate by frequency and is certainly closer to the definition of

[3]https://any23.apache.org

[4]Full dataset is available on-line in the form of Turtle triples: http://ling.go.mail.ru/semanticweb/

"genre".
The corpus of descriptions for these 20 genres contains 9 135 790 word tokens and 147 653 unique word types. Size of genre sub-corpora obviously varies with the genre. As expected, the largest sub-corpus in relation to tokens number is 'drama' with 2 045 430 tokens. However the smallest sub-corpus is not 'anime' but 'educational' with 84 274 tokens.
For all these sub-corpora we detected keywords. That was done using well-tested log-likelihood approach (cf., for example, (El-haj and Rayson, 2013)). It works by comparing word frequencies in smaller corpus and in large reference corpus (in our case, genre sub-corpus and the whole descriptions' corpus). Words which are significantly more frequent relatively in the smaller corpus than in the larger one are keywords, characteristic for this kind of texts (in our case, for descriptions of movies in a particular genre). Exact log-likelihood formula we used is:

$$LL\left(w\right) = 2 * \left(\left(a * \ln\left(a/E_1\right)\right) + \left(b * \ln\left(b/E_2\right)\right)\right)$$

where LL(w) is the "keyness" of a word w, a is its frequency in corpus 1, b is its frequency in corpus 2, E1 and E2 are expected values of this word frequency for each corpus (calculated as a + b multiplied by the size of the corresponding corpus and divided by the total size of both corpora). Thus, keyness is a quantitative measure of a word specificity for a particular genre.
The results were quite convincing. Cf. top five words by their keyness from 'science fiction' sub-corpus:

- планета ("planet", keyness=2285.216)
- земля ("earth", keyness=2041.001)
- космический ("space",keyness=1413.610)
- человечество ("humanity", keyness=1132.876)
- будущее ("future", keyness=1109.299)

For brevity purposes, we extracted only first thousand of top keywords for each genre. Even this threshold seems to be too relaxed, as in the majority of cases only two or three hundred top keywords make sense. To filter out noise we removed keywords with keyness less than 10 and with absolute frequency in the respective sub-corpus less than 10.
This left us with a list of 7990 lemmas. More than half of them (4122) were recognized as keywords for several genres simultaneously. For example, "warrior" is a keyword for both fantasy and anime descriptions (keyness equal to 379.377 and 322.53 respectively).
For each lemma we also calculated frequency (in instances per million tokens, ipm) in each sub-corpus where it is a keyword and coverage, that is, the portion of descriptions in this sub-corpus in which this lemma actually appears. For 'warrior' mentioned above, the data goes as follows:

- fantasy: ipm 1353.98, coverage 0.063
- anime: ipm 1533.75, coverage 0.064,

meaning that if we take a corpus of fantasy movies descriptions 1 million words in size, the word 'warrior' is expected to appear there about 1354 times, while in a similar corpus for anime movies it will appear more often: about 1534 times. At the same time, in both genres coverage of this word is similar: if one takes 100 descriptions of any of these genres, she can expect to encounter 'warrior' in 6 of them. Coverage 0 means that the word does not appear in the sub-corpus at all, coverage 1 means that it appears in all descriptions for this genre without exception.
Thus, for each lemma we got a set of genres, in which it is a keyword, and for each of these genres three numbers: keyness, ipm frequency and coverage. Let us describe the models and vocabularies we used to publish this information as Linguistic Linked Data with the help of 'будущее' ('future') example:

```
@prefix isocat: <http://www.isocat.org/datcat> .
@prefix lemon: <http://lemon-model.net/lemon#> .
@prefix lexinfo: <http://www.lexinfo.net/ontology/2.0/lexinfo#> .
@prefix rdfs: <http://www.w3.org/2000/01/rdf-schema#> .
@prefix xsd: <http://www.w3.org/2001/XMLSchema#> .
isocat:2503 rdfs:label "genreRelation"@en ;
   rdfs:subPropertyOf lemon:property .
isocat:6564 rdfs:label "Keyness"@en ;
   rdfs:subPropertyOf lemon:property .
isocat:6563 rdfs:label "Coverage"@en ;
   rdfs:subPropertyOf lemon:property .
lexinfo:frequency rdfs:label "Instances per million"@en ;
   rdfs:subPropertyOf lemon:property .
<http://ling.go.mail.ru/semanticweb/movielexicon/будущее>
      rdfs:type lemon:entry;
      rdfs:sameAs
      <http://wiktionary.dbpedia.org/resource/Будущее> ;
   isocat:2503 [ isocat:6563 0.0368581002104;
         isocat:6564 92.924;
         lexinfo:frequency 829.519123845;
         rdfs:label "action" ],
      [ isocat:6563 0.0962824284568;
         isocat:6564 1109.299;
         lexinfo:frequency 2352.62367408;
         rdfs:label "science_fiction" ],
      [ isocat:6563 0.0304134985939;
         isocat:6564 20.988;
         lexinfo:frequency 674.027740908;
         rdfs:label "adventure" ],
      [ isocat:6563 0.0418747598924;
         isocat:6564 25.34;
         lexinfo:frequency 854.51982559;
         rdfs:label "anime" ];
   lemon:form [ lemon:writtenRep "будущее"@ru ;
            lemon:writtenRep "future"@en] .
```

We used Lemon model[5] as general framework. Thus, our word (entity of lemon type http://lemon-model.net/lemon#entry located at URI http://ling.go.mail.ru/semanticweb/movielexicon/будущее receives a form predicate, which links two written representations in Russian and in English to it. Then, we define four external predicates as Lemon properties. They are http://www.isocat.org/datcat/

[5] http://lemon-model.net/

2503 for genre relation (property of word being key for a particular genre), http://www.isocat.org/datcat/6564 for keyness of the word in a particular genre, http://www.isocat.org/datcat/6563 for word coverage and http://www.lexinfo.net/ontology/2.0/lexinfo#frequency (Buitelaar et al., 2009) for word frequency in particular sub-corpus.

Thus, the word 'будущее' receives four objects of genreRelation property, each corresponding to a genre where it is a keyword. Each of these objects receives corresponding isocat properties for coverage and keyness, lexinfo property for frequency and rdfs label for genre name.

At last, we link the word to the corresponding entry in DBPedia version of Russian Wiktionary (Hellmann et al., 2013). This allows getting access to full data about the lexeme, available in Wiktionary and any other resources linked there. The process of linking raised some issues, described in the next section.

The whole collection is available as an archive of raw N3 triples (http://ling.go.mail.ru/semanticweb/movielexicon/mailru_movie_keywords2.n3.gz) and as HTTP service at http://ling.go.mail.ru/semanticweb/movielexicon/.

4. Linking the set to Wiktionary

As an attempt to integrate our data with Linked Data Cloud, we linked keywords to entities in Linked Data Wiktionary[6]. For every keyword that existed in it we extracted all triples in Wiktionary RDF with predicate lemon:sense and an object indicating Russian language. After that, each link was added to the keyword RDF description as a triple with rdfs:sameAs relation. In RDF Wiktionary dump we used[7] there were 128 503 unique Russian lexical entries. Intersecting them with 7 990 keywords we got 5 005 links. There are three main reasons for low recall:

- Rare words and neologisms as keywords. A lot of foreign names fall into this type (translations of names Eddie, Annie and so on).
- Lemmatization errors. Some keywords were lemmatized to the wrong first form. These errors should be fixed by using better lemmatization. Freeling library that we used is probably the best freely available morphological analyzer with disambiguation for Russian. Unfortunately, it still sometimes produces erroneous tagging and lemmatization. However it is rather flexible and we were able to manually fix lemmas for about 250 word types, which enhanced quality of keywords detection. In the future we plan to return our fixes to Freeling developers.
- Wiktionary RDF problems. Some words were presented in DBPedia but were not presented in Wiktionary RDF. These errors may be fixed by querying DBPedia directly.

[6]http://dbpedia.org/Wiktionary

[7]Latest at the time of writing: dated 2013-08-29

An important drawback of this interlinking is the lack of word-sense disambiguation. Keywords are linked to lexical entries which may have more than one sense. To disambiguate those senses one should disambiguate them from the beginning, at the keyword extracting phase. This is a direction for future work.

5. Conclusion and future work

We created and published a dataset, which is a collection of Russian lexemes characteristic for descriptions of movies of different genres and their respective statistical properties. Descriptions were extracted from top Russian video content delivery sites using <Schema.org/Movie> class. Dataset is published as Linguistic Linked Data using existing models and vocabularies (Lemon, Lexinfo and Data Category Registry). It can be used for lexicological studies or as a tool within a genre detection framework related to movies. Also, it is another contribution to the cloud of Linguistic Open Data resources, which still seriously lacks resources for Russian language, especially ones dealing with quantitative information.

At the same time, there is an open field for future research. First of all, the extracted keywords should be evaluated by human experts to assess their practical value. To improve the collection, word sense disambiguation and further lemmatization correction should be done. Another way to increase the quality of the dataset is to process not only single words, but also multi-word entities. Finally, the collection can be expanded with data from entities other than <http://schema.org/Movie>, for example, VideoObject and others.

6. References

Tim Berners-Lee. 2004. The semantic web.

Steven Bird, Ewan Klein, and Edward Loper. 2009. Natural language processing with Python. O'Reilly, Beijing; Cambridge [Mass.].

Paul Buitelaar, Philipp Cimiano, Peter Haase, and Michael Sintek. 2009. Towards linguistically grounded ontologies. In Lora Aroyo and others., editors, The Semantic Web: Research and Applications, volume 5554 of Lecture Notes in Computer Science, pages 111–125. Springer Berlin Heidelberg.

Christian Chiarcos, Sebastian Nordhoff, and Sebastian Hellmann, editors. 2012. Linked Data in Linguistics - Representing and Connecting Language Data and Language Metadata. Springer.

Mahmoud El-haj and Paul Rayson. 2013. Using a keyness metric for single and multi document summarisation. In Proceedings of the MultiLing 2013 Workshop on Multilingual Multi-document Summarization, pages 64–71. Association for computational linguistics.

Sebastian Hellmann, Jonas Brekle, and Sören Auer. 2013. Leveraging the crowdsourcing of lexical resources for bootstrapping a linguistic data cloud. In Hideaki Takeda et al., editors, Semantic Technology, volume 7774 of Lecture Notes in Computer Science, pages 191–206. Springer Berlin Heidelberg.

Yong B. Lee and Sung H. Myaeng. 2002. Text genre classification with genre-revealing and subject-revealing features. In Proceedings of the 25th annual international ACM SIGIR conference on Research and development in information retrieval, SIGIR '02, pages 145–150, New York, NY, USA. ACM.

Lluís Padró and Evgeny Stanilovsky. 2012. Freeling 3.0: Towards wider multilinguality. In Nicoletta Calzolari (Conference Chair), Khalid Choukri, Thierry Declerck, Mehmet Uğur Doğan, Bente Maegaard, Joseph Mariani, Jan Odijk, and Stelios Piperidis, editors, Proceedings of the Eight International Conference on Language Resources and Evaluation (LREC'12), Istanbul, Turkey, may. European Language Resources Association (ELRA).

Section 2: Metadata

From CLARIN Component Metadata to Linked Open Data

Matej Ďurčo, Menzo Windhouwer

Institute for Corpus Linguistics and Text Technology (ICLTT), The Language Archive - DANS
Vienna, Austria, The Hague, The Netherlands
matej.durco@oeaw.ac.at, menzo.windhouwer@dans.knaw.nl

Abstract

In the European CLARIN infrastructure a growing number of resources are described with Component Metadata. In this paper we describe a transformation to make this metadata available as linked data. After this first step it becomes possible to connect the CLARIN Component Metadata with other valuable knowledge sources in the Linked Data Cloud.

Keywords: Linked Open Data, RDF, component metadata

1. Motivation

Although semantic interoperability has been one of the main motivations for CLARIN's Component Metadata Infrastructure (CMDI) (Broeder et al., 2010),[1] until now there has been no work on the obvious – bringing CMDI to the Semantic Web. We believe that providing the CLARIN CMD records as Linked Open Data (LOD) interlinked with external semantic resources, will open up new dimensions of processing and exploring of the CMD data by employing the power of semantic technologies. In this paper, we lay out how individual parts of the CMD data domain can be expressed in RDF and made ready to be interlinked with existing external semantic resources (ontologies, taxonomies, knowledge bases, vocabularies).

2. The Component Metadata Infrastructure

The basic building blocks of CMDI are components. Components are used to group elements and attributes, which can take values, and also other components (see Figure 1). Components are stored in the Component Registry (CR), where they can be reused by other modellers. Thus a metadata modeller selects or creates components and combines them into a profile targeted at a specific resource type, a collection of resources or a project, tool or service. A profile serves as blueprint for a schema for metadata records. CLARIN centres offer these CMD records describing their resources to the joint metadata domain. There are a number of generic tools which operate on all the CMD records in this domain, e.g., the Virtual Language Observatory.[2] These tools have to deal with the variety of CMD profiles. They can do so by operating on a semantic level, as components, elements and values can all be annotated with links to concepts in various registries. Currently used concept registries are the Dublin Core metadata terms and the ISOcat Data Category Registry. These concept links allow profiles, while being diverse in structure, to share semantics. Generic tools can use this semantic linkage to overcome differences in terminology and also in structure.

2.1. Current status of the joint CMD Domain

To provide a frame of reference for the proportions of the undertaking, this section gives a few numbers about the data in the CMD domain.

2.1.1. CMD Profiles

Currently[3] 153 public profiles and 859 components are defined in the CR. Next to the 'native' ones a number of profiles have been created that implement existing metadata formats, like OLAC/DCMI-terms, TEI Header or the META-SHARE schema. The individual profiles also differ very much in their structure – next to simple flat profiles there are complex ones with up to 10 levels and a few hundred elements.

2.1.2. Instance Data

The main CLARIN OAI-PMH harvester[4] regularly collects records from the – currently 56 – providers, all in all over 600.000 records. Some 20 of the providers offer CMDI records, the rest provides around 44.000 OLAC/DC records, that are converted into the corresponding CMD profile. Some of the providers of 'native' CMD records expose multiple profiles (e.g. Meertens Institute uses 12 different ones), so that overall instance data for more than 60 profiles is present.

3. CMD to RDF

In the following a RDF encoding is proposed for all levels of the CMD data domain:

- CMD meta model (see Figure 1),
- profile and component definitions,
- administrative and structural information of CMD records and
- individual values in the fields of the CMD records.

[1] http://www.clarin.eu/cmdi/
[2] http://www.clarin.eu/vlo/
[3] All numbers are as of 2014-03.
[4] http://catalog.clarin.eu/oai-harvester/

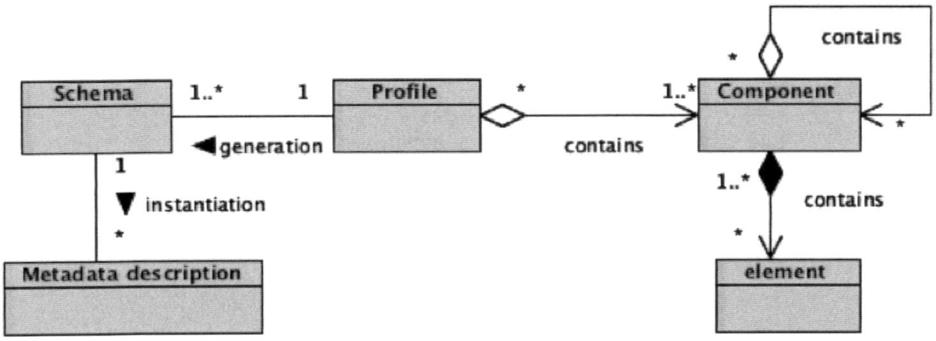

Figure 1: Component Metadata Model (ISO/DIS 24622-1, 2013)

3.1. CMD specification

The main entity of the meta model is the CMD component modelled as a `rdfs:Class` (see Figure 2). A CMD profile is basically a CMD component with some extra features, implying a specialization relation. It may seem natural to translate a CMD element to a RDF property (as it holds the literal value), but given its complexity, i.e., attributes,[5] it too has to be expressed as a `rdfs:Class`. The actual literal value is a property of given element of type `cmdm:hasElementValue`. For values that can be mapped to entities defined in external semantic resources, the references to these entities are expressed in parallel object properties of type `cmdm:hasElementEntity` (constituting outbound links). The containment relation between components and elements is expressed with a dedicated property `cmdm:contains`.

3.2. CMD profile and component definitions

These top-level classes and properties are subsequently used for modelling the actual profiles, components and elements as they are defined in the CR. For stand-alone components, the IRI is the (future) path into the CR to get the RDFS representation for the profile/component.[6] For "inner" components (that are defined as part of another component) and elements the identifier is a concatenation of the nearest ancestor stand-alone component's IRI and the dot-path to given component/element (e.g., Actor: `cr:clarin.eu:cr1:c_1271859438197/rdf #Actor.Actor_Languages.Actor_Language`[7])

```
cmd:collection
  a               cmdm:Profile ;
  rdfs:label      "collection" ;
  dc:identifier   cr:clarin.eu:cr1:p_1345561703620 .
cmd:Actor
  a               cmdm:Component .
```

[5]Although the modelling work has been done, due to space considerations, we will not further discuss attributes.

[6]`http://catalog.clarin.eu/ds/ComponentRegistry/rest/registry/components/clarin.eu:cr1:c_1271859438125/rdf`

[7]For better readability, in the examples we collapse the component IRIs, using just the name, prefixed with `cmd:`

3.2.1. Data Categories

The primary concept registry used by CMDI is ISOcat. The recommended approach to link to the data categories is via an annotation property (Windhouwer and Wright, 2012).

```
dcr:datcat
  a             owl:AnnotationProperty ;
  rdfs:label    "data category"@en .
```

Consequently, the `@ConceptLink` attribute on CMD elements and components referencing the data category can be modelled as:

```
cmd:LanguageName
  dcr:datcat      isocat:DC-2484 .
```

Lateron, this information can be used, e.g., in combination with ontological relationships for these data categories available in the RELcat Relation Registry (Windhouwer, 2012), to map to other vocabularies.

3.3. CMD instances

In the next step, we want to express in RDF the individual CMD instances, the metadata records.

We provide a generic top level class for all resources (including metadata records), the `cmdm:Resource` class and the `cmdm:hasMimeType` predicate to type the resources.

```
<lr1>
  a                   cmdm:Resource ;
  cmdm:hasMimeType    "audio/wav" .
```

3.3.1. Resource Identifier

The PID of a Language Resource (`<lr1>`) is used as the IRI for the described resource in the RDF representation. The relationship between the resource and the metadata record can be expressed as an annotation using the OpenAnnotation vocabulary.[8] (Note, that one MD record

[8]`http://openannotation.org/spec/core/core.html`

```
@prefix cmdm: <http://www.clarin.eu/cmd/general.rdf#>.

# basic building blocks of CMD Model
cmdm:Component          a                   rdfs:Class .
cmdm:Profile            rdfs:subClassOf     cmdm:Component .
cmdm:Element            a                   rdfs:Class .

# basic CMD nesting
cmdm:contains           a                   rdf:Property ;
                        rdfs:domain         cmdm:Component ;
                        rdfs:range          cmdm:Component , cmdm:Element .
# values
cmdm:Value              a                   rdfs:Literal .

cmdm:hasElementValue    a                   rdf:Property ;
                        rdfs:domain         cmdm:Element ;
                        rdfs:range          cmdm:Value .

# add a parallel separate class/property for the resolved entities
cmdm:Entity             a                   rdfs:Class .

cmdm:hasElementEntity   a                   rdf:Property ;
                        rdfs:domain         cmdm:Element ;
                        rdfs:range          cmdm:Entity .
```

Figure 2: The CMD meta model in RDF

can describe multiple resources. This can be also easily accommodated in OpenAnnotation.)

```
_:anno1
  a                 oa:Annotation ;
  oa:hasTarget      <lr1a >, <lr1b>;
  oa:hasBody        _:topComponent1 ;
  oa:motivatedBy    oa:describing .
```

3.3.2. Provenance

The information from the CMD record `cmd:Header` represents the provenance information about the modelled data.

```
<lr1.cmd >
  dc:creator      "John Doe" ;
  dc:publisher    <http://clarin.eu>;
  dc:created      "2014-02-05"^^xs:date .
```

3.3.3. Collection hierarchy

In CMD, there are dedicated generic elements – the `cmd:ResourceProxyList` structure – used to express both the collection hierarchy and to point to resource(s) described by the CMD record. The collection hierarchy can be modelled as an OAI-ORE Aggregation.[9] (The links to resources are handled by `oa:hasTarget`.) :

```
<lr0.cmd >   a               ore:ResourceMap .
<lr0.cmd>    ore:describes   _:agg0 .
_:agg0       a               ore:Aggregation ;
             ore:aggregates  <lr1.cmd>, <lr2.cmd>.
```

3.3.4. Components – nested structures

For expressing the tree structure of the CMD records, i.e., the containment relation between the components, a dedicated property `cmd:contains` is used:

```
_:actor1        a              cmd:Actor .
_:actor1lang1   a              cmd:Actor.Language .
_:actor1        cmd:contains   _:actor1lang1 .
```

3.3.5. Elements, Fields, Values

Finally, we want to integrate also the actual values in the CMD records into the linked data. As explained before, CMD elements have to be typed as `rdfs:Class`, the actual value expressed as `cmdm:ElementValue`, and they are related by a `cmdm:hasElementValue` property.

While generating triples with literal values seems straightforward, the more challenging but also more valuable aspect is to generate object property triples (predicate `cmdm:hasElementEntity`) with the literal values mapped to semantic entities. The example in Figure 3 shows the whole chain of statements from metamodel to literal value and corresponding semantic entity.

[9] `http://www.openarchives.org/ore/1.0/primer#Foundations`

```
cmd:Person                         a                          cmdm:Component .
cmd:Person.Organisation            a                          cmdm:Element .
cmd:hasPerson.OrganisationElementValue
                                   rdfs:subPropertyOf         cmdm:hasElementValue ;
                                   rdfs:domain                cmd:Person.Organisation ;
                                   rdfs:range                 xs:string .
cmd:hasPerson.OrganisationElementEntity
                                   rdfs:subPropertyOf         cmdm:hasElementEntity ;
                                   rdfs:domain                cmd:Person.Organisation ;
                                   rdfs:range                 cmd:Person.OrganisationElementEntity .
cmd:Person.OrganisationElementEntity
                                   a                          cmdm:Entity .

  # person (mentioned in a MD record) has an affiliation (cmd:Person/cmd:Organisation)
_:pers                             a                          cmd:Person ;
                                   cmdm:contains              _:org .
_:org                              a                          cmd:Person.Organisation ;
                                   cmd:hasPerson.OrganisationElementValue     'MPI'^^xs:string ;
                                   cmd:hasPerson.OrganisationElementEntity    <http://www.mpi.nl/>.
<http://www.mpi.nl/>               a                          cmd:OrganisationElementEntity .
```

Figure 3: Chain of statements from metamodel to literal value and corresponding semantic entity

4. Implementation

The transformation of profiles and instances into RDF/XML is accomplished by a set of XSL-stylesheets. In the future, when the mapping has been tested extensively, they will be integrated into the CMD core infrastructure, e.g., the CR. A linked data representation of the CLARIN joint metadata domain can then be stored in a RDF triple store and exposed via a SPARQL endpoint. Currently, a prototype interface is available for testing as part of the Metadata repository developed at CLARIN Centre Vienna[10].

5. CMDI's future in the LOD Cloud

The main added value of LOD (Berners-Lee, 2006) is the interconnecting of disparate datasets in the so called LOD cloud (Cyganiak and Jentzsch, 2010).

The actual mapping process from CMDI values (see Section 3.3.5.) to entities is a complex and challenging task. The main idea is to find entities in selected reference datasets (controlled vocabularies, ontologies) corresponding to the literal values in the metadata records. The obtained entity identifiers are further used to generate new RDF triples, representing outbound links. Within CMDI the SKOS-based vocabulary service CLAVAS,[11] which will be supported in the upcoming new version of CMDI, can be used as a starting point, e.g., for organisations. In the broader context of LOD Cloud there is the Open Knowledge Foundations Working Group on Linked Data in Linguistics, that represents an obvious pool of candidate datasets to link the CMD data with.[12] Within these lexvo seems a most promising starting point, as it features URIs like `http://lexvo.org/id/term/eng/`, i.e., based on the ISO-639-3 language identifiers which are also used in CMD records. lexvo also seems suitable as it is already linked with a number of other LOD linguistic datasets like WALS, lingvoj and Glottolog. Of course, language is just one dimension to use for mapping. Step by step we will link other categories like countries, geographica, organisations, etc. to some of the central nodes of the LOD cloud, like dbpedia, Yago or geonames, but also to domain-specific semantic resource like the ontology for language technology LT-World (Jörg et al., 2010) developed at DFKI.

Next to entities also predicates can be shared across datasets. The CMD Infrastructure already provides facilities in the form of ISOcat and RELcat. RELcat, for example, has already sets to relate data categories to Dublin Core terms. This can be extended with the ontology for metadata concepts described in (Zinn et al., 2012), which does not provide common predicates but would allow to do more generic or specific searches.

6. Conclusions

In this paper, we sketched the work on encoding of the whole of the CMD data domain in RDF, with special focus on the core model – the general component schema. In the future we will extend this with mapping element values to semantic entities.

With this new enhanced dataset, the groundwork is laid for a full-blown *semantic search*, i.e., the possibility of exploring the dataset indirectly using external semantic resources (like vocabularies of organizations or taxonomies of resource types) to which the CMD data will then be linked.

7. References

Tim Berners-Lee. 2006. Linked data. online: http://www.w3.org/DesignIssues/LinkedData.html.

[10] `http://clarin.oeaw.ac.at/mdrepo/cmd?operation=cmd2rdf`

[11] `https://openskos.meertens.knaw.nl/`

[12] `http://linguistics.okfn.org/resources/llod/`

Daan Broeder, Marc Kemps-Snijders, et al. 2010. A data category registry- and component-based metadata framework. In Nicoletta Calzolari, Khalid Choukri, et al., editors, *LREC*, Valletta, May. ELRA.

Richard Cyganiak and Anja Jentzsch. 2010. The linking open data cloud diagram. online: http://lod-cloud.net/.

ISO/DIS 24622-1. 2013. Language resource management – component metadata infrastructure – part 1: The component metadata model (cmdi-1).

Brigitte Jörg, Hans Uszkoreit, and Alastair Burt. 2010. LT World: Ontology and reference information portal. In Nicoletta Calzolari and Khalid Choukri et al., editors, *LREC*, Valletta, Malta, May. ELRA.

Menzo Windhouwer and Sue Ellen Wright. 2012. Linking to linguistic data categories in ISOcat. In *Linked Data in Linguistics*, pages 99–107. Springer.

Menzo Windhouwer. 2012. RELcat: a relation registry for ISOcat data categories. In Nicoletta Calzolari, Khalid Choukri, et al., editors, *LREC*, Istanbul, May. ELRA.

Claus Zinn, Christina Hoppermann, and Thorsten Trippel. 2012. The isocat registry reloaded. In Elena Simperl, Philipp Cimiano, Axel Polleres, Oscar Corcho, and Valentina Presutti, editors, *The Semantic Web: Research and Applications*, volume 7295 of *Lecture Notes in Computer Science*, pages 285–299. Springer Berlin Heidelberg.

A Brief Survey of Multimedia Annotation Localisation on the Web of Linked Data

Gary Lefman[1], Dave Lewis[1], Felix Sasaki[2]
[1]CNGL the Centre for Global Intelligent Content, Trinity College Dublin, Ireland
[2]Language Technology Lab, German Research Centre for Artificial Intelligence (DFKI), Germany
E-mail: lefmang@tcd.ie, dave.lewis@cs.tcd.ie, felix.sasaki@dfki.de

Abstract

Multimedia annotation generates a vast amount of monolingual data that can help to describe audio, video, and still images. These annotations are, however, unlikely to be useful to people that cannot communicate through the same language. Annotations may also contain insufficient context for people coming from different cultures, so there is a need for localised annotations, in addition to localised multimedia. We have performed a brief survey of multimedia annotation capabilities, choosing Flickr as a representative candidate of open social media platforms. The focus of our examination was on the role of localisation in multimedia ontologies and Linked Data frameworks. In order to share annotated multimedia effectively on the Web of Linked Data, we believe that annotations should be linked to similar resources that have already been adapted for other languages and cultures. In the absence of a Linked Data framework, monolingual annotations remain trapped in silos and cannot, therefore, be shared with other open social media platforms. This discovery led to the identification of a gap in the localisation continuity between multimedia annotations and the Web of Linked Data.

Keywords: Localisation, Multimedia Annotation, Linguistic Linked Open Data, Multimedia Ontology, RDF, OWL, Flickr

1. Introduction

We carried out this survey to determine if there are gaps in the continuity between multilingual annotated multimedia and open social media platforms across the Web of Linked Data. We selected Flickr[1], as an example of an open social media platform for sharing images and videos, because it provides users with an annotation feature. Since the lexical and semantic value of ontology localisation has already been well-defined (Cimiano et al., 2010), our approach was to examine the *practicality* of multimedia annotation localisation. In this paper we concentrate only on still images, even though Flickr supports video as well. Our definition of multimedia localisation is the adaptation of audio and visual media resources to meet the specific requirements of different cultures and natural languages.

When people annotate images, videos, and graphics on the Web, they are describing their observations and experiences in a manner that can be shared and retrieved. Multimedia annotations may contain observable and clearly recognisable characteristics of a scene, such as a tree on a grassy hill, and metaphysical properties, like emotions, that may be derived from the same scene. Multimedia annotations on an open social media platform may be written in different languages, and by people who might represent completely different cultures. A user from England might look at our scene in Figure 1 and add an annotation with the term "tree", a user from Wales sees the tree and annotates it with "coeden" (Welsh:tree), and another user from Wales adds "bren" (Welsh:wood). Each annotation represents the same object in this image, and a search for any of these terms would probably show this resource. However, if each annotation is added to a different image on different platforms, for example, we want to ensure a resource for all three images is extracted if we search for the term "coeden" (Figure 2).

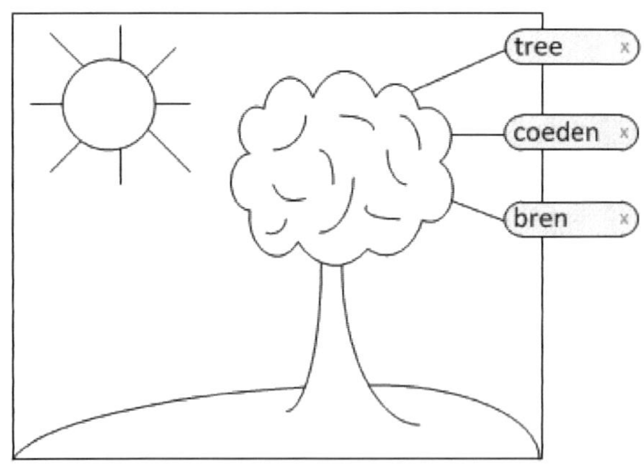

Figure 1 - Annotating objects in an image

Multimedia is usually annotated in one language; the user's primary language, or the language commonly used by a community of users. Regardless of the language used, an open social media platform may index these annotations in a monolingual manner. There will be no simple way to index or search for an annotation by language if, for example, there is no language tag in the resource URI to explicitly identify it. Nor will it be easy to link it to other monolingual resources. These multilingual annotations are effectively mixed within a single container. Any attempt to link this data would be pot luck

[1] http://www.flickr.com/

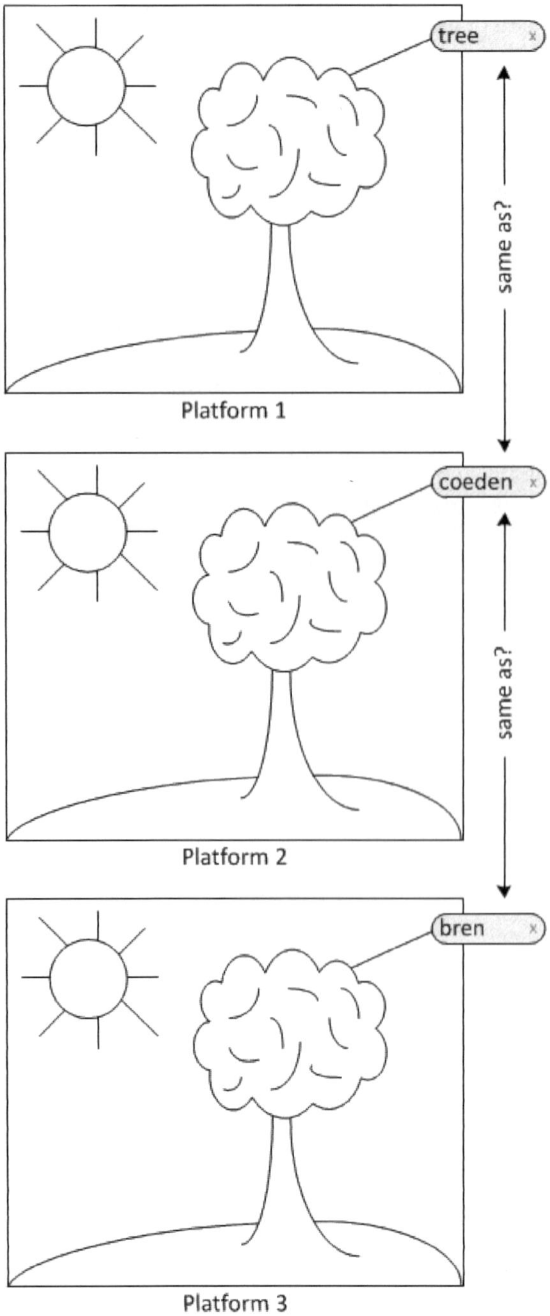

Figure 2 - Comparing cross-platform annotations of the same image

because the target language of an annotation cannot be guaranteed without the intervention of a translation. This applies equally to intra- and inter-platform environments. Gracia et al. (2012) suggest that users expect access to the Web of Data to be *intuitive, appealing, and effortless*. We believe this is also true for Linguistic Linked Open Data. Linking semantically related resources across the Web of Data *can improve the situation* (Sasaki, 2013) of, what would otherwise be, disparate linguistic platforms. The alternative is to replicate and directly adapt every annotation. This can be expensive and time-consuming. Whereas linking related media annotation utilises existing multilingual resources.

2. Related Work

There has been a considerable amount of research into the extraction of multimedia annotations, and linking them semantically with other resources (Konkova et al., 2014) (Im & Park, 2014) (Sjekavica et al., 2013) (Nogales et al., 2013) (Ballan et al., 2013) (Stegmaier et al., 2012). However, none of the studies appear to have examined the relevance of localised annotations and their impact on the Web of Data. The most recent work (Im & Park, 2014) exploited the semantic relationship between the tags of image pairs using RDF (W3C, 2004) and OWL (W3C, 2012c), whilst utilising the link analysis algorithm HITS to rank comparable annotations. They also used the Linked Open Data provider DBpedia[2] for its heuristics and ontology classes in order to provide disambiguation between tags. Their "Linked Tag" approach appears to have operated in isolation of other open social media platforms. This would have decreased the opportunity for access to resource annotations in languages other than the language used in their experiments.

On 1 November 2013, a project called LIDER[3] was set up to study Linguistic Linked Open Data (LLOD) and its applicability to multilingual and multimedia content. Among other items, its two-year mission is to provide guidelines and best practices for building and exploiting resources in this area on the Web. This paper aims to provide input to the W3C Linked Data for Language Technology[4] (LD4LT) community group. LD4LT is the front-end to LIDER, which has a remit spanning the wider linguistic linked data arena.

3. Multimedia Annotations

In this survey we made a distinction between annotations and embedded metadata. An annotation is a separate layer of information that is associated with a multimedia object, such as a keyword or note describing an image, and temporal or spatial mark-up of a video. An annotation may be created manually by a user, or automatically by a computer-based agent. Embedded multimedia metadata, on the other hand, is less subjective, providing technical attributes of the media format it represents and how it was created. However, this does not discredit the usefulness of cataloguing metadata for multimedia search and retrieval.

Multimedia annotation data is typically stored in an external resource, such as databases like the Microsoft Research Annotation System (Grudin & Bargeron, 2005), and freeDB[5]; although a limited amount of relevant information may be wrapped-up inside a media file

[2] http://dbpedia.org/
[3] http://www.lider-project.eu/
[4] http://www.w3.org/community/ld4lt/
[5] http://www.freedb.org/

container, such as a Scalable Vector Graphics (SVG) file (W3C, 2011). Self-contained annotations are portable, but they are, however, silos of information that must be extracted and stored externally if they are to be useful to the Web of Linked Data. This is because self-contained annotations require a specific content format parser to extract data for use in indexing and search etc. The use of an open media annotation format, however, makes it easier to extract and index data. Externalising self-contained annotations simplifies the process of mapping its resources into a common vocabulary, and linking it to other data. Therefore indexing, searching, and integration with other content become easier, too.

Current multimedia content description formats like MPEG-7 or ID3 ((W3C, 2012b) provides an overview) mostly do not rely on Semantic Web technologies and were developed before the Semantic Web itself was conceived (Sjekavica et al., 2014). This leads us to believe that the first hurdle to cross is the standardisation of multimedia annotation techniques. This challenge might be exaggerated when we also consider that multimedia annotation techniques in use today are essentially monolingual in nature. This isn't necessarily a concern from a linguistics standpoint, because effective internationalisation allows for the adaptation for other languages. But it does present a potential problem when examining the rest of the localisation process. During localisation, images can also be adapted. Thus objects may move or change shape, and the spoken language might change, too. One could compensate for this problem by using the Media Fragments URI specification (W3C, 2012a), which allows for the adaptation of spatial and temporal values. It is also important to provide a means for the same (or similar) resource to be linked, so that they may all be included in the wide scope of queries.

4. Ontologies and Linked Open Data Frameworks for Multimedia

Multimedia ontologies provide a formal vocabulary for the identification and arrangement of audio and visual resources. They support the semantics of images in a manner that is consistent, permitting successful storage and retrieval of multimedia properties. General ontologies like schema.org provide domain-specific areas for media. Schema.org relies on a simple taxonomic model. This can be serialised as microdata or in the linked data RDFa Lite 1.1 (W3C, 2012d) form, but lacks the expressive power of OWL ontologies, that does not go beyond subClassOf relations. It is possible, though, to generate Linked Data from microdata. Nonetheless, there has been a movement towards mapping it to the Web of Data (Nogales, Sicilia et al., 2013). Dublin Core (DCMI, 2012) is another generic ontology that describes documents. It can be applied to several models; the Resource Description Framework (RDF), and the more simplified RDF in attributes (RDFa). Dublin Core supports the multimedia types (classes) `Image`, `MovingImage`, `Sound`, and `StillImage`. Some of the properties for these classes that can be localised, such as `dc:description`, `dc:title`, and `dc:subject`.

Dedicated multimedia ontologies, on the other hand, are more conducive to describing image resources. The W3C Ontology for Media Resources (MediaONT) (W3C, 2012b) was purposefully designed with the Web of Data in mind. It provides a level of abstraction to interrelate the aforementioned, not Semantic Web based multimedia content description formats like MPEG-7 or ID3.

MediaONT is essentially monolingual in nature, pertaining to a single semantic concept per element or property. Some ontologies provide a way of identifying the natural language of the data that is applied to it. But they do not necessarily cater for data provided in multiple languages within the same property. Dublin Core and MediaONT, for example, use `Language` and `language`, respectively. The value of the language code applied to them is invariably BCP47 (IETF, 2009) or the less granular RFC-3066 (IETF, 2001) format. Since the ontologies do not directly support multiple variations within the same property, they rely upon a wrapper to contain the linguistic variations.

5. An Example: Multimedia Annotation in Flickr

Flickr is an open social media platform for sharing images and video. We selected Flickr as an example because it is a popular platform where users can apply spatial annotations to selected regions of images shared by others, as well as their own. Flickr annotations are called tags, which are heterogeneous folksonomies that mostly contain unstructured data (Concas et al., 2014). This kind of tagging requires users to interpret image contents (Konkova, Göker et al., 2014). Interpretations may be personal or biased, depending upon the users' social context and language. In addition to tags, structured Exif (CIPA, 2012) embedded metadata in the form of camera, lens, and exposure attributes may be recorded. Devices fitted with a GPS receiver may also record geospatial data in the form of longitude and latitude coordinates.

The lack of tag structure in Flickr presents a problem, in the sense that there is no ontology to which users can apply their tags. All of the terms are essentially collected in a single container or set (Marlow et al., 2006), without any form of classification. Therefore, it is unlikely that the semantic value of these tags can be determined from the relationships between images, alone. To compound this issue, many users can tag the same image with a variety of terms that have the same meaning. This becomes apparent when considering users may apply tags in different natural languages, as observed by (Allam, 2013). For example, user A tags an image of a cat with the English word "cat" and user B tags a different image of a cat in Norwegian as "katt". Since no ontology is employed, a search for "katt" will show only the images of cats that were tagged with the Norwegian term. Images that were tagged with the English term will not be shown due to this *disagreement in vocabulary* (Marlow, Naaman et al., 2006). Furthermore, images of people with the personal name "Katt" will be returned, emphasising the ambiguity that is introduced with the lack of ontological structure. Therefore localised tags are *meaningless to a global audience* (Konkova, Göker et al., 2014) if there is no facility to link heterogeneous tags.

Managing localised multimedia annotations on the Web of Data appears to be a challenge that may stem from the source of the annotations. In Flickr's case, ambiguity is introduced through the absence of ontology and language identification. There have, however, been several successful attempts to extract relationships between Flickr tags across the Web of Data. One example is LinkedTV. This was a project that presented a URI-based RESTful Linked Services Infrastructure (Nixon, 2013), which used a model for aggregating tags from Flickr, and leveraged MediaONT to classify them. They also used RDF to bridge the gap between tagged images in Flickr and the Web of Data. This allowed for the extraction of related content from other online services like YouTube[6] and Instagram[7]. However, they explicitly ignored RDF labels that were not in English. So there was a missed opportunity to utilise a Linguistic Linked Open Data source (Chiarcos et al., 2012), such as DBpedia, to extract resource URIs from relationships with other languages.

Flickr also recognises machine tags (Flickr, 2014), which are annotations with text that conforms to the syntax `namespace:predicate=value`. To carry out a search, the machine tag is appended to a Flickr URL and submitted. The `namespace` and `predicate` properties can be any term with the only restriction being that they must match the regular expression `^[a-zA-Z0-9_].*`. The value may consist of a double-quote encapsulated string containing any percent-encoded character. Both `namespace` and `predicate` are uncontrolled, so the user is free to enter whatever they like (Yee, 2008), although Flickr does offer a few suggestions. Interestingly, one of these suggestions refers to Dublin Core, using the form `dc:title=value`. This namespace, however, appeared to be rarely used. A quick experiment applied to a Web browser demonstrated this through the use of the wildcard URI `http://www.flickr.com/photos/tags/dc:title=*`. This resulted in only 78 images tagged with the title property, which is a considerably small number considering that over 580 million photos were added to the service in 2013 alone (Michael, 2014). The wildcard URI `http://www.flickr.com/photos/tags/dc:*` for the entire Dublin Core name space resulted in 132,789 images spanning 10 properties. Those properties included `dc:identifier` and `dc:author`, and `dc:subject`. It's worth noting that `dc:author` is not an authoritative Dublin Core term, which highlights the lack of control over the use of namespace and predicates.

[6] http://www.youtube.com/

[7] http://instagram.com/

The ability to annotate Flickr multimedia with machine tags, albeit unstructured and loosely controlled, does provide an open channel to resources that would be beneficial to the Web of Data. The challenge is a lack suggestion when users annotate resources. Better management of machine tags could be gained through the recognition of annotations starting with `dc:`. Users could then be presented with a choice of authoritative Dublin Core properties from which to choose. This would result in a hybrid of the "set" and "suggestive" classifications proposed by (Marlow, Naaman et al. (2006)). Of particular interest is `dc:language`, which would offer greater flexibility in matching related resources in Linguistic Linked Open Data. This feature could also be extended to the MediaONT namespace `ma:` to support several additional properties that are absent from Dublin Core, although, there is no reason why users cannot use it now. It was observed that Flickr documentation of machine tags was sparse, which may have contributed to poor adoption of the Dublin Core namespace.

6. Conclusion

We have examined the role of localisation in multimedia annotation and how annotation data relates to multimedia ontologies and Linked Open Data. The focus of our survey has been on the open social media platform called Flickr. The goal was to identify gaps in the continuity between multilingual annotated images and the Web of Linked Data. To the best of our knowledge, there has been no consideration of localisation in the multimedia annotation technologies examined in this paper. Where multimedia ontologies are present, they are not inherently multilingual. This provides an opportunity for Linguistic Linked Open Data to bridge the gap between multimedia annotation in social media and the Web of Linked Data. Linguistic Linked Open Data provides a way to semantically link annotations between languages, and also link annotations across other open social media platforms.

7. Future Work

Exposing multimedia annotations to the Web of Linked Data will increase accessibility to multilingual information, for machines and people alike. With this in mind, we would like to continue research into linking social media folksonomies across languages and across social media platforms, with a view to integrating information with Linked Open Data resources. We will consider MediaONT to formalise multimedia annotations in social media, using RDF/OWL, and investigate whether Media Fragments URI can play a role or not.

8. Acknowledgements

This research is partially supported by the European Commission as part of the LIDER project (contract number 610782) and by the Science Foundation Ireland (Grant 12/CE/I2267) as part of the CNGL Centre for Global Intelligent content (www.cngl.ie) at Trinity College Dublin.

9. References

Allam, H. (2013). Social, Technical, and Organizational Determinants of Employees' Participation in Enterprise Social Tagging Tools: A Conceptual Model and an Empirical Investigation. PhD Thesis, Dalhousie University.

Ballan, L., Bertini, M., Uricchio, T. & Del Bimbo, A. (2013). Social media annotation. In Content-Based Multimedia Indexing (CBMI), 2013 11th International Workshop on, 2013. IEEE, 229-235.

Chiarcos, C., Hellmann, S. & Nordhoff, S. (2012). Linking linguistic resources: Examples from the open linguistics working group. Linked Data in Linguistics. Springer.

Cimiano, P., Montiel-Ponsoda, E., Buitelaar, P., Espinoza, M. & Gómez-Pérez, A. (2010). A note on ontology localization. *Applied Ontology,* **5**, 127-137.

CIPA (2012). Exchangeable image file format for digital still cameras: Exif Version 2.3, December 2012. Available: http://www.cipa.jp/std/documents/e/DC-008-2012_E.pdf [Accessed 23 January 2014].

Concas, G., Pani, F. E., Lunesu, M. I. & Mannaro, K. (2014). Using an Ontology for Multimedia Content Semantics. Distributed Systems and Applications of Information Filtering and Retrieval. Springer.

DCMI (2012). DCMI Metadata Terms, 14 June 2012. Available: http://dublincore.org/documents/dcmi-terms/ [Accessed 23 January 2014].

Flickr. (2014). Flickr Tags FAQ [Online]. Available: http://www.flickr.com/help/tags/ [Accessed 02 February 2014].

Gracia, J., Montiel-Ponsoda, E., Cimiano, P., Gómez-Pérez, A., Buitelaar, P. & McCrae, J. (2012). Challenges for the multilingual web of data. *Web Semantics: Science, Services and Agents on the World Wide Web,* **11**, 63-71.

Grudin, J. & Bargeron, D. (2005). Multimedia annotation: an unsuccessful tool becomes a successful framework. *Communication and Collaboration Support Systems. TH a. TIEK Okada. Ohmsha.*

IETF (2001). Tags for the Identification of Languages, RFC 3066, January 2001. Available: http://www.ietf.org/rfc/rfc3066.txt [Accessed 14 February 2014].

IETF (2009). Tags for Identifying Languages, BCP47, September 2009. Available: http://tools.ietf.org/search/bcp47 [Accessed 14 February 2014].

Im, D.-H. & Park, G.-D. (2014). Linked tag: image annotation using semantic relationships between image tags. *Multimedia Tools and Applications*, 1-15.

Konkova, E., Göker, A., Butterworth, R. & MacFarlane, A. (2014). Social Tagging: Exploring the Image, the Tags, and the Game. *Knowledge Organization,* 41.

Marlow, C., Naaman, M., Boyd, D. & Davis, M. (2006). HT06, tagging paper, taxonomy, Flickr, academic article, to read. In Proceedings of the seventeenth conference on Hypertext and hypermedia, 2006. ACM, 31-40.

Michael, F. (2014). How many photos are uploaded to Flickr every day, month, year? [Online]. Available: http://www.flickr.com/photos/franckmichel/6855169886/ [Accessed 05 February 2014].

Nixon, L. (2013). Linked services infrastructure: a single entry point for online media related to any linked data concept. In Proceedings of the 22nd international conference on World Wide Web companion, 2013. International World Wide Web Conferences Steering Committee, 7-10.

Nogales, A., Sicilia, M.-A., García-Barriocanal, E. & Sánchez-Alonso, S. (2013). Exploring the Potential for Mapping Schema. org Microdata and the Web of Linked Data. Metadata and Semantics Research. Springer.

Sasaki, F. (2013). Metadata for the Multilingual Web. *Translation: Computation, Corpora, Cognition,* 3.

Sjekavica, T., Gledec, G. & Horvat, M. (2013). Multimedia annotation using Semantic Web technologies. In Proceedings of the 7th WSEAS European Computing Conference (ECC'13), 2013. 228-233.

Sjekavica, T., Gledec, G. & Horvat, M. (2014). Advantages of Semantic Web Technologies Usage in the Multimedia Annotation and Retrieval. *International Journal of Computers and Communications,* **8**, 41-48.

Stegmaier, F., Bailer, W., Mannens, E., Champin, P., Evain, J., Doeller, M. & Kosch, H. (2012). Unified Access to Media Metadata on the Web: Towards Interoperability Using a Core Vocabulary.

W3C (2004). Resource Description Framework (RDF), W3C Recommendation, 10 February 2004. Available: http://www.w3.org/TR/rdf-schema/ [Accessed 21 January 2014].

W3C (2011). Scalable Vector Graphics (SVG) 1.1 (Second Edition), W3C Recommendation, 16 August 2011. Available: http://www.w3.org/TR/SVG11/ [Accessed 24 January 2014].

W3C (2012a). Media Fragments URI 1.0 (basic), 22 January 2012. Available: http://www.w3.org/TR/media-frags/ [Accessed 22 January 2014].

W3C (2012b). Ontology for Media Resources 1.0, W3C Recommendation, 09 February 2012. Available: http://www.w3.org/TR/mediaont-10/ [Accessed 21 January 2014].

W3C (2012c). OWL 2 Web Ontology Language Document Overview (Second Edition), W3C Recommendation, 11 December 2012. Available: http://www.w3.org/TR/owl2-overview/ [Accessed 22 January 2014].

W3C (2012d). RDFa Lite 1.1, W3C Recommendation, 07 June 2012. Available: http://www.w3.org/TR/rdfa-lite/ [Accessed 02 February 2014].

Yee, R. (2008). Understanding Tagging and Folksonomies. *Pro Web 2.0 Mashups: Remixing Data and Web Services*, 61-75.

Towards a Linked Open Data Representation of a Grammar Terms Index

Daniel Jettka, Karim Kuropka, Cristina Vertan, Heike Zinsmeister

Universität Hamburg
Hamburg, Germany
{daniel.jettka, cristina.vertan, heike.zinsmeister}@uni-hamburg.de
karim.kuropka@studium.uni-hamburg.de

Abstract

In this paper, we report ongoing work on HyperGramm, a Linked Open Data set of German grammar terms. HyperGramm is based on a print-oriented, manually created resource containing different types of internal and external linking relations that are either explicitly marked by formatting or only implicitly encoded in the language. The initial aim of the HyperGramm resource was the on-line visualization of the terms. However, because this resource could be used in a variety of other scenarios, both for research and learning purposes, it is desirable for the representation to capture as much information as possible about the internal structure of the original resource. We first motivate the data's conversion into an intermediate, well-defined XML presentation, which serves as the basis for the RDF modeling. Subsequently, we detail the RDF model and demonstrate how it allows us to encode the internal structure and the linking mechanisms in an explicit and interoperable fashion. In addition, we discuss the possible integration of HyperGramm into the LOD Cloud.

Keywords: RDF, XML, grammar terms, German, Linguistic Linked Open Data

1. Introduction

This paper describes work in progress on the modeling of a terminological resource in an interoperable, graph-based fashion. The underlying motivation is that the hypertextualization of the existing manually created list of grammar terms would make its additional content – definitions, examples, and other types of related information – more easily accessible for users than is possible with a tabular printed version. The terms index is modeled as Linked Open Data (LOD), thus representing it in an interoperable and sustainable manner for future applications. In particular, our "HyperGramm" index offers (i) multiple perspectives on the data, including the option to start from linguistic examples that provide links to all relevant concepts, (ii) sustainable links for internal reference and to external resources, and (iii) support of multiple output formats. In this paper, we will first outline the motivation for creating the new Grammar Terms Index and describe properties of the manually created document (Section 2). The next section will detail the conversion to XML, which we argue is a relevant intermediate representation in our transformation workflow from inconsistent input to the targeted semantic representation, both because it is human-readable and editable, and also because it guarantees a high degree of consistency and generates an ideal base format for further processing (Section 3). In Section 4, we will specify our LOD model for the grammar terms, which captures internal and external links in an interoperable fashion. Finally, we conclude the paper with a brief outlook towards future work.

2. The German Grammar Terms Index

The German Grammar Terms Index is the result of a long-term collaborative effort of a group of German linguists and didacticians, including one of the co-authors of this paper (Hennig, 2012; Ossner, 2012).[1] The foundational German grammar terminology used in schools and for teacher training in Germany is based on an index recommended in 1982 by the Standing Conference of the Ministers of Education and Cultural Affairs of the Länder. The quality and consistency of this standard has been the subject of much debate ever since. The new German Grammar Terms Index has not been officially ratified, but nevertheless seeks to provide a substantial basis for an alternative to the old standard. Its current version targets teachers and teacher training. Revised versions will be created for students of various ages, and a list of core terms will be defined as a minimum standard.

The format of choice for the group developing the new index was Microsoft Word, as this was the common format with which all members of the group could work. In iterative rounds of discussion, the group identified relevant terms and created definitions with explanations and examples. The result of this conceptual work was represented in terms of thematic sublists in tabular form. In 2013, three lists (*Word*, *Simple Clause*, *Complex Sentence*) with about 170 term entries were published online as PDF documents. Additional lists will be published in 2014.

When these lists were used in university seminars on German grammar, it was discovered that they were not easy to work with, due to their bulky format. It became evident that the lists must be hypertextualized in order to make their content more easily accessible. Another motivation for creating an online searchable version of the index was to make the group's efforts more visible in the community, thereby helping to establish the index as the basis for a new standard over the long run.

Before we explain the conversion into a structured XML format and the RDF modeling, we will briefly introduce

[1] `http://www.grammatischeterminologie.de/` [All URLs in this paper were last retrieved in April 2014].

the structure of the term entries. The table in Appendix A depicts a complete (very short) sample entry, exemplifying the seven-column structure and the referential properties of the entry.

The **term name** is displayed together with its index number, e.g., *4.3 Intensitätspartikel* 'intensity particle'. Under **other common names** for the concept, we present established labels in linguistics and in the teacher-training community that are dispreferred in the terms index. The **definition** briefly defines the concept. Often, this includes references to other terms in the index (marked by '→'). The **explanations** are illustrated by examples that are listed in the **examples** column. The crucial parts of the example strings are set in bold and are referenced by numbers in parentheses, e.g., '(1)'. **Problem solving** details the detection process by means of tests that help to identify the concept in texts. Finally, **comments** complement the characterization of the term. The comments are structured in a variety of types: motivation, further information, other opinions, and borderline cases. They may also introduce additional examples.

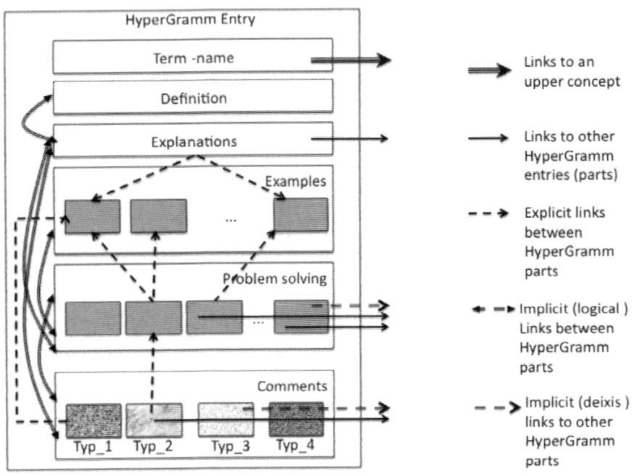

Figure 1: Logical structure of a HyperGramm entry.

Figure 1 depicts the logical structure of the entry more abstractly, in a format that ultimately serves as the basis for the HyperGramm realization. In addition to explicitly marked links (e.g., '→' and '(1)'), there are also text-deictic links (such as 'see above'), as well as implicit links that are only encoded in the table structure in the sense that the explanations explain the current definition, and the problem solving and comments are logically associated with the current definition and explanation. Links to an "upper concept" are also only implicitly encoded in the original file (in the form of the term's index number).

3. Preparation of the Semi-structured Data

3.1. WORD to XML conversion

In the first step towards creating an LOD representation for the German Grammar Terms Index, measures had to be taken to ensure the consistency of the underlying data. For this purpose, a machine-processable but human-readable XML format was defined using an XML schema (cf. Appendix B). This allowed the automatic validation of the underlying data, but still facilitated further manual correction and editing. The format reflects the hierarchical structure and to some extent the referential structure that is more or less explicitly present in the organization and textual content of the Word tables. Before converting Word's XML export format into the intermediate XML format, some manual corrections had to be made in order to rectify obvious inconsistencies in the data. Many of these would otherwise have led to unnecessary errors in the later validation of the generated XML.

A minor issue that could largely be dealt with automatically was the inconsistent use of whitespaces between term numbers and term names, term reference arrows and the immediately following names of referenced terms, and at the beginnings and ends of paragraphs within the table's cells. More glaring inconsistencies included references to terms where abbreviations such as *vgl.* ('cf.') and *s.* or *siehe* ('see') had been inserted instead of a leading arrow. Because abbreviations like these were also used for other types of references (e.g., text-deictic or external), because not all strings after reference arrows directly matched existing term names, and because different kinds of arrow characters were used to signal term references, a manual check was necessary. In addition, we had to address certain minor inconsistencies concerning the formatting of examples to obtain a data set that was as consistent as possible.

3.2. Inferring hierarchical structure and internal linking mechanisms

The conversion of the tables into the intermediate XML format involved the automatic annotation of the term hierarchy and the links between certain parts of the grammar terms. Because the hierarchical structure is indicated by the term index numbers, it was possible to automatically identify and annotate parent-child relations between terms using XML attributes and the ID/IDREF mechanism; e.g., the term numbered '4.3' could be annotated as having the parent/super-term numbered '4'.

In addition, a simple algorithm was used to resolve references to terms from within the textual content indicated by a leading arrow character. On the basis of a generated list of all existing terms (including an ID for each individual term), in most cases it was possible to map the text directly following the arrow to the corresponding term name and create a link to the corresponding term.

A similar approach was applied to identify and resolve references to individual examples. In a first step, the examples were automatically identified and assigned IDs consisting of the corresponding term name and the number of the example. In the textual content, references to examples are signaled by strings such as '(2)', '(3-5)', and '(1, 3-6)'. These could be located using a simple regular expression; they were then linked to the existing examples.

However, these automatic processes exhibited certain limitations:

- When term index numbers were incorrect or inconsistent (e.g., the same number was used twice or the wrong number format was used), the corresponding term could not be located in the term hierarchy.

- Some term references could not be resolved automatically because the reference text did not clearly indicate the referenced term.
- Some example references could not be resolved because the example did not exist in the data, or there was a problem identifying and annotating the example correctly.

Problems like these were easily identified by validating the transformed XML document; afterwards, they had to be corrected manually. Other important phenomena, such as references to external entities (e.g., *siehe §58, 3.2 ARW*)[2] and text-deictic references (e.g., *siehe oben* 'see above') were covered by the automatic preprocessing of the data. However, these played a crucial role in creating a valuable LOD resource, an issue that will be addressed in the next section.

4. Towards LOD Conversion

The tree structure behind the XML representation described in Section 3 cannot capture all of the explicit and implicit connections between the different parts of a HyperGramm entry, nor can it show references between two or more HyperGramm entries.
As introduced in Section 2, the initial aim of the HyperGramm resource was the on-line visualization of the terms. However, this resource could potentially be used in a variety of other scenarios, both for research and learning purposes. Thus, it is desirable for the representation to capture as much information as possible about the internal connections. A "hard-core" approach might entail the introduction of attributes within the relevant XML elements, allowing us to simulate references and confer a URI to each element. Such an approach would transform the rather transparent tree structure of the resource into a complicated, unlabeled graph that would be difficult to integrate into or connect with other resources.
The Semantic Web Layer Cake (Berners-Lee et al., 2001) offers the possibility to built two additional layers on top of the XML representations: the resource modeling by means of RDF triples, and the ontological representation of the RDF labels within these triples by means of OWL. This representation enables not only a transparent and meaningful description of the resource, but also its connection with other open resources.
The Linked Open Data (LOD) movement intends to make use of such three-layer cakes (XML, RDF, and OWL) to enable data publishing and querying over the Internet. This requires the modeling of the new resource to follow certain principles (Berners-Lee, 2007):

1. Existent vocabularies should be used as much as possible.
2. Each new label should be well documented as an RDF triple and have its own URI.
3. The access to the resource must be provided via HTTP.

[2] Amtliches Regelwerk vom Rat für deutsche Rechtschreibung – Official Spelling Rules of the Council for German Orthography: `http://rechtschreibrat.ids-mannheim.de/download/regeln2006.pdf`.

Linguistic Linked Open Data is a recent development that seeks to enable access to various linguistic resources by providing them in the form of LODs. As described in Chiarcos et al. (2013), the first step in modeling a linguistic resource as an LOD is to represent its structure as a directed labeled graph. Furthermore, one must select existent RDF vocabularies that correspond to the labels of the directed graph. In Section 4.1, we describe the graph-modeling of the HyperGramm resource; in Section 4.2, we list and explain the RDF vocabularies that are adequate for our resource.

4.1. RDF representation

The model we describe in this section is depicted in Figure 2. For reasons of readability, we did not include in this representation the `DataTypeProperty` "hasID", which is obligatory for each class. IDs will be represented as URIs compliant with the LOD representation principles described above.

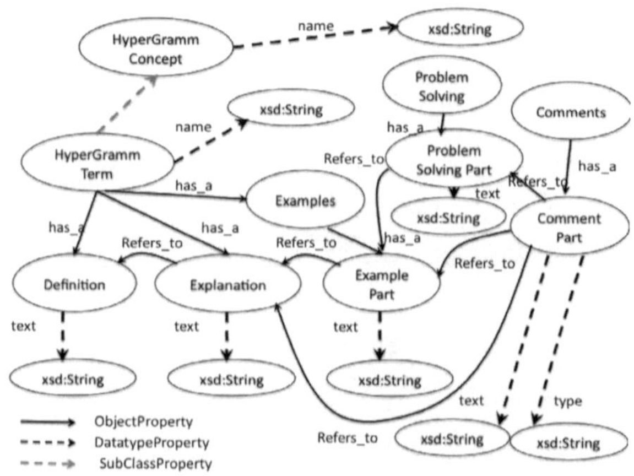

Figure 2: Conceptual representation of HyperGramm terms.

The main differences between this representation and the strictly hierarchical structure depicted in Figure 1 are:

1. The component parts of a HyperGramm term are no longer encapsulated in it, but instead act as independent classes related to the term by an `ObjectProperty` relation `has_a`. In this way, each `Example Part`, `Problem Solving Part`, or `Comment Part` can be addressed via its URI.
2. Through the `ObjectProperty Refers_to`, it is possible that, e.g., a `Comment Part` will refer to one or more `Example Parts` of the same term or from different terms.
3. Links between parts are specified (labeled).

In a second step, we intend to further refine the `ObjectProperty Refers_to` by means of subproperties:

1. `refersToSameTerm`
2. `refersToDifferentTerm`
3. `refersImplicit`

Consequently, this modeling allows complex queries across data, such as identifying all terms for which one example is relevant

4.2. LOD and linking with other data sets

Two aspects should be differentiated here: (i) suitable available vocabularies that will be involved in the data representation, and (ii) existing linguistic LOD sets that could be linked with the HyperGramm data set.
With respect to the first issue, at this stage of the representation, we have selected DC[3], RDF-Schema[4], OWL[5], and SKOS[6], as shown in Table 1.

Scope	Example	Vocabulary
Metadata for the resource	`creator`	DC
Concept hierarchies	`subClassOf`	RDF-Schema
Relation types or classes	`ObjectProperty, Class`	OWL
Specific conceptualization	`Concept, hasTopConcept, definition`	SKOS

Table 1: Examples of vocabularies used for the representation of HyperGramm.

The Linguistic LOD Cloud[7] offers a good overview of the available linguistic resources. We should mention once again that HyperGramm is a resource describing linguistic terminology and not a linguistically annotated data set. Thus, there are four types of links that can be exploited:

1. Links with other descriptive LOD data sets: isocat, OliA
2. Links with linguistically annotated resources in German that include terms for HyperGramm: Leipzig Corpora Collection
3. Links at the word level, i.e., words appearing in examples in HyperGramm that could be linked to words in DBpedia-de or the Leipzig Corpora Collection
4. Links to multilingual collections; this would link HyperGramm to similar collections for other languages and make contrastive queries possible: World Atlas of Language Structures (WALS)

5. Conclusion and Future Work

In this paper, we have presented ongoing work on the development of HyperGramm, a Linguistic LOD set based on the German Grammar Terms Index (a linguistic resource that is currently available in print-oriented formats). We motivated the first step of the conversion of the existing Word format into a well-defined XML structure, described its limitations, and presented the RDF modeling that will allow us to publish the terms set as LOD. In addition, we introduced the vocabularies used for the LOD representation, as well as the possible integration of HyperGramm into the LOD Cloud. HyperGramm is currently a German-language resource, but integration with similar resources in other languages is possible; this will facilitate contrastive analyses of grammar terms (e.g., to what extent a noun in German is similar to a noun in Dutch or Italian. In the future, HyperGramm will be hosted by the Institut für Deutsche Sprache (IDS),[8] where it will be integrated into the IDS's grammar information platform "grammis2.0".[9] This platform already hosts a number of grammar resources, including another grammar terms index created in a separate IDS project. However, our new resource is more comprehensive and specifically targets teachers and teacher training. Future efforts will be required to relate the newly integrated teacher training-oriented terms to the existing grammis2.0 resources. We also envisage a link with the ontology available at IDS.

6. Acknowledgements

We would like to thank Claire Bacher for improving the English. All remaining errors are ours.

7. References

T. Berners-Lee, J. Hendler, and O. Lassila. 2001. The Semantic Web: A new form of Web content that is meaningful to computers will unleash a revolution of new possibilities. *Scientific American*, 284(5):34–43.

T. Berners-Lee. 2007. Linked Data: Design Issues. http://www.w3.org/DesignIssues/LinkedData.html.

C. Chiarcos, J. McCrae, and C. Fellbaum. 2013. Towards Open Data for Linguistics: Linguistic Linked Data. http://www.lemon-model.net/papers/open-data-for-linguistics.pdf.

M. Hennig. 2012. Grammatische Terminologie. Einladung zur Diskussion. *Zeitschrift für Germanistische Linguistik*, 40:443–450.

J. Ossner. 2012. Grammatische Terminologie in der Schule. Einladung zur Diskussion. *Didaktik Deutsch*, 32:111–127.

[3] `http://dublincore.org/`
[4] `http://www.w3.org/RDF/`
[5] `http://www.w3.org/2001/sw/wiki/OWL`
[6] `http://www.w3.org/2004/02/skos/`
[7] `http://linguistics.okfn.org/resources/llod/`
[8] `http://www1.ids-mannheim.de/gra/schulgramm-terminologie.html`
[9] `http://hypermedia.ids-mannheim.de`

Appendix A: Sample term entry in the original list

Terminus 'term'	**Andere gebräuchliche Termini** 'other common terms'	**Definition** 'definition'	**Erläuterung** 'explanations'	**Beispiele** 'examples'	**Problemlöseverfahren** 'problem solving'	**Kommentare** 'comments'
4.3 Intensitätspartikel	Gradpartikel Steigerungspartikel	Intensitätspartikeln bestimmen den Grad der durch ein → Adjektv bezeichneten Eigenschaft	Intensitätspartikeln können eine Eigenschaft verstärken (1) oder abschwächen (2). Die Abschwächung kann sich auch auf eine durch ein Adjektiv bezeichnete Menge beziehen (3).	(1) Das Konzert war **sehr/ besonders/ voll/ irre** gut. (2) Das Konzert war **einigermaßen/ ziemlich/ etwas** gut. (3) Wir brauchen **etwa** drei Kilo Zucker.	Verstärkende Intensitätspartikeln sind immer durch *sehr*, abschwächende durch *nicht sehr* ersetzbar	**Weiterführendes** Intensitätspartikeln können sich auch auf einige → Adverbien und → Verben beziehen: (4) ***So** allein hat er sich lange nicht gefühlt.* (5) *Peter hat **sehr** getrauert.*
'intensity particle'	'degree particle enhancement particle'	'Intensity particles determine the degree of a property denoted by an → adjective.'	'Intensity particles can strengthen (1) or weaken (2) a property. The weakening can also refer to a set denoted by the adjective (3).'	'(1) The concert was very/ particularly/... good. (2) The concert was somewhat/... good. (3) We need about three kilos of sugar.'	'Strengthening intensity particles can always be replaced by very, weakening particles by not very.'	'Further information: Intensity particles can also be associated with some → adverbs and → verbs: (4) *He had not felt this lonely for a long time.* (5) *Peter had grieved deeply.*'

Table 2: Sample entry of term *Intensitätspartikel* 'intensity particle' in the original list (with English translations).

Appendix B: Excerpt from the XML schema for the intermediate XML format

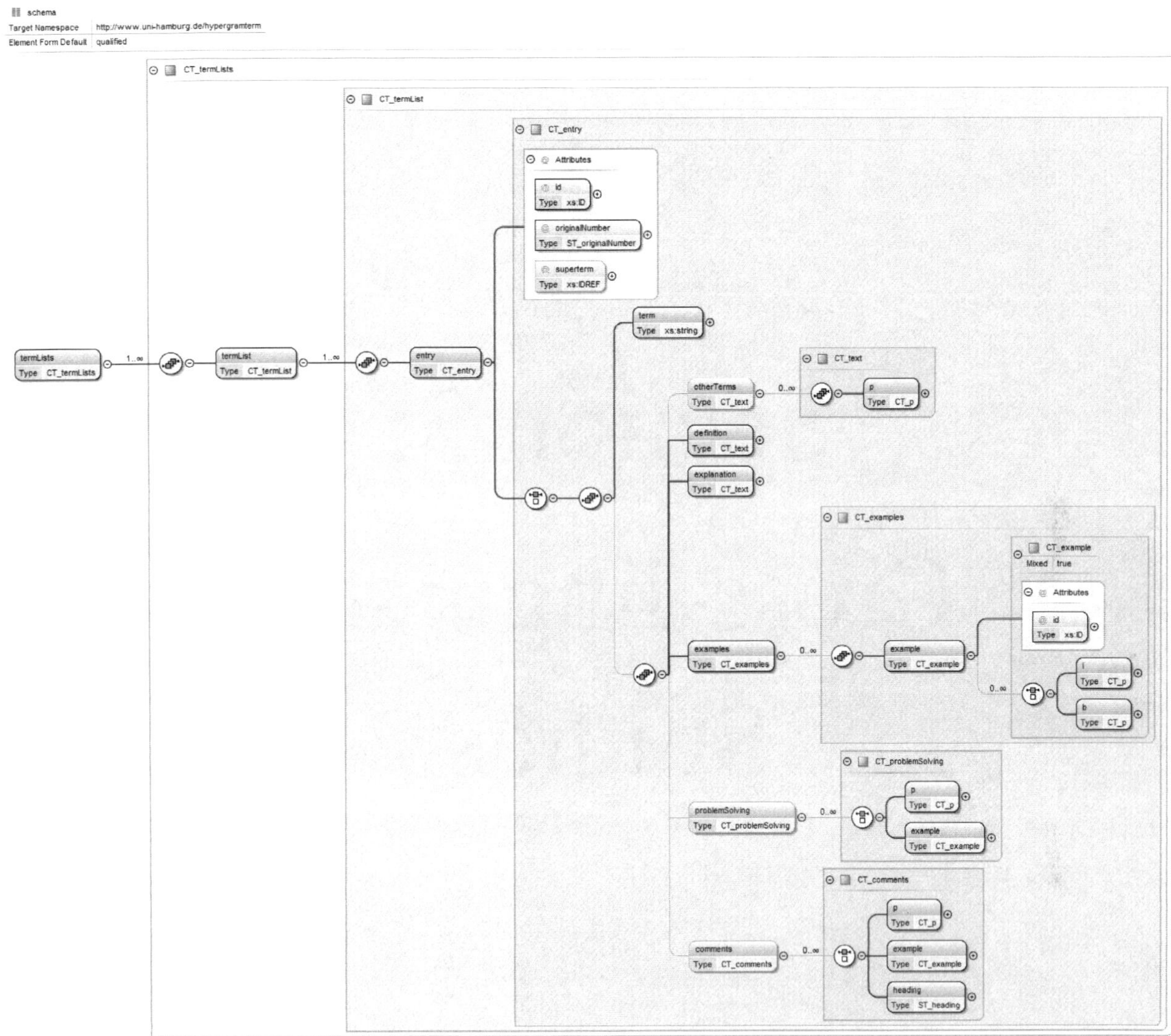

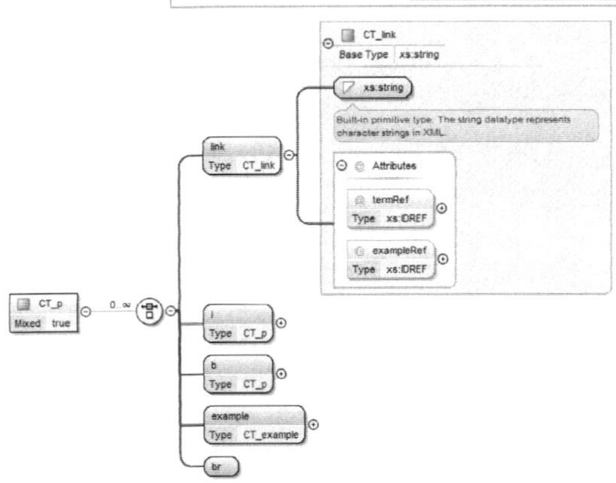

Section 3: Cross-linguistic Studies

Linking Etymological Databases. A Case Study in Germanic

Christian Chiarcos and Maria Sukhareva

Goethe-Universität Frankfurt am Main, Germany
{chiarcos|sukharev}@em.uni-frankfurt.de

Abstract

This paper deals with resources for the study of older Germanic languages that are currently developed at the Goethe-Universität Frankfurt am Main, Germany. Here, we focus on etymological dictionaries that provide explicit information about diachronic phonological correspondences between lexemes at different language stages. We present pilot studies on (a) their modeling in RDF, (b) their linking with other resources, and (c) possible applications of the resulting resource.
To our best knowledge, this data represents the first attempt to bring together etymological databases with the world of (Linguistic) Linked Open Data. This is surprising, as the application of the Linked Data paradigm in this domain is particularly promising, as the basic nature of etymology involves cross-references between different language-specific dictionaries.

Keywords: Linked Data, etymology, Germanic, *lemon*

1. Background

The Goethe Universität Frankfurt has been a center for the digitally supported study of historical and comparative linguistics in Germany, particularly with respect to Indo-European languages. A noticeable early resource established in this context is the 'Thesaurus of Indo-European Text and Language Materials' (Gippert, 2011, TITUS), a database providing digital editions of texts in old Germanic, other Indo-European and selected non-Indo-European languages since already 25 years.[1]
The 'Old German Reference Corpus' (Mittmann, 2013) is a subsequent project (2009-2014) in cooperation between the Humboldt University Berlin and the universities of Frankfurt and Jena, conducted in the wider context of a national initiative aiming to provide deeply-annotated reference corpora of all historical stages of German. The Old German Reference Corpus comprises all preserved texts from the oldest stages Old High German and Old Saxon, dating from ca. 750 to 1050 CE, with a total of 650,000 tokens, annotated for (hyper)lemmas, morphosyntax, inflectional morphology and shallow syntax, further augmented with metadata and published via the ANNIS database (Linde and Mittmann, 2013).
Several projects in the LOEWE cluster 'Digital Humanities' (2011-2014)[2] complement these efforts by creating additional resources for Germanic (and other) languages, including the conversion of a dataset of etymological dictionaries, previously available in PDF only, to XML and the development of a database prototype to query this data in a user-friendly fashion (Price, 2012).[3]
The resulting dataset comprises etymological dictionaries for Old Saxon (**OS**), Old High German (**OHG**), Old English (**OE**), Gothic (**Got**), Old Norse (**ON**), Old Frisian (**OFr**), Old Low Franconian (**OLF**), Proto-Germanic (**PGmc**); also Proto-Indo-European (**PIE**) and represents the basis for our pilot study to model a etymological database in a Linked Data compliant way: Section 2. describes the conversion of the dictionaries to RDF; Sect. 3. describes the linking with two other data sets, translational dictionaries automatically constructed from parallel text in older Germanic languages, and an RDF edition of German and English Wiktionary.
Finally, Sect. 4. sketches case studies on how this data can be used in NLP-supported research in Digital Humanities.

[1]http://titus.uni-frankfurt.de/

[2]http://www.digital-humanities-hessen.de

[3]Along with the etymological dictionaries, lexicons and glossaries for Old High German and Old Saxon have been digitized and prepared for a database edition in the Old German Reference Corpus project and further enriched within LOEWE. But as we will not receive copyright clearance for redistributing this data, we focus on this data in our conversion studies.

2. Linked Etymological Dictionaries

Etymological dictionaries aim to provide information on the evolution of words and their meaning, their origin and development. They are thus characterized by a heavy linkage across different languages, so that etymological lexicons for different languages are very likely to refer to the same protoforms, and thus complement each other. RDF provides the means to represent cross-language links using a uniform formalism, and subsequently, to facilitate information aggregation over multiple etymological lexicons as well as language-specific lexical resources. Applying the Linked Data paradigm (Bizer et al., 2009) to etymological lexicons is thus particularly promising.
In this section, we describe an experimental RDF conversion of a set of interlinked etymological dictionaries. These dictionaries are already available with rich XML markup, concept-oriented and machine-readable, but a document-centered representation. As opposed to this, a Linked Data edition provides a data-centered view on the information delivered by the etymological dictionaries, and our use of established vocabularies also provides an interoperable representation of the *semantics* of the markup.
Aside for studies in historical linguistics, philology and history, we consider such a machine-readable representation particularly relevant for developing algorithms in Natural Language Processing that *exploit* diachronic relatedness between different languages in order to facilitate their

analysis. Examples from Digital Humanities research on older West Germanic languages are given in Sect. 4..
The RDF conversion follows the three main objectives:

linkability The existing XML representation of the etymological dictionaries is optimized for document-centered search using XPath and XQuery. However, as these lexicons complement each other, it would be desirable to provide explicit cross-references between these entries, and to allow them to be queried efficiently. Within the RDF data model, the relations within and beyond a single lexicon can be represented and queried with equal ease, surmounting constraints imposed by the tree-based XML data model.

interoperability Instead of resource-specific abbreviations for languages and grammatical categories, we represent linguistic information and meta data by reference to community-maintained vocabularies publicly available as part of the (Linguistic) Linked Open Data cloud, namely lexvo (de Melo, 2013, ISO 639-3 language codes), Glottolog (Nordhoff and Hammarström, 2011, language families) and OLiA (Chiarcos, 2008, linguistic categories). Reusing vocabularies shared among many parties over the Web of Data has the advantage that resources dealing with related phenomena in the same language can be easily identified and their information integrated without additional conversion steps.

inference XML representation was created as a faithful representation of the original PDF document, augmented with markup for relevant linguistic features. These documents, however, provided complementary information, so that, say, a lexicon entry in the OS dictionary provided a reference to an etymological corresponding OHG entry, but this reference was not found in the OHG dictionary. Such gaps can be easily detected (and filled) through symmetric closure in the RDF data model.

2.1. Lexicon Data

As mentioned above, the LOEWE cluster 'Digital Humanities' provided us with an XML version of Gerhard Köbler's etymological dictionaries of Germanic languages (Tab. 1, first row).[4] Price (2012) describes the conversion of the original PDF data to an XML representation, resolving cross-references and publishing the results via an XML database. Further, a web interface had been developed that provides user-friendly means of comparing etymologically related forms between historical dialects and their daughter languages: Queries are transformed into XQuery, run against the database and the results conveniently visualized using XSLT. Eventually, a platform was created that allows philologists and historical linguists to search, browse and visualize the content of the etymological dictionaries in a convenient and intuitive way.
The XML version of the etymological dictionaries is illustrated in Fig. 1. It should be noted that the markup was

[4]See http://www.koeblergerhard.de/ahdwbhin.html. Although more advanced etymological dictionaries do exist, this data is particularly suitable for technological pilot experiments as described here, as it is the *only* machine-readable data set of its kind that is available for the Germanic languages at the moment.

Table 1: Statistics on the etymological dictionaries, see Sect. 1. for abbreviations

	West Germanic					other		reconstr.	
lexicon	OE	OHG	OS	OLF	OFr	ON	Got	PGmc	PIE
entries (XML, in K)									
	25	24	9	2	13	12	5	9	7
triples (RDF, in M)									
	1.2	1.6	.6	.2	.6	.7	.4	.2	.2
lemon:Words & links (in K)									
OE	25					1			
OHG	2	26	7	2	3	1			
OS	1	4	9	1	2	1			
ON	1				1	14			
Got	1	1			1	1	6		
PGmc	5	3	3	1	2	4	2	8	
PIE	2	1	1	1	1	1	1		8
German	16	23	8	4	10	12	7	6	3
English		10	4	2	5		9		2
symmetric closure of etym. links (triples *per lang.* in K)									
	+11	+14	+11	+5	+9	+8	+5	+21	+9
links to (L)LOD data sets (triples *per data set* in K)									
OLiA	24	22	8	2	12	11	5	8	7
lexvo	132	186	82	21	68	82	49	14	15
Glottolog	15	11	8	3	7	11	6	9	13

```
<Entry>
 <HEADWORD>                        <!-- lexical entry -->
  <LEMMA>sweltan</LEMMA> <morph>swel-t-an</morph>,
  <LANG>ae.</LANG>,  <pos>st. V. (3b)</pos>:
 </HEADWORD>
 <TRANSLATION>                      <!-- German gloss -->
  <LANG>nhd.</LANG>
  <LOOKUP lang='nhd.'>sterben</LOOKUP>,   (...)
 </TRANSLATION>
 <sub type="ÜG.">         <!-- translation glosses -->
  <LANG>lat.</LANG>
  <LOOKUP lang='lat.'>interire</LOOKUP>,
  <LOOKUP lang='lat.'>mori</LOOKUP> (...)
 </sub>   (...)
 <sub type="E.">                        <!-- etymology -->
  <LANG>germ.</LANG>
  *<LOOKUP lang='germ.'>sweltan</LOOKUP>,
  <pos>st. V.</pos>,
  <LOOKUP lang='nhd.'>sterben</LOOKUP>; (...)
 </sub>
 <sub type="L.">                       <!-- literature -->
  <lit>Hh 335, Hall/Meritt 330b, Lehnert 198b</lit>
 </sub>
</Entry>
```

Figure 1: Partial lexical entry from the XML version of the Old English dictionary

added to the original text. The mapping of content elements was almost exhaustive, although certain pieces of information, e.g., explicitly marking a form as a reconstruction (* in front of a word) was not captured in the markup. The XML markup was developed specifically for these dictionaries, and designed to be easily interpretable for speakers of German, hence, the use of conventional abbreviations such as ÜG 'translational gloss' (*Übersetzungsglosse*). However, XML does not provide us with the means to formalize the (language-independent) meaning of such tags, which is one motivation to investigate alternative, and more interoperable means of representation in a machine-readable way. Linked Data and its potential to re-use existing vocabularies represent one possibility.

```
# lexical entry
wen:WktEN_lexicalEntry_100154 a lemon:LexicalEntry
 #  sense
  lemon:sense wen:WktEN_sense_158899;
 #  form
  lemon:canonicalForm wenLE100154:CanonicalForm.
# form
wenLE100154:CanonicalForm a lemon:Form;
  lemon:writtenRep "swelt"@en.
# sense
wen:WktEN_sense_158899> a lemon:LexicalSense;

# sense definition
  lemon:definition :Statement1.

# sense definition for "swelt"
:Statement1 a lemon:SenseDefinition;
  uby:statementType "etymology";
  lemon:value "(obsolete) To die."@en;
  lemon:value "Old English sweltan."@en.
```

Figure 2: Partial information on English "swelt" in the English Wiktionary part of lemonUby

2.2. State of the Art

At the moment, we are not aware of any publicly available data set representing an RDF edition of an existing etymological dictionary. Related efforts do exist, of course, most noteably the publicly accessible linked etymologies of Starostin's portal.[5] This data is, however, distributed in a proprietary database format, and hence, neither capable of being reliably referred to from the web, nor being trivially processable independently from its original technical infrastructure.

Also, Brill's Indo-European Etymolological Dictionaries Online[6] seem to be comparable in intent, as they do not just provide a digital edition of printed dictionaries, but also cross-references across these. However, a machine-readable interface to the database is not available, and commercial interests contradict any prospects of having this data published in an LOD-compliant way within the next, say, 25 years.

Hence, the only available dataset comparable in structure, scope and origin can be found in Linked Data editions of community-maintained digital dictionaries, most noteable, the different language-specific Wiktionaries. Although this is not the focus of a general-purpose dictionary, several Wiktionaries also provide occasional information on etymology. A fragment of an entry from the lemonUby edition of the English Wiktionary (Eckle-Kohler et al., to appear) is given in Fig. 2. It is formalized in accordance to *lemon*, the *LExicon Model For ONtologies* (McCrae et al., 2011), an established vocabulary to represent machine-readable lexicons by using Semantic Web standards.

lemon has been developed as an interchange format for publishing machine-readable lexical resources. It is not restricted to the data model of a specific lexical resource, but aims at giving an opportunity to represent and publish multiple models (McCrae et al., 2012). Consequently, it became a widely accepted representation formalism for machine-readable lexicons in RDF, it is actively developed by a W3C community group, and can be considered as a counterpart for the Lexical Markup Framework (LMF) (Eckle-Kohler et al., 2013) in the RDF world. LMF was developed with primary emphasis on XML representations, and an RDF adaptation of LMF represents the historical origin of *lemon*. For an RDF representation of etymological dictionaries, it is thus the most likely point to start with. However, in lemonUby, etymological information is not given in a machine-readable way, but hidden in string values (Fig. 2). Hence, developing a specialized vocabulary to formalize this information is required.

2.3. Converting the Etymological Dictionaries

Based on the XML representation of the Köbler etymological dictionaries, we show how conversion into *lemon* format assist to creation of a useful, interoperable and machine-readable resource and, even more, we present an approach that can be applied to further etymological datasets, which may form the basis for a massively interlinked etymological datasets in the future LLOD cloud.

We began our experiment with an in-depth study of *lemon* core,[7] using Protégé as a standard tool for ontology browsing. As indicated by Fig. 2, *lemon* currently covers the mapping of lexical decomposition, phrase structure, syntax, variation, morphology, and lexicon-ontology mapping, but not etymology. In the following, extensions with respect to etymological dictionaries are assigned the namespace `lemonet`.

We focused on identifying a minimal subset of concepts and relations that could be applied for our purpose. The fine-grained distinction between `lemon:LexicalSense` and `lemon:SenseDefinition`, for example, is well-suited for resources such as WordNet that provides word senses as a pre-defined datatype. However, this is not the case for a resource structured like classical print editions of etymological dictionaries, with independent traditions rooting deep in the 19th century. In an etymological dictionary, we only find glosses, often extended by clarifying comments.

An even more important difference between classical machine-readable dictionaries and etymological dictionaries is the strong focus on *forms* rather than *senses*. In particular, etymological relations only exist on the formal level, whereas relations between senses are established indirectly through reference to forms that stand in a particular relationship (e.g., diachronic identity).

At the same time, we are dealing with historical texts, with partially deficient, or at least diverging orthographies. In an etymological dictionary, these are usually normalized, but this normalization does not necessarily distinguish homophones consistently. For Middle Low German (MLG), for example, long *o* and long *e* represent both a broad variety of vowels and diphthongs that were clearly different in earlier language stages (Old Saxon), but also in modern language (Modern Low German) – nevertheless, the standard MLG orthography did not distinguish them (regional orthographies or individual writers may have done so, however).

Accordingly, we face a great number of homographs (which may or may not be homophones), often distinguished by different definition numbers. As these

[5] `http://starling.rinet.ru`

[6] `http://iedo.brillonline.nl/dictionaries`

[7] `http://lemon-model.net/lemon.rdf`

homographs may be homophones, at the same time, we decided not to identify them with `lemon:LexicalSense`, but rather to distinguish them on the level of `lemon:LexicalEntrys`, or, more precisely, `lemon:Words` (a subclass of `lemon:LexicalEntry`). Where multiple homographs exist, these are distinguished by definition numbers, and if this was the case, one `lemon:Word` per number was created, in addition with a `lemon:Word` that represents all homophones as a group. In this way, cross-references to forms from another language can be resolved even if no definition number is provided. A subproperty of `lemon:lexicalVariant` is used to link every homograph with the `lemon:Word` that represents a group of homonyms.[8]

To represent the language of a form, we used `lemon:language` with string arguments. This was necessary because we wanted to preserve the original language abbreviations (including any typos and variants) for later reference. That `lemon:language` is not applicable to `lemon:LexicalSense` was another reason not to (ab)use the latter for distinguishing homographs.

For intra-language links, we used `lemon:lexicalVariant`, without distinguishing, however, which kind of variation this pertained to. For links between languages, we introduced the relation `lemonet:etym` as a subproperty of `lexicalVariant`. A typical entry in an etymological dictionary merely lists etymologically related forms for an entry without systematically providing structured information about historical relationships; `lemonet:etym` is thus undirected and can thus be interpreted as symmetric (and transitive). Both relations were directly derived from the XML representation; where additional information on the relation between two forms was given as a textual comment in the original PDF, for example, was not represented in the XML and hence not taken into consideration for the RDF conversion. Accordingly, the RDF representation abstracts away many aspects captured in unstructured text as part of the original XML.

To achieve a compact representation with minimal overhead, we were aiming to provide a structure as flat as possible. Without a formal model of word senses from the original dictionaries, we treat the glosses provided, again, as `lemon:LexicalEntrys`, and introduced `lemonet:translates` as a relation between both entries. Of course, this specific aspect needs to be refined in subsequent research. For the moment, however, it also accommodates another purpose, namely that of translational equivalence provided by historical glossaries. Substantial parts of older Germanic languages are known through glosses that indigenous writers added to Latin manuscripts. The Köbler dictionaries partially provide this information, so that historical explanations can

```
<http://purl.org/acoli/lex/koebler/ang#sweltan>
  a lemon:Word ;                    #       OE "sweltan"
  lemon:language "ae."@deu ;  #       orig. abbrev.
  lexvo:language <http://lexvo.org/id/iso639-3/ang> ;
                              #    -> language URI
  lemonet:hasPos "st. V. (3b)" ; # orig. gramm. feats
  a olia:Verb ;                     #   -> word class URI
  lemonet:hasMorph "swel-t-an".  #   orig. morphology

# cross-references to German (deu), (Proto-)Germanic
# (germ1287) and form
<http://purl.org/acoli/lex/koebler/ang#sweltan>
  lemonet:translates koebler_deu:sterben ; # ->   deu
  lemonet:etym koebler_germ1287:sweltan;    # germ1287
  lemon:lexicalForm _:node18eltqeccx119402.#  -> form

_:node18eltqeccx119402 a lemon:Form ;       #     form
                   lemon:representation "sweltan"@ang .
```

Figure 3: Partial representation of OE "sweltan" in the RDF conversion of the etymological dictionaries

be treated like modern glosses (for which the Latin glosses may be the only source).

Each of the original XML files was converted separately, but a unified naming scheme was applied: URIs for lexical entries were formed with a common prefix, then a language tag, then the form. Where a numbered definition was referenced (for homographs), the numerical id was added. Hence, wherever a specific form is mentioned, we generate the same URI to identify it. In this way, textual cross-references were automatically converted into RDF links.

For the moment, other links than those between the resulting RDF graphs are limited to references to vocabularies for metadata and linguistic terminology. We extracted all language identifiers, and by a hand-crafted mapping from the original abbreviations, we assigned ISO 639-3 codes wherever possible. These are represented with `lexvo:language`. For language URIs, we employed lexvo (de Melo, 2013). Unfortunately, many abbreviations could not be resolved against lexvo, in particular, this included hypothetical forms for reconstructed historical language stages, e.g., Proto-Germanic. For these, etymological dictionaries represent the main body of data, so their technical support is currently weak. In typology and language documentation, more fine-grained language taxonomies have been developed, most notably Glottlog (Nordhoff and Hammarström, 2011). These do, however, not compensate this lack, because they are focusing on language *data* – reconstructed forms are generally unattested. In this case, Glottolog identifiers for the language families whose hypothetical origin is the reconstructed language under consideration was used, instead. This mapping is, however, imprecise, and the extension of existing terminologies with respect to historical language stages would be a great desideratum. In addition, the etymological dictionaries provide rudimentary grammatical information. In a similar fashion, these abbreviations were mapped to the Ontologies of Linguistic Annotation (Chiarcos, 2008, OLiA) using hand-crafted rules. The degree of variability among these abbreviations was, however, substantially greater than for language codes, and partially implicit (e.g., where only an inflection class was provided, which allows the specialist to infer word class, gender, etc.). Therefore, only the 1000 most frequent abbreviations were taken into consideration.

[8]To distinguish homonymy and homography in the dictionaries is extremely complicated, also because the dictionaries operate on an idealized orthography, where, in reality, different graphical representations could have been applicable, too. Hence, not every dictionary homograph actually *is* a homograph in the documents. Hence, we chose the more frequently used `homonym` as relation label. This notion of homonymy is, however, much less-well defined than 'homonymy' in general use.

The morphological segmentation shown in Fig. 1 was included as an opaque string via `lemonet:hasMorph`, a subproperty of `lemon:value`.

2.4. Results

The results of this conversion are summarized in Tab. 1. In the original XML (first row), every entry corresponds to a lemma of the language under consideration, with different etymologies (and/or senses) being associated with it. In RDF (second row), each of these homographs (together with its definition number) is defined as a `lemon:Word` with a homonymy relation with the homonym set (represented by a `lemon:Word` *without* definition number). The number of `lemon:Words` is thus slightly higher than the number of entries in the original dictionaries. Differently from the XML, however, information from different data sets can be easily aggregated, and triples originating from one document can be complemented with triples from another, shown here for the symmetric closure of etymological relations (third row) that can be easily generated using a simple SPARQL pattern like `CONSTRUCT { ?o ?p ?s } WHERE {?s ?p ?o}`. In Sect. 4., we describe an application of these dictionaries where parallel phrases in quasi-parallel (freely translated) text are to be spotted. One of the factors considered there is the presence of a link between two forms in the etymological dictionary. Here, the symmetric closure of etymological links from etymological dictionaries dedicated to different languages yields a substantial extension of coverage (Tab. 1, third row).

The last row shows links to other data sets from the (Linguistic) Linked Open Data cloud. Most original lexicon entries had grammatical information using different (and not fully consistent) abbreviations. For the most frequent abbreviations used, a link to the corresponding OLiA concept was generated. The grammatical specifications are thus *interoperable* beyond the lexicons and can be compared, e.g., with those of lexical-semantic resources for Modern German and English compiled by Eckle-Kohler et al. (to appear). Similarly, language abbreviations were mapped to ISO 639-3 codes (in lexvo), or, where these were not available, to Glottolog. Unfortunately, fine-grained language codes for historical language stages, especially, reconstructed languages, are available from neither of these resources, so that a link to the corresponding language family (provided by Glottolog) was used instead.

3. Extending and Enriching the Etymological Database

Etymological dictionaries provide information about diachronic counterparts of related words from different languages – etymological relatedness is established, however, primarily on phonological grounds (albeit constrained by semantic plausibility). Hence, etymological dictionaries tend to focus on the linguistic *form*, and neglect the *function* of the lexemes. (There are glosses, of course, but rarely examples.) To address this gap, we compiled an additional set of dictionaries based on *translation equivalence* in parallel text (Sect. 3.1.), and link these with the etymological dictionaries (Sect. 3.2.). In addition, we investigate the linking of the etymological dictionaries with the English and German Wiktionary (Sect. 3.3.).

3.1. Compiling and modeling translational dictionaries

The basis for this experiment is a corpus of parallel biblical texts from most historical stages of all Germanic languages. Using standard techniques for statistical word alignment, we compiled bilingual word lists, modeled them analogously to the etymological dictionaries and linked them with these. The resulting data set is published under a CC-BY license, see `http://datahub.io/dataset/germlex`.

Since about two years, we are in the process of compiling a massive parallel corpus of modern and historical language stages for all Germanic languages, mostly consisting of biblical text. This data is intended for experiments on annotation projection and the study of diachronic differences in syntax and phonology (orthography) – both for studies in the humanities (philology, historical linguistics) and the development of NLP algorithms exploiting diachronic relatedness. As an intermediate result of this research, we compiled multi-lingual word lists of translation equivalents. Bible data represents the majority of parallel data available for historical Germanic languages, and for the case of Old Saxon and Old High German, gospel harmonies represent even the majority of data currently known. Hence, we began compiling a corpus of Bible texts, excerpts and fragments for all Germanic languages marked up with IDs for verse (if possible), chapter and books. To represent the data, we employed an XML version of the CES-scheme developed by (Resnik et al., 1997). Having outgrown the scale of Resnik's earlier project by far, we are currently in transition to state-of-the-art TEI XML. At the moment, 105 texts with about 47M tokens have already been processed (Tab. 2). Copyright prevents redistributing most of this data under a free or an academic license, but we share extraction and conversion scripts we used. Except for automatically parsed Bibles in modern English, German and Swedish, and data drawn from the Old German Reference Corpus, the texts in this collection are not annotated. Where partial annotations are available from other corpora, however, these were aligned with our Bibles.

A parallel corpus in for a language family with well-documented phonological and syntactic properties is a perfect testbed for experiments involving statistical word alignment that make explicit use of the parameter of diachronic relatedness. So far, we acquired statistical word alignment of most of the Germanic Bibles to their modern descendant and/or English using GIZA++ (Och and Ney, 2003) as a standard toolset for the purpose. We aim to provide alignments between all language pairs, but due to the huge amount of data, this is still in progress at the time of writing.

GIZA++ produces two files of lexical translation probabilities: conditional probabilities of $P(w_s|w_t)$ and $P(w_t|w_s)$ where w_s is a source word and w_t is a target word. These lexical translation tables serves as a basis for the extracted word lists. The quality of alignment varies depending on the language pair and the amount of parallel data (many

Table 2: Verse-aligned texts in the Germanic parallel Bible corpus (parentheses indicate marginal fragments)

	after 1800	1600-1800	1400-1600	1100-1400	before 1100
			Insular West Germanic		
English	19	3	6	4	2
Creols	4				
Scots	(6)		(1)		
Low German	5		**Continental West Germanic**		
Dutch	2	1	5		(1)
Afrikaans	3				
Frisian	1			(1)	
German	4	(19)	2	1	1
dialects	3				
Yiddish	1				
Danish	1		**North & East Germanic**		
Swedish	3		(1)		
Bokmål	2				
Nynorsk	2				
Icelandic	1		1		
Faroese	1				
Norn		(2)			
Gothic					1
tokens	33M	3.1M	9.3M	1.1M	190K

Table 3: Selected translational dictionaries extracted from parallel Bibles

language pairs			entries with filter	
			>1	>5
Old High German	vs.	Latin	1772	714
Old English		Gothic	6372	4530
	vs.	German	10878	5865
		Early Modern High German	3495	1266
English		Dutch	9270	3803
	vs.	Middle English	1076	443
		Middle Icelandic	1184	446
		Early Modern High German	3369	1304

older Germanic languages are fragmentary attested, only). To eliminate possible outliers, we eliminated all hapax legomena from the alignment table (filter >1 in Tab. 3).

However, manual inspection showed that even words with higher frequencies were occasionally mis-aligned, so that in the second setting, we pruned the word list from all entries with frequencies less or equal than 5. At the moment, translational dictionaries for unidirectional probability table $P(w_t|w_s)$ have been compiled, with sensible results for most language pairs. A more rigid pruning, and thus, more reliable results can be achieved by limiting the result set to bidirectionally maximally probable word pairs ($P(w_t|w_s) \cdot P(w_s|w_t)$). These lists are being compiled at the moment, we do expect, however, that the gain in accuracy is accompanied by a substantial loss of coverage.

The conversion of the translational dictionaries follows the modeling of the Köbler dictionaries (Sect. 2.3.), we convert the extracted translational equivalent word pairs into the *lemon*. As shown in Fig. 4, `lemon:Words` here are linked by `lemonet:translates`.

```
germlex_ang:sweltan a lemon:Word;
  rdfs:label "sweltan"@ang ;
  lemon:language "ang" ;
  lexvo:language <http://lexvo.org/id/iso639-3/ang> ;
  lemonet:translates germlex_eng:die ;
  lemon:lexicalForm _:nodeE3B049A4C1 .

_:nodeE3B049A4C1 a lemon:Form ;
  lemon:representation "sweltan"@ang .
```

Figure 4: Old English “sweltan” in the Old English/Modern English translational dictionary

3.2. Linking translational and etymological dictionaries

The word lists we compiled from parallel text can be used in applications in a similar way as the etymological dictionaries (Sect. 4.). Nevertheless, there are important differences between both data sets:

quality the etymological dictionaries were manually compiled, the translational dictionaries are error-prone

depth the etymological dictionaries are augmented with rich grammatical information

lexical coverage the etymological dictionaries are compiled from the literature and thus, relatively exhaustive, the translational dictionaries are limited by our pruning algorithm

formal coverage the etymological dictionaries only contain base forms, the translational dictionaries also comprise inflected forms

language coverage the etymological dictionaries provide links between selected language pairs only, translational dictionaries can be built for any language pair. In particular, this includes language stages not attested in the Köbler dictionaries but available in our corpus.

availability at the moment, the licensing conditions for the etymological dictionaries are still being clarified, the translational dictionaries can be redistributed under an open license

Accordingly, both resources complement each other, and to exploit prospective synergies, we developed a simple linking based on a mapping between `LexicalEntrys`: For every `LexicalEntry` in the translational dictionary, we created a link to a Köbler `LexicalEntry` if an identical `lemon:representation` can be found. As homography cannot be resolved on the side of the translational dictionaries, we employ `rdfs:seeAlso`. In a qualitative evaluation, we are currently investigating whether these can be replaced by `owl:sameAs`.

3.3. Linking Wiktionary

Although the lemonUby editions of German and English Wiktionary currently available from the LLOD cloud lack formalized etymological information, a linking with our dictionaries can be performed.
We linked the Old English Köbler dictionary with the English Wiktionary and the Old High German dictionary with the German Wiktionary using the following heuristics:

```
germlex_ang:sweltan
  rdfs:seeAlso koebler_ang:sweltan ,
<http://.../WktEN_lexicalEntry_100154> .
```

Figure 5: Linking OE "sweltan"

(i) For every `lemon:Statement` in the Wiktionaries, whose `lemon:values` contain the String 'Old English' (resp. '[Aa]lthochdeutsch'), extract the following word as a hypothetical Old English (resp. Old High German) lexeme.

(ii) Normalize the hypothetical lexeme according to manually defined rules.

(iii) If this lexeme is found as a `lemon:representation` in the etymological dictionary, create an `rdfs:seeAlso` link between both `LexicalEntrys`.

As a result, we established 189 links for Old English and 117 for Old High German for the Köbler dictionaries. Although this is a marginal fraction only of both Wiktionary and the etymological data, it complements the etymological dictionaries with elaborate descriptions of etymologically related modern forms in the same way as it complements Wiktionary with formal etymologies previously expressed in unstructured text, only.
Fig. 5 shows the linking of Old English `sweltan`.

4. Application: Aligning quasiparallel text in old Germanic

Finally, we sketch a prospective application for the linked etymological database described before, i.e., the detection of corresponding phrases in quasi-parallel text.
During the middle ages, the language of lithurgy in the Germanica has been Latin, and hence, biblical texts were more often freely *retold* rather than translated. Accordingly, the majority of the data we possess are free adaptations of biblical texts, often in poetic form, and thus quasiparallel (they describe the same events, but with very different wording). For some languages, such free adaptations of Bible text represent the majority of data we possess, e.g., for Old Saxon with the *Heliand*, a gospel harmony in the form of an heroic poem. Comparing these texts with their biblical sources is a field of research in historical and comparative linguistics,[9] philology,[10] history,[11] or theology.
For such studies, it is necessary to identify corresponding passages in the different versions. As an example, we compare the OS Heliand with an OHG gospel harmony, a translation of an earlier work of *Tatian the Assyrian*.
Although not direct translations of the Bible and hence not directly alignable with the gospel translations we have for Old English, Gothic, and later stages of English, German, Dutch and North Germanic, a thorough, qualitative comparison between these texts has been conducted and a section-level alignment of Tatian and Heliand has been manually extrapolated from the literature (Price, 2012). While Tatian is indeed verse-alignable with the Bible, the situation for OS is complicated by the fact that only a thematical alignment of Heliand with Tatian and the gospels could be established.
We thus investigate parallel phrase detection between Heliand and Tatian, to refine the existing section-level alignment, with an NLP-supported identification of comparable verse groups. We explore different types of similarity metrics for every Old Saxon word w_{OS} and its potential Old High German cognate w_{OHG}. Over a web interface, a user (linguist, historian or philologist) can manually combine these metrics in a formula and evaluate whether it fits his needs. (We expect different user groups to have different criteria.) In subsequent studies, different algorithms to combine individual features will be explored.
Old Saxon and Old High German are genetically closely related, and thus, two important groups of features to identify cognate phrases include *etymological links* and *character substitution probabilities*:

lexicon-based $\delta_{lex}(w_{OS}, w_{OHG}) = 1$ iff $w_{OHG} \in W$ (0 otherwise) where W is a set of possible OHG translations for w_{OS} suggested by a lexicon, i.e., either

- **etym** linked by (the symmetric closure of) `lemonet:etym`
- **etym-indirect** transitive-symmetric closure of `lemonet:etym`
- **translational** linked by `lemonet:translates`
- **translational-indirect** indirectly linked by `lemonet:translates` through a third language

character-based similarity measure based on character replacement likelihood:

- **statistical** character replacement probability as approximated by a character-based statistical machine translation system (Neubig et al., 2012), trained on lemmas connected by `lemonet:etym`
- **weighted Levenshtein-distance** $\delta_{norm}(w_{OS}, w_{OHG}) = \delta_i(w'_{OS}, w_{OHG})$, with w'_{OS} being the OHG 'normalization' of the original w_{OS}. Here, normalization uses a weighted Levenshtein distance, trained on lemmas drawn from `lemonet:etym`, and a fixed list of OHG target words (Bollmann et al., 2011)

For any two thematically aligned OS and OHG word vectors, we thus span up a similarity matrix between both word vectors on the basis of these metrics. On the matrices, different operations can be applied to calculate similarity derived metrics, including point-wise multiplication or addition, thresholds and a smoothing operator, that aligns words

[9] Research question: Which constructions/lexemes are applied under comparable circumstances?

[10] Research question: How did the different texts/traditions influence each other?

[11] Research question: Which elements of the original text have been maintained or altered, and what does conclusions about society and ideology of the intended audience can be drawn from these alterations?

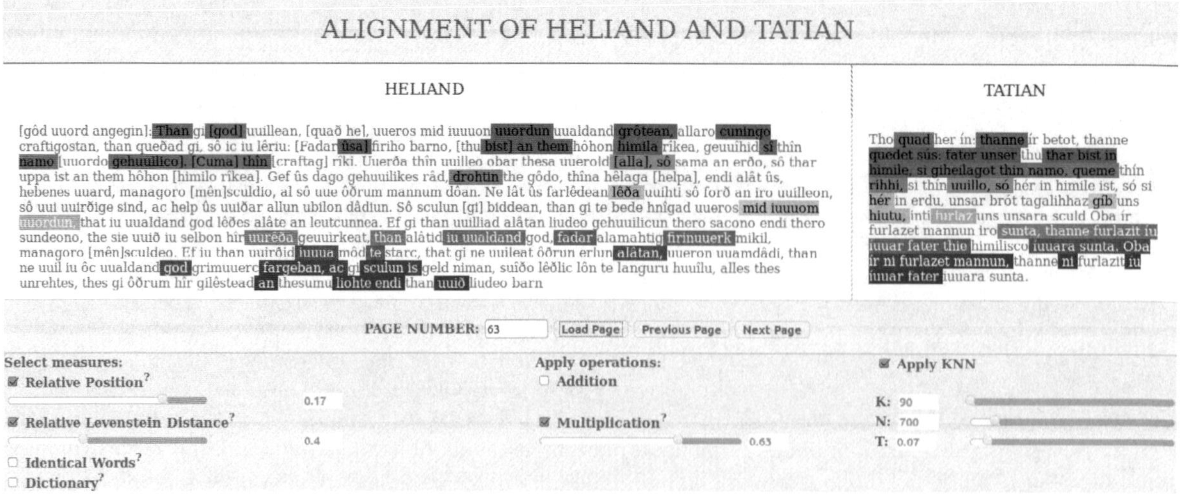

Figure 6: Visualization and fine-tuning of parallel segment detection metrics for OS and OHG Tatian

due to the similarity of its neighbors. The resulting matrix is decoded by a greedy algorithm that aligns the words with the highest score, and then iterates for the remaining words. At the moment, we provide a graphical interface over a webpage that allows a philologist to dynamically define an alignment function and that provides a graphical visualization of the result (Fig. 6).

A partial qualitative evaluation by historical linguists indicates that the best results can be achieved by combining multiple metrics, with lexicon- and normalization-based approaches being particularly successful. Extending these metrics with positional alignment criteria appears to be particularly promising. Systematic experiments to automatically explore this feature space being prepared at the moment, they depend on the availability of a gold alignment for selected verses that is currently being produced.

5. Discussion

In the last years, the RDF and Linked Data got in the focus of the language resource community, and the vision of a Linguistic Linked Open Data (LLOD) cloud began to emerge (Chiarcos et al., 2012). As the RDF format is not only very flexible in terms of information type presented, it also opens the potential of universal data representation in a machine readable way that offers a convenient way of data integration, the number of resources that use RDF is constantly increasing.

Here, we described the application of the Linked Data paradigm to the modeling of etymological dictionaries for the older Germanic languages, a particularly promising field of application due to its abundance of cross-language links that have direct ties to language-specific lexical-semantic resources. As a basis, we adopted *lemon* core, and identified two properties that were necessary for the specifics of our data, i.e., `etym` (as subproperties of `lemon:lexicalVariant`), and `translates`. In addition, `hasMorph` and `hasPos` were introduced as subproperties of `lemon:value` to include string representations of grammatical features and morphological analysis. In subsequent studies, these should be replaced by *lemon*-conformant representations.

With these minor adjustments, the Köbler dictionaries could be modeled in *lemon* and successfully linked with other resources. We also described a prospective application of this data in parallel phrase detection. Here, etymological links can be employed (along with translational equivalence) to identify corresponding words. Moreover, they provide training data for alignment approaches that emulate phonological change, e.g., in normalization-based alignment models.

An interesting feature of the RDF modeling is that the symmetric closure of unidirectional etymological links in the dictionary can be obtained through a simple SPARQL statement which yields an improvement in coverage over the original XML documents. Moreover, by representing etymological dictionaries, translational dictionaries, and lexical-semantic resources for modern languages in RDF, and linking them, it is possible to extend queries beyond individual resources (e.g., an etymological dictionary for English) and query across multiple etymological resources at the same time, thereby facilitating easy information aggregation.

We aim to make our data available under an open license. For the Köbler dictionaries themselves, the license terms of the original data allow us only to make these lexical resources available among the LOEWE cluster 'Digital Humanities' and its collaborators. However, the original compiler of the dictionary himself provides an openly accessible web version of his data,[12] and we are currently in contact to figure out details with respect to licensing and distribution of our version, possibly under a similar modus operandi. The translational dictionaries and their Wiktionary links available under a CC-BY license (see `http://datahub.io/dataset/germlex`).

[12] `http://www.koeblergerhard.de/wikiling/`

6. References

Christian Bizer, Tom Heath, and Tim Berners-Lee. 2009. Linked Data – The story so far. *International Journal on Semantic Web and Information Systems (IJSWIS)*, 5(3):1–22.

Marcel Bollmann, Florian Petran, and Stefanie Dipper. 2011. Rule-based normalization of historical texts. In *Proceedings of the Workshop on Language Technologies for Digital Humanities and Cultural Heritage*, pages 34–42, Hissar, Bulgaria, September.

Christian Chiarcos, Sebastian Nordhoff, and Sebastian Hellmann, editors. 2012. *Linked Data in Linguistics. Representing Language Data and Metadata*. Springer, Heidelberg. companion volume of the Workshop on Linked Data in Linguistics 2012 (LDL-2012), held in conjunction with the 34th Annual Meeting of the German Linguistic Society (DGfS), March 2012, Frankfurt/M., Germany.

Christian Chiarcos. 2008. An ontology of linguistic annotations. *LDV Forum*, 23(1):1–16.

Gerard de Melo. 2013. Lexvo.org: Language-related information for the linguistic linked data cloud. *Semantic Web Journal*, 0(1):1–7.

Judith Eckle-Kohler, Iryna Gurevych, Silvana Hartmann, Michael Matuschek, and Christian M. Meyer. 2013. Uby-lmf – exploring the boundaries of language-independent lexicon models. In Gil Francopoulo, editor, *LMF: Lexical Markup Framework*, chapter 10, pages 145–156. London: Wiley-ISTE, March.

Judith Eckle-Kohler, John McCrae, and Christian Chiarcos. to appear. lemonUby – A large, interlinked, syntactically-rich resource for ontologies. *Semantic Web Journal: Multilingual Linked Open Data*.

Jost Gippert. 2011. The titus project. 25 years of corpus building in ancient languages, in: Perspektiven einer corpusbasierten historischen linguistik und philologie. internationale tagung des akademienvorhabens „altägyptisches wörter. In *Internationale Tagung des Akademienvorhabens "Altägyptisches Wörterbuch" an der Berlin-Brandenburgischen Akademie der Wissenschaften*, pages 169–192, Berlin, Dec.

Sonja Linde and Roland Mittmann. 2013. Old german reference corpus. digitizing the knowledge of the 19th century. In Paul Bennett, Martin Durrell, Silke Scheible, and Richard J. Whitt, editors, *New Methods in Historical Corpus Linguistics = Korpuslinguistik und interdiziplinäre Perspektiven auf Sprache – Corpus linguistics and Interdisciplinary perspectives on language (CLIP)*, volume 3 of *Korpuslinguistik und interdiziplinäre Perspektiven auf Sprache – Corpus linguistics and Interdisciplinary perspectives on language (CLIP)*, Tübingen. Narr.

John McCrae, Dennis Spohr, and Philipp Cimiano. 2011. Linking lexical resources and ontologies on the semantic web with lemon. In *The Semantic Web: Research and Applications*, pages 245–259. Springer.

John McCrae, Elena Montiel-Ponsoda, and Philipp Cimiano. 2012. Integrating wordnet and wiktionary with lemon. In *Proceedings of the Workshop on Linked Data in Linguistics 2012 (LDL-2012)*.

Roland Mittmann. 2013. Digitalisierung historischer glossare zur automatisierten vorannotation von textkorpora am beispiel des altdeutschen. In Armin Hoenen and Thomas Jügel, editors, *Altüberlieferte Sprachen als Gegenstand der Texttechnologie – Text Technological Mining of Ancient Languages = Journal for Language Technology and Computational Linguistics (JLCL)*, volume 27 [2/2012] of *Journal for Language Technology and Computational Linguistics (JLCL)*, pages 39–52, Berlin. Gesellschaft für Sprachtechnologie und Computerlinguistik (GSCL).

Graham Neubig, Taro Watanabe, Shinsuke Mori, and Tatsuya Kawahara. 2012. Machine translation without words through substring alignment. In *Proc. 50th Annual Meeting of the Association for Computational Linguistics (ACL-2012)*, pages 165–174, Jeju Island, Korea, July.

Sebastian Nordhoff and Harald Hammarström. 2011. Glottolog/langdoc: Defining dialects, languages, and language families as collections of resources. In *Proceedings of the First International Workshop on Linked Science 2011 (LISC2011)*.

Franz Josef Och and Hermann Ney. 2003. A systematic comparison of various statistical alignment models. *Computational Linguistics*, 29(1):19–51.

Timothy Blaine Price. 2012. Multi-faceted alignment: Toward automatic detection of textual similarity in gospel-derived texts. In *Proceedings of Historical Corpora 2012*, Frankfurt, Germany.

Philip Resnik, Mari Broman Olsen, and Mona Diab. 1997. Creating a parallel corpus from the book of 2000 tongues. In *Proc. of the Text Encoding Initiative 10th Anniversary User Conference (TEI-10)*.

Using *lemon* to Model Lexical Semantic Shift in Diachronic Lexical Resources

Fahad Khan, Federico Boschetti, Francesca Frontini
CNR-ILC
Pisa, Italy
{name.surname}@ilc.cnr.it

Abstract

In this paper we propose a model, called *lemonDIA*, for representing lexical semantic change using the *lemon* framework and based on the ontological notion of the perdurant. Namely we extend the notion of sense in *lemon* by adding a temporal dimension and then define a class of perdurant entities that represents a shift in meaning of a word and which contains different related senses. We start by discussing the general problem of semantic shift and the utility of being able to easily access and represent such information in diachronic lexical resources. We then describe our model and illustrate it with examples.

Keywords: lemon, linked data, OWL, ontologies, perdurants, semantic shift

1. Introduction

In this paper we propose a model for representing lexical semantic change using the *lemon* framework. More precisely, we want to be able to track the shifts in meaning undergone by the lexical entries contained in some lexical resource (or resources), and to represent and access information about these meaning shifts in an intuitive way. We will limit our focus in this paper to changes in the meanings of lexemes (although in our examples we will focus on single words only) rather than trying to deal with so called grammatical semantic change – although this is a very closely related topic, see (Hollmann, 2009) for an overview.

The lexical resources that we particularly have in mind in this paper are those that contain etymological and/or other diachronically relevant information, as well as lexica for historical languages like Latin or ancient Greek in which the different stages of the language's development have to be taken into consideration. On the other hand the ideas we discuss are also applicable to any kind of general purpose lexicon and especially for wordnets.

We will work with the *lemon* model for lexical resources using the "semantics by reference" principles defined in (Cimiano et al., 2013). We will assume, given a lexicon L, that we have access to an ontology O which provides the semantics for L. Each lexical entry l in L (or at least the lexical entries we are interested in) will be associated with one or more ontology vocabulary items c in O that serve as extensions for l. In addition in this work we will assume that there is a time interval t associated with each correspondence between an entry and a vocabulary item.

We will employ the notion of *perdurant* commonly used in ontology modelling for representing change over time, to represent the shift in meaning of a lexical entry l from an original meaning c_0. For us this process of meaning shift becomes a perdurant entity to which we can explicitly refer. A perdurant here can be thought of as an event or a process that may be composed of different temporal as well as spatial parts.

We have called our new model *lemonDIA*.

In the next section, Section 2 we discuss the general problem of semantic shift with a particular emphasis on historical languages. Then in Section 4 we present our proposed model and give examples to illustrate its use, before finally discussing ideas for further work in the conclusion.

2. Lexical Semantic Change

The meaning of words in a language can often shift quite drastically over time, sometimes even over relatively short time scales. For example until a few decades ago the adjective *gay* was used to refer to someone as 'happy' or 'carefree', whereas this meaning is no longer in common currency and the word is now primarily used to refer to someone as a homosexual. To take another example, the word *fantastic* was once used to mean that something was a product of the imagination, but now refers to something as being very positive.

Theoretical linguistic research in this area has identified a number of different typologies of semantic change, e.g., there are semantic shifts where the meaning of a word becomes more general, and others where the meaning becomes more specific. The thesis that there exists a general pattern whereby semantic changes tend to lead to words becoming less *objective* and more *subjective* (with these words being used in a special technical sense closely related to their everyday meaning), the so called process of subjectification, has also been proposed and found widespread acceptance, again see (Hollmann, 2009).

Moreover in the case of modern lexica for ancient Greek or Latin there is a clear need for tools to assist philologists and historical linguists in the study and representation of lexical semantic shift.

For example it was quite common in the ancient world, after a major change in a predominant epistemic paradigm (e.g., from pre-socratic to post-socratic) or in a governing religious or socio-cultural framework (e.g. from pagan to Christian), that terms in numerous important domains would be affected by semantic change – even if in many cases a prior general purpose meaning and a new more domain specific meaning were able to coexist for a certain period of time.

The Latin word *otium* (leisure, rest time) offers an excellent example of such a semantic shift, which in this case

occurred over several different, clearly defined, stages. The original meaning as attested in archaic texts can be understood as "the state prevailing during the absence of war", and referred to the state of leisure enjoyed by soldiers in an army camp, especially in winter.
During the classical age, the word assumed a very positive connotation and related to the absence of political duties: "time that is free from duties or responsibilities", "time available for hobbies and other activities that you enjoy" (which especially meant in this case the study of philosophy). Later in the Middle Ages, *otium* gained a double meaning. The first was positive: in the case when this "freedom from activity (work or strain or responsibility)" was devoted to God. The second was negative: when it meant "leisure time away from work devoted to rest or pleasure", and thus corresponded to the deadly sin of sloth. This latter meaning was to prevail during the medieval ages. Finally, Renaissance era Latin restored the classical meaning of *otium* according to which it meant freedom from social and political duties with the extra time instead being devoted to philosophical studies.
All of the meanings of *otium* quoted above are represented in Latin WordNet but as, we hope, the above demonstrates, there is a real need for a tool that can assist in the discovery and representation of this kind of semantic-conceptual evolution over different time periods.
Along with Latin there are currently wordnets in development for ancient Greek (Bizzoni et al., 2014) as well as for several other languages - such as Sanskrit (Kulkarni et al., 2010) - with long and well documented histories of use and for which the representation of semantic shift would be particularly useful for different groups of researchers such as historians and philologists.

3. The *lemon* model

As more and more lexical resources are added to the linguistic linked open data cloud, it becomes increasingly important to develop tools and methodologies to exploit the data contained within them. *lemon* (Mccrae et al., 2012) is currently one of the most popular models for publishing lexical resources as linked open data in RDF/OWL and so we decided to work with it as a foundation. Along with its popularity *lemon* also has a clearly defined semantics which made its use in this work even more attractive.
In the *lemon* model we can represent the relation between a lexicon L and a ontology $O = (\Lambda_0, V_0)$ whose vocabulary items provide the semantics for the lexical entries in L using sense objects as follows. Each lexical entry l is related to a vocabulary item $c \in V_0$ via a (reified) sense object $s = \sigma^{(l,c)}$ if there exists evidence for a use of l in which it can be taken to mean c. We represent this state of affairs using the `sense` and `reference` relations as defined in *lemon*: `sense`(l, s), `reference`(s, c).
lemon does make provision for adding temporal information to lexica by defining a property `usedSince` of *lemon* sense objects. `usedSince` is a subproperty of the *lemon* context property and allows the addition of information specifying when a term was first used in a particular sense[1].

[1]See the lemon cookbook for further details at `http://lemon-model.net/lemon-cookbook/`.

The work in the rest of this paper however explores a more extensive modelling of word sense shifts using *lemon*.

4. Using Perdurants to Model Word Senses

Let us assume that the word *punk* is an entry in our lexicon, L. Here it is taken as both a noun that from the 1970s onwards came to refer to a follower of a certain youth culture, and also as a noun that from around the 1590s until the 1700s meant a prostitute[2]. We want to be able to represent both of these meanings along with their relevant periods of use.
We will take these two meanings to correspond to two different concepts c, c', respectively, in an ontology O. Under the *lemon* semantics by reference framework we define a sense $s = \sigma^{(punk,c)}$ that represents the meaning of *punk* as c, and another sense $s' = \sigma^{(punk,c')}$ representing the meaning of *punk* as c'. In addition let t represent a time interval [1976 - Current] and t' represent the 'fuzzy' interval [1590 - ?1750] (we will mention issues relating to the representation of intervals whether qualitatively or quantitatively, i.e., without fixed endpoints, in the next subsection).
The time intervals we are working with here could represent any number of things such as the first and last attested uses of that particular meaning of a word or they could represent an educated guess as to the relevant time period in which that meaning was current. So then we would like to be able to state something like the following: $\texttt{sense}(punk, s, t)$, $\texttt{reference}(s, c)$ and $\texttt{sense}(punk, s', t')$, $\texttt{reference}(s', c')$[3].
In other words we want to make the sense relation a fluent. The question then arises, how can we model this and keep within what is broadly speaking still the *lemon* framework? An obvious solution and the one which we will pursue in the rest of this paper is to model each sense s as a perdurant, namely as an object with a time interval associated with it[4]. Then the correspondence between a lexical entry l and vocabulary entry c represented by a given *lemon* sense object has a certain time dimension representing, say, the validity of this correspondence or the time during which it was commonly in use.
Clearly adding this temporal dimension is helpful because it enables us to plot the different meanings of a word over a given time period and also to see if and when these meanings overlap. It would also be very helpful to be able to track how a specific meaning changes or evolves over a certain time period and in this case it makes sense to talk about the sense of a word, when viewed as an event or a process, as something that has different temporal parts, some of which may have different lexical references (although to

[2]For the purposes of the example we do not assume that these two meanings are related by a process of semantic shift, although this may well be the case.

[3]We could also of course add an extra argument for the reference relation instead, and model the relation between a sense and reference as varying with time; this way of modelling change over time could be handled in a similar way to the methodology we propose below.

[4]As we briefly discuss later, redefining the sense relation as a 3-place relation in OWL brings a host of problems with it.

avoid confusion with *lemon* sense objects we will refer to a sense viewed diachronically as a diachronic shift object).

For example the word *girl* originally referred to a young person of either male or female gender before shifting meaning so that it ended up referring only to young females, see (Hollmann, 2009).

So imagine that in our lexicon we have a entry $girl$ which during the interval $t1$ means "young human being" and that this class of entities is represented in our ontology by the concept c_1, and that during another, later, time interval t_2 it means "young female human being", and that this class is represented by the concept c_2 in our ontology. We want to be able to relate the senses $s_1 = \sigma^{(girl,c_1)}$ and $s_2 = \sigma^{(girl,c_2)}$ together as parts of another event 'object' representing the historical shift in meaning that took place from the word *girl* having the meaning of c_1 to its having the meaning c_2 along with other further shifts that might have also have taken place over time. In the next section we discuss how to do this using perdurants.

4.1. Perdurants, Endurants and Time Slices

When modelling fluents, i.e., relations and functions that change over time, common use is made in ontology design of the notion of a perdurant. By perdurants here we mean entities that have a temporal dimension and which we can indeed view as being composed of different temporal parts. Perdurants may have different properties which hold at some times during the time span associated with them but which do not hold at others; significantly enough, though, there will also be other, essential, properties which hold throughout the whole life span of the perdurant and by which they can be identified.

The notion of perdurant is often contrasted with the notion of an endurant by which we mean an entity that also has an associated life span but which is in some sense wholly present at each time point of its life span; so that unlike with perdurants we do not view endurants as being actually composed of different temporal segments. Another core idea which is related to that of perdurant is that of the *time slice*, which is a snapshot of a perdurant representing all (or perhaps a relevant subset) of the properties which hold of a perdurant at a given point in time.

Perdurants are a particularly popular method for representing fluents in OWL since they avoid the main pitfalls associated with the strategy of representing fluents using n-ary relations in OWL. In an influential paper (Welty and Fikes, 2006) Welty and Fikes describe these pitfalls in detail as well as laying out an approach in which all entities are represented as perdurants – although we do not pursue this approach in the current paper.

4.2. Description of the *lemonDIA* Model

Now we will give a description of *lemonDIA* our new model based on *lemon*. We define a new subclass of sense objects, so called lexical p-sense objects, which are defined similarly to normal *lemon* sense objects except that we define them as perdurants with a temporal dimension. These p-sense objects can be understood as follows.

Given a lexical entry l, an ontology vocabulary item c, and a time interval t, we propose the following criteria for determining the existence of a lexical p-sense object $s = \sigma^{(l,c,t)}$:

- We have evidence that the lexical item l was interpreted as c during the time period t.
- There exists evidence of a number of uses of the entry l being used to mean c during the time period t; and the set of these uses is represented by s.
- We are able to hypothesize the existence of a concept s giving the full lexical meaning of l when it was used to mean c during t.

Here the time intervals should be understood as being maximal in the sense that they represent the whole time interval in which l is interpreted as c.

So to return to the *punk* example we have the following `pSense`$(punk, s)$, `reference`(s, c) and `pSense`$(punk, s')$, `reference`(s', c') where the senses s, s' are now perdurants. We then add the following statements `temporalExtent`(s, t) and `temporalExtent`(s', t') where `temporalExtent` is a relation between a perdurant and its associated time span given by a time interval.

How can we model the *girl* example given above, this time explicitly modelling the shift in meaning that took place between the two senses of *girl*? This will involve the definition of a class of diachronic shift objects.

Meanings or senses, like ideas, are not three- or even four-dimensional objects: that is although a meaning can be manifested in a physical format, the meaning itself has no spatial dimensions, similarly it can be argued that meanings are in some sense timeless. However as we mentioned above meanings can be associated with temporal intervals (and also with spatial dimensions if we think in terms of the geographical regions in which the language communities occur for which these meanings are common although we do not discuss this here). We will use these temporal intervals along with the 'dimension' of meaning provided by an ontology in order to view meanings as perdurants. We can motivate this solution in a (hopefully) intuitive way as follows.

Say there exists an initial correspondence between a lexical item l with a ontology concept c_0 at time t_0 and imagine we have a graph where the x-axis represents time (the time line is represented as a real line) and the y-axis is an enumeration of the concepts in our ontology O. We can visualize meaning shift by plotting the vocabulary items $c^i_1, ...c^i_k$ at each succeeding time point t_i on the basis of whether l means c^i_j at time t_i and where these meanings are related by the process of meaning shift to the original meaning at time t_0. Let $C_{(l,c_0,t_0)}$ be the set of all such c^i_j.

It is important to emphasise that the meanings in $C_{(l,c_0,t_0)}$ all derive from the original pairing of l and c_0 by a process of historical meaning shift, but that the lexical entry l may mean other unrelated things at each of these time points, if for example the word is homonymous and the other senses are not etymologically related to the meaning of l as c. (Also we will assume in this paper that if a lexical entry l means two different but related things, that the distinction is not made between these two things in our ontology but that there is one 'closest' single vocabulary item c capturing the two meanings, we are allowed to assume these two senses are one – although this might be problematic in practice.)

In Fig 1 we give a chart representing the situation where a lexical entry has meaning c at time points $t0$ to time $t4$ and meaning c' at time $t4$ and $t5$. This chart and the succeeding one in Fig 2 are based on similar charts in (Bittner and Donnelly, 2004).

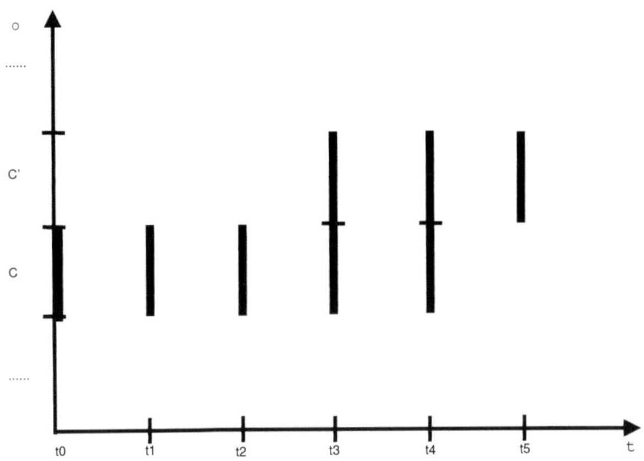

Figure 1: The meaning of a lexical entry l over time.

Taken together, at each time point t_i, the meanings c_j^i can be thought of as constituting a time slice of a perdurant object, d such that d represents the process of meaning shift of the lexical entry l with original meaning c_0.

In other words, given an ontology item $c \in C_{(l,c_0,t_0)}$ each p-sense $s = \sigma^{(l,c,t_c)}$, where t_c is the appropriate time interval, is related to d via a (perdurant) `partOf` relation (since a perdurant can have both time slices and other perdurants as parts, see (Bittner and Donnelly, 2004)); on the other hand we can think of d as the 'sum' of all the p-senses $s = \sigma^{(l,c,t_c)}$ where $c \in C_{(l,c_0,t_0)}$. We will refer to d as a diachronic shift object, for want of a better word, and use it to represent the meaning shift that words undergo over time. We will define a relation `diachronicShift` that holds between l and d.

In Fig 2 we represent the diachronic shift object for the example in the previous figure.

To return to the *girl* example, given our previous definitions we have that $\texttt{pSense}(girl, s_1)$ with $\texttt{reference}(s_1, c_1)$, $\texttt{temporalExtent}(s_1, t_1)$, and $\texttt{pSense}(girl, s_2)$ with $\texttt{reference}(s_2, c_2)$, $\texttt{temporalExtent}(s_2, t_2)$. Accordingly we can define a diachronic sense object d with $\texttt{diachronicShift}(girl, d)$ such that there exists a `partOf` relation between d and s_1 and d and s_2. In Figure 3 we represent the *girl* example with a diagram.

Note again that the diachronic shift object d captures the meaning shift of a lexical item from an initial meaning of c_0 by encompassing meanings that are related historically. The word *page*, for example, has two historically unrelated senses which we wouldn't want to include in a single diachronical sense object, at least not from an etymological point of view.

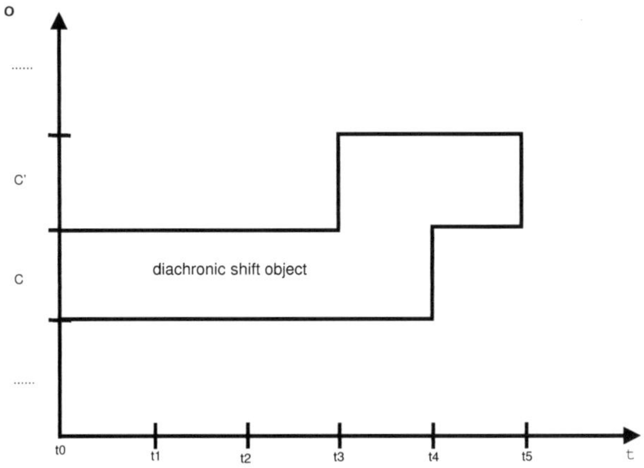

Figure 2: The meaning of a lexical entry l over time represented as a perdurant.

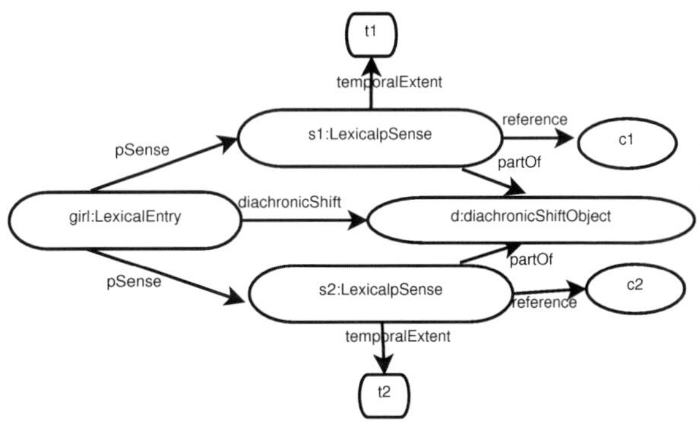

Figure 3: The *girl* example.

In Figure 4 we present a diagram of the *lemonDIA* model.

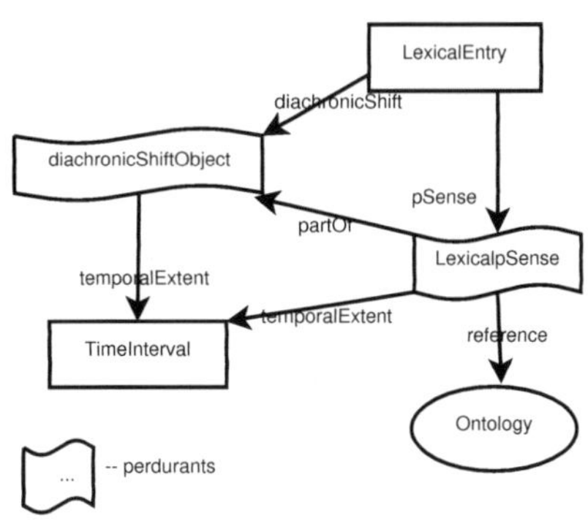

Figure 4: The *lemonDIA* model.

5. Conclusions

We have outlined a model, called *lemonDIA*, for representing lexical semantic change using the *lemon* framework and the ontological notion of the perdurant. The description of the model given above needs to be considerably fleshed out.

One of the most important issues relates to how to represent the time intervals associated with the periods corresponding to a lexical item's having a given meaning. It is often the case that due to a lack of evidence we cannot give an exact year, decade or even century specifying when a certain meaning first started to be used, nor for when it stopped being commonly used. Fortunately, there has been work done recently on representing so called qualitative time intervals, namely intervals which do not have specified start or end dates, defining relationships between them using Allen's temporal relations (e.g., Before, After, Meet), and on building reasoning tools using SWRL and special querying tools (Batsakis and Petrakis, 2011). This kind of work seems to be an important starting point for the further development of *lemonDIA*.

It would also be useful to add further properties that specify for a given time period which of the senses of a word are used predominantly, which of them are rarely used, though not yet obsolete, and which senses are at least still understood if not used. In addition it is important to be able to specify information relating to context or literary genre, especially when it comes to working with resources such as ancient Greek or Latin wordnets, where certain words may be obsolete or rarely used in one literary genre or in every day speech but still common in another.

At this stage of the development of the *lemonDIA* model these issues need to be explored in much greater depth. The most important thing of course is to see how the model works in practice, namely, when it is used on an actual lexical resource, something we have still to undertake.

6. Acknowledgements

The research in this paper was undertaken within Memorata Poetis, an Italian national project and part of the Programma di Ricerca di Rilevante Interesse Nazionale program for 2010/2011.

7. References

Batsakis, S. and Petrakis, E. (2011). Representing temporal knowledge in the semantic web: The extended 4d fluents approach. In Hatzilygeroudis, I. and Prentzas, J., editors, *Combinations of Intelligent Methods and Applications*, volume 8 of *Smart Innovation, Systems and Technologies*, pages 55–69. Springer Berlin Heidelberg.

Bittner, T. and Donnelly, M. (2004). The mereology of stages and persistent entities. In de Mántaras, R. L. and Saitta, L., editors, *ECAI*, pages 283–287. IOS Press.

Bizzoni, Y., Boschetti, F., Del Gratta, R., Diakoff, H., Monachini, M., and Crane, G. (2014). The making of Ancient Greek WordNet. In Calzolari, N., Choukri, K., Declerck, T., Loftsson, H., Maegaard, B., Mariani, J., Odijk, J., and Piperidis, S., editors, *Proceedings of the Ninth International Conference on Language Resources and Evaluation (LREC-2014), Reykjavik, Iceland, May 28-30, 2014*, Reykjavik, Iceland. European Language Resources Association (ELRA).

Cimiano, P., McCrae, J., Buitelaar, P., and Montiel-Ponsoda, E. (2013). On the role of senses in the ontology-lexicon. In *New Trends of Research in Ontologies and Lexical Resources*, pages 43–62. Springer.

Hollmann, W. B., (2009). *English language: description, variation and context*, chapter Semantic change. Basingstoke: Palgrave.

Kulkarni, M., Dangarikar, C., Kulkarni, I., Nanda, A., and Bhattacharya, P. (2010). Introducing sanskrit wordnet. In *The 5th International Conference of the Global WordNet Association (GWC-2010)*.

Mccrae, J., Aguado-De-Cea, G., Buitelaar, P., Cimiano, P., Declerck, T., Gómez-Pérez, A., Gracia, J., Hollink, L., Montiel-Ponsoda, E., Spohr, D., and Wunner, T. (2012). Interchanging lexical resources on the semantic web. *Lang. Resour. Eval.*, 46(4):701–719, December.

Welty, C. and Fikes, R. (2006). A reusable ontology for fluents in owl. In *Proceedings of the 2006 Conference on Formal Ontology in Information Systems: Proceedings of the Fourth International Conference (FOIS 2006)*, pages 226–236, Amsterdam, The Netherlands, The Netherlands. IOS Press.

Typology with graphs and matrices

Steven Moran[*†], **Michael Cysouw**[†]

[*] University of Zurich
Plattenstrasse 54, 8032 Zürich
steven.moran@uzh.ch

[†] Philipps University Marburg
Deutschhausstrasse 3, 35037 Marburg
cysouw@uni-marburg.de

Abstract

In this paper we show how the same data source can be represented in three different data formats – graphs, tables and matrices. After extracting table data from aggregated graphs data sources in the Linguistic Linked Open Data cloud, we convert these tables into numerical matrices to which we can apply mathematical formulations of linear algebra. As one example of the application of matrix algebra for language comparison, we identify clusters of association between disparate typological databases by leveraging the transformation of different data formats and Linked Data.

Keywords: linguistics, typology, language comparison

1. Introduction

In this paper we show how to access federated linguistic databases through Linked Data graphs so that we can extract data for typological analyses and then apply efficient computation for association measures through linear algebra on matrix structures to do language comparison. First we demonstrate how to leverage Semantic Web technologies to transform data in any number of typological databases, e.g. WALS (Haspelmath et al., 2008), AUTOTYP (Bickel and Nichols, 2002), PHOIBLE (Moran, 2012), ODIN (Lewis, 2006), or language-specific databases – along with metadata from Ethnologue (Lewis et al., 2013), LLMAP (LINGUIST List, 2009a), Multitree (LINGUIST List, 2009b) and Glottolog (Nordhoff et al., 2013) – into Linked Data. This is the vision of the Linguistic Linked Open Data Cloud (LLOD; (Chiarcos et al., 2012)).

Once data from these databases are converted into a homogeneous format, i.e. RDF graph data structures, the contents of these disparate datasets can be merged into one large graph, which allows for their data to be queried in a federated search fashion, in line with how we currently search the content of the Web through popular search engines. We illustrate how users can query and retrieve information about a particular language, from multiple databases, e.g. via a languages ISO 639-3 code. For example, a user might be interested in accessing all typological variables described by various databases for a particular language, e.g. word order data from WALS, genealogical information and phonological word domains from AUTOTYP, and phoneme inventory data from PHOIBLE.

Further, we show how the results of such queries can be combined and output into a matrix format that mirrors recent work in multivariate typology (cf. (Witzlack-Makarevich, 2011; Bickel, 2011a)). By outputting the results of user's queries across different databases into table-based matrix formats, the results can be directly loaded into statistical packages for statistical analyses, and published algorithms can be directly applied to them and tested, e.g. statistical sampling procedures (cf. (Cysouw, 2005)) and statistical approaches to determine universal (language) preferences, e.g. Family Bias (Bickel, 2011b). Furthermore, when typological data are output into tables, state-of-the-art approaches using linear algebra to transform matrices into new datasets can be applied (Mayer and Cysouw, 2012; Cysouw, 2014).

2. Graphs and matrices

Graphs and matrices are two representations of data that can encode the same things. We use the term *graph* in its mathematical sense, i.e. an ordered pair comprising of a set of vertices together with a set of edges, or in other words, a set of objects in which some objects are connected by links. By *table* data, we simply mean data in a table format. And by *matrix*, we mean purely numerical table data. Some illustrations will make these definitions clear.

Table 1 illustrates what we mean by table data; it provides a set of data, here observations about the last symbol in several words, where each word's class is also given.

observations	word class	last symbol
some	adjective	e
words	noun	s
as	preposition	s
example	noun	e

Table 1: Table data

If we want to transform the table data in Table 1 into a matrix, we can use numerical values to indicate the presence or absence of features, as illustrated in Table 2.[1]

[1] We provide the headers for convenience, but strictly speaking, a matrix in this work contains purely numerical data in a tabular structure.

observations	adj	noun	prep	final e	final s
some	1	0	0	1	0
words	0	1	0	0	1
as	0	0	1	0	1
example	0	1	0	1	0

Table 2: Matrix data

Table 2 can algorithmically be transformed into a graph by assigning the row and column labels as vertices and connecting them via edges for cells that have a "1". The result of this transformation is illustrated in Figure 1.

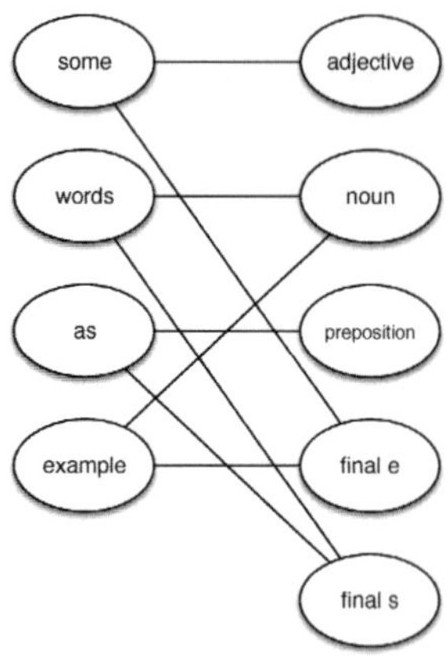

Figure 1: Matrix transformed into a graph

3. Connection to Linked Data

Linked Data refers to Semantic Web framework practices for publishing and connecting structured data.[2] Linked Data uses a graph-based model for data interchange, whereby data, specifically Web content, is connected using the Resource Description Framework (RDF), uniform resource identifiers (URIs) and content negotiation. Using graphs, anyone can describe "knowledge" in statements encoded in subject-predicate-object triples; a hypothetical example is given in Figure 2 of a concept "language" having several phonological "segment(s)".

The aims of a Semantic Web are to attain syntactic and semantic interoperability of data (cf. (Ide and Pustejovsky, 2010)). Syntactic interoperability means a consistent interpretation of exchanged data, which is achieved through graph data structures that allow for data access, aggregation and manipulation. Semantic interoperability is the ability to automatically interpret exchanged information meaningfully. Content must be unambiguously defined and is dependent on common definitions and concepts in a vocabulary or ontology. In this paper we are mainly concerned with syntactic interoperability for data aggregation and transformation.

[2]`http://linkeddata.org`

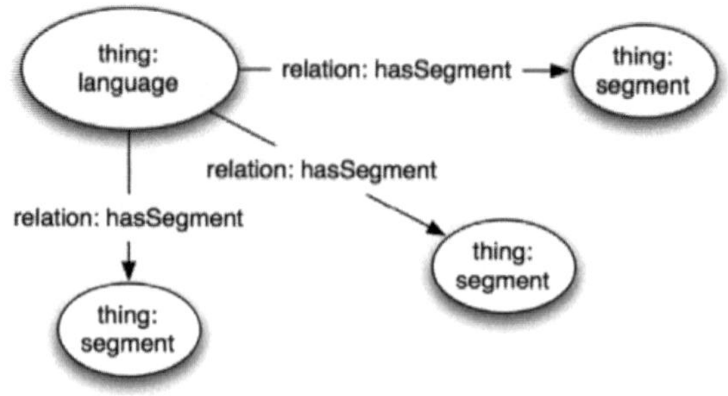

Figure 2: Linked Data example

There are several technological issues with Linked Data that are worth pointing out. First, anyone can say anything about anything, i.e. anyone can define their own naming conventions, devise their own models, etc. This is of course problematic when striving to attain semantic interoperability between resources. Another issue is the open world assumption that is built into the design of the Semantic Web. This assumption states that the truth value of a statement is independent of whether or not it is known to be true. Or in other words, not knowing whether or not a statement is explicitly true, does not imply that the statement is false. Although this stipulation is an important factor in attaining semantic interoperability of data sources, it is also directly relevant to academic research that uses Linked Data. Data as it currently stands in resources like the Linguistics Linked Open Data cloud (LLOD)[3] cloud must be problematically taken at face-value.

There are also practical problems with Linked Data, such as the difficulty to deploy, host and maintain it. Furthermore, accessing the underlying structures is not necessarily transparent (i.e. most resources, say, in the LLOD are not published with information about their underlying data models). Technology to federate queries across endpoints is still immature, so that in reality Linked Data sets typically have to be hosted on the same server.[4]

Using an endpoint, such as one set up by the Open Working Group on Open Data in Linguistics (OWLG),[5] we can query data sources already in the LLOD, such as Glottolog, WALS, PHOIBLE, Wordnet (Fellbaum, 1998), IDS (Key and Comrie, 2014), WOLD (Haspelmath and Tadmor, 2009) and Lexvo (de Melo, 2014). By querying the LLOD via an endpoint, users can extract data from disparate but connected Linked Data graphs, to get information (metadata, typological data, etc), aggregated data (e.g. extract wordlists from different lexical sources such as WOLD,

[3]`http://linguistics.okfn.org/files/2013/10/llod-colored-current.png`

[4]The SPARQL query language is the standard technique to match sets of triple patterns that match concepts and their relations by binding variables to match graph patterns. An online query service can be made accessible through the browser via a so-called SPARQL "endpoint".

[5]`http://linguistics.okfn.org/`

IDS and QuantHistLing[6]) and to contrast data from different sources, e.g. published language geo-coordinates or language genealogical classifications.
Extracting information from Linked Data graphs is as simple as the SPARQL-query given in Example 1,[7] which says 'show me all sources linked in the cloud'.[8] Some results of this query are shown in Table 3.

1.
```
select distinct ?graph
where {GRAPH ?graph {?s ?p ?o}}
```

graph
http://wiktionary-en.dbpedia.org/
http://linked-data.org/resource/wals/
http://lexvo.org/
http://linked-data.org/resource/ids/
http://quanthistling.info/lod/
http://mlode.nlp2rdf.org/resource/ids/
http://mlode.nlp2rdf.org/resource/wals/
http://wold.livingsources.org/
http://example.org/
http://wiktionary.dbpedia.org/
http://lemon-model.net/

Table 3: Some results from a simple query

Moving a step forward towards querying linguistic data, we can ask for all data sources linked in the LLOD that have information for a given WALS code (as associated with an ISO 639-3 language name identifier) with the query given in Example 2 for WALS code chr (language name Chrau; ISO 639-3 crw). Some query results are given in Table 4.

2.
```
PREFIX wals:
<http://mlode.nlp2rdf.org/
resource/wals/language/>
PREFIX dcterms:
<http://purl.org/dc/terms/>
select distinct ?relation where {
wals:chr dcterms:relation ?relation . }
```

relation
llmap.org/maps/by-code/crw.html
ethnologue.com/show_language.asp?code=crw
en.wikipedia.org/wiki/ISO_639:crw
lexvo.org/data/iso639-3/crw
sil.org/iso639-3/documentation.asp?id=crw
multitree.org/codes/crw
scriptsource.org/lang/crw
language-archives.org/language/crw
odin.linguistlist.org/igt_urls.php?lang=crw
glottolog.org/resource/languoid/id/chra1242

Table 4: Some results from an aggregated query

Digging deeper, we can extend this query so that we return all information for a given WALS code, as shown in Example 3. Example results are given in Table 5.

3.
```
PREFIX wals: <http://mlode.nlp2rdf.org/
resource/wals/language/>
PREFIX walsVocab: <http://mlode.nlp2rdf.org/
resource/wals/vocabulary/>
PREFIX wgs84: <http://www.w3.org/2003/01/geo/
wgs84_pos#>
PREFIX dcterms: <http://purl.org/dc/terms/>

select distinct ?label ?descr ?ref
?area ?lat ?long ?genus where {
?s dcterms:subject wals:chr .
?s walsVocab:hasValue ?value .
?value dcterms:description ?descr .
wals:chr wgs84:lat ?lat ;
         wgs84:long ?long ;
         ?feature ?datapoint ;
         rdfs:label ?label ;
         walsVocab:hasGenus ?genus ;
         walsVocab:altName ?name .

?datapoint dcterms:references ?ref .
?feature dcterms:isPartOf ?chapter .
?chapter walsVocab:chapterArea ?area .
}
```

The idea of federated queries across Linked Data graphs allows us to combine different data sources and not only aggregate the results, but to use information from different linked sources to filter results. In Example 4, we leverage the World Geodetic System (WGS) standard to query for language data within specific geographic coordinates, a common task and useful function in cross-linguistic investigations.

4.
```
PREFIX phoible:
<http://mlode.nlp2rdf.org/resource/phoible/>
PREFIX wgs84:
<http://www.w3.org/2003/01/geo/wgs84_pos#>
select distinct ?iso ?segRes where {
GRAPH <http://mlode.nlp2rdf.org/
resource/phoible/> {
?langRes phoible:hasSegment ?segRes;
phoible:iso639-3 ?iso;
wgs84:lat ?lat;
wgs84:long ?long.
FILTER(?lat < 12.57 && ?lat > -56.24 &&
?long > -81.57 && ?long < -34.15) }
}
```

This query returns data on information about phonological inventories, from the PHOIBLE database, for languages spoken in South America. Some results are illustrated in Table 6.

[6]http://quanthistling.info/

[7]Due to page restrictions, we will not explain the details of how to formulate SPARQL-queries here. The W3C Recommendation can be found at http://www.w3.org/TR/sparql11-overview/, but many more gentile and accessible introductions can be found online.

[8]This is a simplification because Linked Data federated queries do not yet work across disparately hosted data sources. As is, we query data sources *hosted* on a single server and accessible through an endpoint. In this work we use the endpoint hosted by Martin Brümmer: linked-data.org/sparql. There is a URL to access the LLOD's endpoint at http://llod.info, but again, hosting Linked Data sources and true federate query is difficult.

label	description	reference	area	lat	long	genus
Chrau	The language has no morphologically dedicated second-person imperatives at all	Thomas 1971	Verbal Categories	10.75	107.5	bahnaric
Chrau	Differentiation: one word denotes ‘hand’ and another, different word denotes ‘finger’ (or, very rarely, ‘fingers’)	Thomas 1971	Verbal Categories	10.75	107.5	bahnaric
Chrau	Identity: a single word denotes both ‘hand’ and ‘arm’	Thomas 1971	Verbal Categories	10.75	107.5	bahnaric

Table 5: Some results from aggregated query

iso	segRes
teh	http://mlode.nlp2rdf.org/resource/phoible/segment/j
teh	http://mlode.nlp2rdf.org/resource/phoible/segment/a
teh	http://mlode.nlp2rdf.org/resource/phoible/segment/k
teh	http://mlode.nlp2rdf.org/resource/phoible/segment/o

Table 6: Some results from aggregated query

4. Extract and convert

We have demonstrated how to extract table data from the Linked Data graph and explained how table data can be transformed into numerical matrices. An illustration is given in Figure 3, which contrasts the graph, table and matrix formats.

LLOD

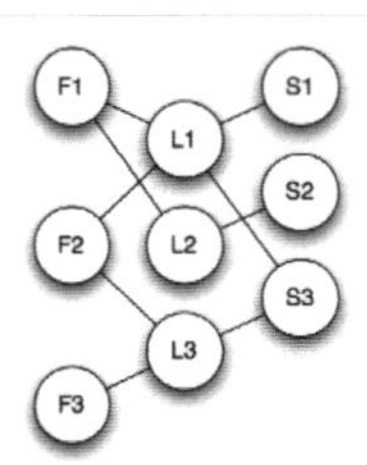

Extracted tables

L1	S1
L1	S3
L2	S2
L3	S3

L1	F1
L1	F2
L2	F1
L3	F2
L3	F3

Matrices

	S1	S2	S3
L1	1	0	1
L2	0	1	0
L3	0	0	1

	F1	F2	F3
L1	1	1	0
L2	1	0	0
L3	0	1	1

Figure 3: Toy example of a graph with the equivalent table and matrix formats. The graph has two kinds of links: between nodes of kind ‘F’ and ‘L’, and between nodes of kind ‘L’ and ‘S’. So, there are two tables with links, and two corresponding matrices.

Once graph data have been extracted into table format and transformed into numerical matrices, a straightforward transformation in statistical packages, matrix algebra calculations can be applied for the comparison of languages (Cysouw, 2014). One example of matrix manipulation is to take the dot product of two matrices, as illustrated in Figure 4. Here the transposed matrix LS (Languages by Symbols) is multiplied with the matrix LF (Languages by Features), resulting in newly derived data in the Segment by Features matrix (SF).[9] This result of this dot product represents the number of paths connecting S-nodes to F-nodes.

$LS^T \cdot LF = SF$

	S1	S2	S3
L1	1	0	1
L2	0	1	0
L3	0	0	1

	L1	L2	L3
F1	1	1	0
F2	1	0	1
F3	0	0	1

	F1	F2	F3
S1	1	1	0
S2	1	0	0
S3	1	2	1

Figure 4: Dot product

The application of linear algebra on matrices (vectors) has numerous applications across many fields, inside and outside of linguistics. The reformulation of various research methods from the field of language comparison into matrix algebra highlights many parallels across methods and we believe it promises a deeper understanding of the methodology of language comparison in general. Additionally, the available implementations of matrix algebra are highly efficient and fast. This makes computation on large datasets, like those that can be extracted from the LLOD, easier to manage and to perform. Furthermore, using matrix algebra computations can be straightforwardly formulated and explained in the form of formulas, which can both simplify instantiations in computer code as well as documentation of the research in published papers.

For example, using matrices, measures of association (similarity) can be computed. For association measures, we can compute the association between all rows of, say, matrix A and matrix B by taking the dot product of the two. Depending on the form of normalization applied, we can for example take Pearson's correlation coefficient, with or without weighting, or we can calculate Cosine similarity (Cysouw, 2014). Identifying missing data, a substantial problem in linguistics, is also relatively easy using matrices and matrix manipulations hold promise for adding data correction methods, such as normalization or estimating expected values by taking into account the distribution of missing information. All these possibilities will unfortunately take too much space here to discuss in detail.

[9]Here we use superscript <^{T}> to denote the transposed matrix.

5. Testing the approach

To exemplify our approach, we first extracted data from WALS and PHOIBLE from the LLOD.[10] There are a total of 117,279 links between WALS codes and linguistic characteristics in PHOIBLE. Extraction from the LLOD goes quick – a few seconds with a good internet connection. Transformation from the extracted tables into sparse matrices is also very fast.[11] Correlation using a weighted cosine similarity of all pairs of characteristics (3263x3263) via sparse matrix manipulation is extremely fast (0.18 sec. on a MacBook Air). The biggest problem we encounter is how to analyze such large correlation matrices in a way that makes sense to a non-mathematically inclined linguist.

We decided to try and identify major clusters of association between WALS and PHOIBLE. Using a weighted cosine similarity, we identify levels of high association between clusters of features in WALS chapters and PHOIBLE phonological inventory data. These are visualized as heat maps in Figures 5, 6 and 7.[12] The point of these figures is mainly to illustrate the possible observation of clusters. The detailed extraction of linguistically sensible clusters and their interpretation will have to wait for another paper. We will here only comment on a few possible interpretations.

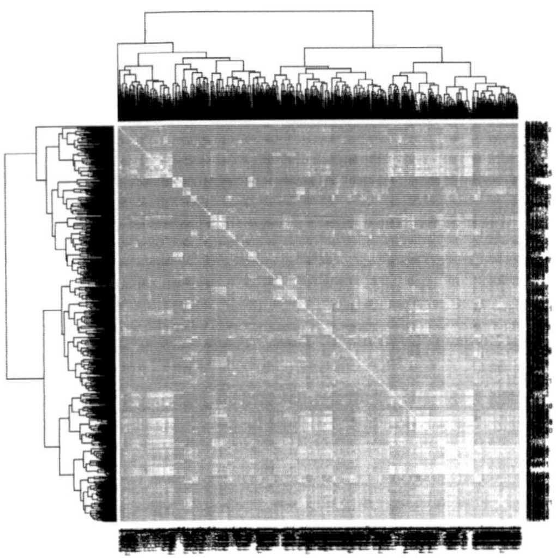

Figure 5: Heat map for all characteristics with frequency more than 10 (~1000 characteristics)

What we find are several clusters between data in WALS chapters and sets of segments from cross-linguistic phonological inventory data in PHOIBLE. For example, there are various (unsurprising) clusters of characteristics like

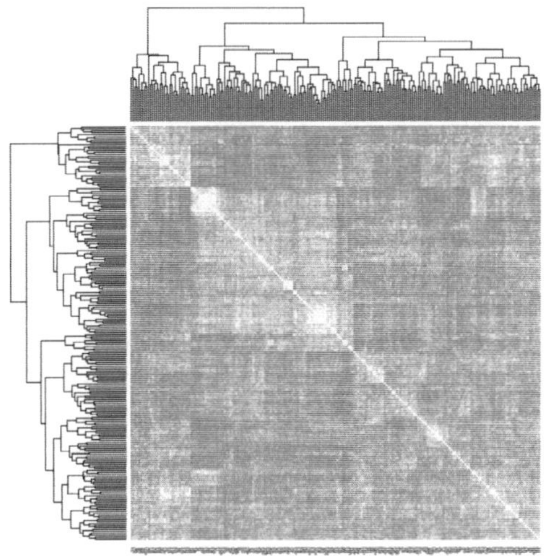

Figure 6: Heat map for languages with most data in WALS only

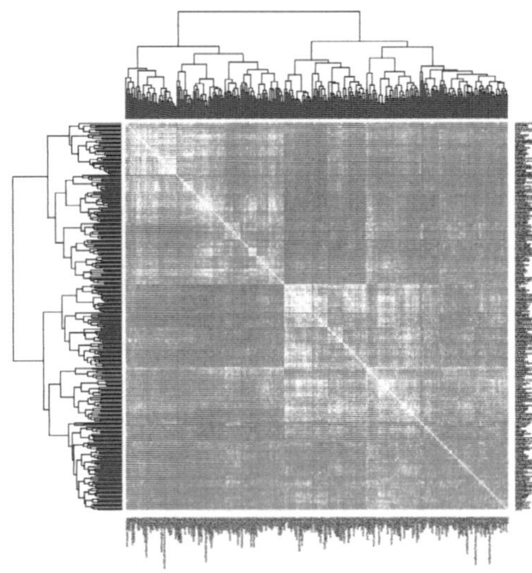

Figure 7: Heat map for genera with most data in WALS only

an association between WALS feature 13A-3 (complex tone system) and high and low tone segments (a subset of tones) found in PHOIBLE's 1600+ languages. In another highly associated cluster, WALS feature 7A-2 (glottalized consonants, ejectives only) corresponds with languages in PHOIBLE that contain ejective segments /k', p', q', ts', tʃ'/. Our approach also identifies similarity between WALS feature 10A-1 (vowel nasalization present) and the set of languages in PHOIBLE that contain the cardinal nasalized vowels /ã, ẽ, ɛ̃, ĩ, õ, ɔ̃ , ũ/.

This is just a simple demonstration of identifying association using similarity measures between two richly-annotated typological databases. One can imagine expanding the search for associations across other data sources,

[10] Raw data from WALS and PHOIBLE is also available online: `http://wals.info/` and `http://phoible.org`.

[11] We use R for the conversion and most of the time is spent reading in the data.

[12] These visualizations are of course just that: visualizations. There are numerous other approaches that can be used to identify structure in the data, e.g. clustering, partitioning, dimensional reduction, etc.

and even more exciting, apply the wealth of possibilities afforded by matrix algebra for language comparison, such as normalization of entities to be compared, the application of other measures of association, applying normalizations for genealogical overrepresentation and correction for missing data through evaluation of expected and observed results.

6. Conclusion

We have shown that the same data source can be represented in different data structures. Linguistic data often starts its life stored in tables, e.g. database tables. Table data can be converted into mathematical graphs, which can be used to overcome the problem of syntactic interoperability for data aggregation. Linked Data is the classic example. Linked Data graphs can be combined into larger graphs with links between them, thus enhancing data aggregation. In this paper we have illustrated how combined data graphs in the form of the LLOD can be queried and how data can be extracted and transformed into matrices. Matrix data gives us a data format to leverage mathematic formulations of matrix algebra, the surface of which we have only scratched in this paper. We have provided a simple example of how to manipulate data and to find clusters of association in combined datasets for research in language comparison and typology.

7. Acknowledgements

This work was supported by the ERC starting grant 240816: 'Quantitative modeling of historical-comparative linguistics'. Many thanks to Martin Brümmer and several anonymous reviewers.

8. References

Balthasar Bickel and Johanna Nichols. 2002. Autotypologizing databases and their use in fieldwork. In *Proceedings of the LREC 2002 Workshop on Resources and Tools in Field Linguistics*.

Balthasar Bickel. 2011a. Grammatical relations typology. In J J Song, editor, *The Oxford Handbook of Language Typology*, Oxford Handbooks in Linguistics, pages 399 – 444. Oxford University Press, Oxford.

Balthasar Bickel. 2011b. Statistical modeling of language universals. *Linguistic Typology*, 15(2):401–413.

Christian Chiarcos, Sebastian Nordhoff, and Sebastian Hellmann. 2012. *Linked Data in Linguistics*. Springer.

Michael Cysouw. 2005. Quantitative Methods in Typology. In Gabriel Altmann, Reinhard Köhler, and Rajmund G. Piotrowski, editors, *Quantitative Linguistics: An International Handbook*, pages 554–578. Berlin: Walter de Gruyter.

Michael Cysouw. 2014. Matrix algebra for language comparison. Unpublished manuscript.

Gerard de Melo. 2014. Lexvo. org: Language-related information for the linguistic linked data cloud. *Semantic Web Journal*.

Christiane Fellbaum, editor. 1998. *WordNet: An Electronic Lexical Database*. MIT Press, Cambridge, MA.

Martin Haspelmath and Uri Tadmor, editors. 2009. *WOLD*. Max Planck Institute for Evolutionary Anthropology, Leipzig.

Martin Haspelmath, Matthew S. Dryer, David Gil, and Bernard Comrie. 2008. The world atlas of language structures online. Munich: Max Planck Digital Library. Available online at `http://wals.info/`.

Nancy Ide and James Pustejovsky. 2010. What does interoperability mean, anyway? toward an operational definition of interoperability for language technology. In *Proceedings of the Second International Conference on Global Interoperability for Language Resources. Hong Kong, China*.

Mary Ritchie Key and Bernard Comrie, editors. 2014. *The Intercontinental Dictionary Series*. Max Planck Institute for Evolutionary Anthropology, Leipzig.

M. Paul Lewis, Gary F. Simons, and Charles D. Fennig, editors. 2013. *Ethnologue: Languages of the World, Seventeenth edition*. SIL International, Dallas, Texas.

William D Lewis. 2006. ODIN: A model for adapting and enriching legacy infrastructure. In *e-Science and Grid Computing, 2006. e-Science'06. Second IEEE International Conference on*, pages 137–137. IEEE.

LINGUIST List. 2009a. LL-MAP: Language and location - map accessibility project. Online: `http://llmap.org/`.

LINGUIST List. 2009b. Multitree: A Digital Library of Language Relationships. Institute for Language Information and Technology (LINGUIST List), Eastern Michigan University. Ypsilanti, MI. Online: `http://multitree.org/`.

Thomas Mayer and Michael Cysouw. 2012. Language comparison through sparse multilingual word alignment. In *Proceedings of the EACL 2012 Joint Workshop of LINGVIS & UNCLH*, pages 54–62. Association for Computational Linguistics.

Steven Moran. 2012. *Phonetics information base and lexicon*. Ph.D. thesis, University of Washington.

Sebastian Nordhoff, Harald Hammarström, Robert Forkel, and Martin Haspelmath (eds.). 2013. Glottolog 2.2. Leipzig: Max Planck Institute for Evolutionary Anthropology. Available online at `http://glottolog.org`.

Alena Witzlack-Makarevich. 2011. *Typological variation in grammatical relations*. Ph.D. thesis, University of Leipzig.

The Cross-Linguistic Linked Data project

Robert Forkel

Max Planck Institute for Evolutionary Anthropology
Deutscher Platz 6, D-04103 Leipzig
robert_forkel@eva.mpg.de

Abstract

The *Cross-Linguistic Linked Data project (CLLD –* `http://clld.org`*) helps record the world's language diversity heritage by establishing an interoperable data publishing infrastructure. I describe the project and the environment it operates in, with an emphasis on the datasets that are published within the project. The publishing infrastructure is built upon a custom software stack – the* `clld` *framework – which is described next. I then proceed to explain how Linked Data plays an important role in the strategy regarding interoperability and sustainability. Finally I gauge the impact the project may have on its environment.*

Keywords: *Linked Data, Linguistics, Software, Typology*

1. Cross-Linguistic data – the status quo

For the purposes of this paper I define cross-linguistic data as either data on many languages, or as data about under-resourced languages. I also restrict it to textual data.[1] Thus, this data will mostly come in the form of wordlists, dictionaries, phoneme inventories, typological surveys, small collections of glossed text, grammars, or bibliographies.

This kind of data is the result or forms the basis of much of the work being done at the department of linguistics of the Max Planck Institute for Evolutionary Anthropology (MPI EVA) in Leipzig which is one of the centers of what may be called "language diversity research".

Since data collection via fieldwork is well respected in this community there is not a shortage of data; often this data is not very complex but even more often it is unpublished. And even if this data is published, it may have ended up as a printed grammar or dictionary,[2] which – given the fact that these are reference works – is clearly inferior to a digital medium.[3]

Similar observations can be made for typological databases. While many presentations at ALT 10[4] used data from WALS[5] and complemented it with the author's own data, typically this complementary data is not published.

So there is quite a bit of seemingly low-hanging fruit out there: simple data waiting to get published.

2. The CLLD project

Cross-Linguistic Linked Data (CLLD) is a project funded by the Max Planck Society for four years, setting out to pick this fruit by establishing data publishing infrastructure.

We try to do so by:

- closing the gap between data creation and data publication by making publication easy and attractive,
- overcoming the disconnect between data creators and data consumers,[6]
- providing the infrastructure in a sustainable way.

2.1. The datasets

Most datasets under consideration right now have been compiled by or in association with the department of linguistics at the MPI EVA:

WALS The World Atlas of Language Structures is now online in its third implementation.

APiCS The Atlas of Pidgin and Creole Language Structures is a typological database modeled after WALS but focussing on pidgins and creoles.

ASJP (to be published in 2014) The Automated Similarity Judgement Program has collected almost 7000 small wordlists of languages and varieties from all over the world.

IDS (to be published in 2014) The Intercontinental Dictionary Series is a collection of extensive wordlists (ca. 1300 items) collected for a curated set of meanings covering more than 220 languages.

AfBo A world-wide survey of affix borrowing describes 101 cases of affix borrowing from one language into another.

WOLD The World Loanword Database contains extensive vocabularies (similar to IDS) for 41 languages annotated for loanword status and source words (Haspelmath and Tadmor, 2009).

Glottolog Glottolog is a language catalog and bibliographical database, comprising close to 8000 languages and more than 200000 bibliographical records (Nordhoff, 2012).

[1] There does not seem to be much of a Linked Data story for multimedia content anyway.

[2] Publishing printed grammars and dictionaries seems to get more and more difficult, though (Haspelmath, 2014).

[3] Re-publication or aggregation of data from printed media in digital form is fraught with all the license and copyright issues and the interpretations thereof in the community (Austin, 2011).

[4] The 10th Biennial Conference of the Association for Linguistic Typology, Leipzig August 2013

[5] The World Atlas of Language Structures

[6] It is an interesting observation that at ALT 10 the typical presenters of papers working with quantitative methods on linguistic datasets were disjoint from the people creating such databases.

But CLLD also provides infrastructure to publish datasets originating outside the MPI EVA:

- Two data journals (one for dictionaries and one for typological databases) will be started in 2014 which are open to submissions. These journals will serve the double purpose of
  - allowing publication of datasets referenced in "traditional" publications (as is increasingly required by funders),
  - applying the traditional model of peer-reviewed publications to data, thereby incentivizing researchers through recognition.
- Bigger datasets can become part of CLLD following an "edited series" publication model. There are already two datasets in this category:

  eWAVE The electronic World Atlas of Varieties of English is a typological database containing information on 76 varieties of English.[7]

  PHOIBLE (to be published in 2014) The Phonetics Information Base is a large collection of phoneme inventories for languages from all over the world.
- Last but not least the `clld` framework,[8] upon which all publications are built, is open source software and can be freely reused; i.e. institutions or individuals can build applications based on the `clld` framework to host and publish their own databases.

2.2. The `clld` framework

Recognizing that the field of interoperable linguistic data publication is still in its beginnings[9] adaptability and in general an iterative approach is called for. Thus, we aim to "standardize" on a lower level, namely on the publication platform; in doing so we hope to make published resources – i.e. the interface to the data – more adaptable.[10] So our aim is at the same time more modest than semantic interoperability and more ambitious, because the platform is open to serving non-RDF serializations of resources should these become de-facto standards.
In the first year of the project[11] a cross-linguistic database framework – the `clld` framework[12] – has been developed, which will be the focus of the following sections. Publishing datasets as `clld` applications should be seen as a perfect basis for publishing it as Linked Data while at the same time publishing it in a more traditional way (with respect to Web-publishing). It is also a good way to extend the uniformity of the interface from the machine readable data to the user interface accessed with the browser. While I understand the strength of the Linked Data approach to publishing, being able to also put an attractive human user interface on top of a dataset must not be underestimated when it comes to convincing linguists to open up their data. Thus the `clld` framework provides

- a common core data model,
- a basic API built on Linked Data principles
- and what could be termed a "reference implementation" of a dataset browser as user-friendly interface for humans.

2.2.1. The data model

The design of the data model was guided by three principles:

1. All the target datasets have to "fit in" without loss.
2. The data model must be as abstract as necessary, as concrete as possible.
3. The data model must be extensible.

Note that these guidelines mirror the requirements set forth in Section 6.1 of Monachesi et al. (2002) for a *linguistic "metalanguage"*, ensuring unified access to typological databases. It turns out that most of the datasets we encountered thus far can be modeled using the following concepts.[13]

Dataset holds metadata about a dataset like license and publisher information.

Language often rather a languoid in the sense of Good and Cysouw (2014).

Parameter a feature that can be coded or determined for a language – e.g. a word meaning, or a typological feature.

ValueSet set of values measured/observed/recorded for one language and one parameter, i.e. the points in the Language-Parameter-matrix.

Value a single measurement (different scales can be modeled using custom attributes).[14]

Unit parts of a language system that are annotated, such as sounds, words or constructions.

UnitParameter a feature that can be determined for a unit.

UnitValue measurement for one unit and one unitparameter.

[7] Datasets like eWAVE highlight the fact that ISO 639-3 is not sufficient to identify language varieties.

[8] `https://github.com/clld/clld`

[9] Although this may have been so for almost 10 years.

[10] It should be noted that this is not the first attempt at standardization of a software stack for cross-linguistic databases (Monachesi et al., 2002); but today's options for community driven development of open source software promise to make a real difference.

[11] `http://clld.org/2014/01/03/new-year.html`

[12] Spelled in lowercase conforming to common rules for names of Python software packages

[13] Or as Dimitriadis (2006) put it (further corroborating our experience): "survey databases are all alike".

[14] The only assumption the core data model makes about values is that they have a name, i.e. a textual description; datatypes for values can be implemented as application-specific extensions of this core model.

Source pointer to secondary literature – e.g. bibliographical records.

Sentence a small piece of text, preferably in the form of interlinear glossed text[15] according to the Leipzig Glossing Rules.[16]

Contribution a collection of ValueSets that share provenance information, e.g. authorship.[17]

The relations between these entities are shown in Figure 1. Note that Dimitriadis' *Construction* maps to our *Unit* and *Example* to *Sentence* (Dimitriadis, 2006, p. 15).

Figure 1: Entity-relationship diagram of the CLLD core data model

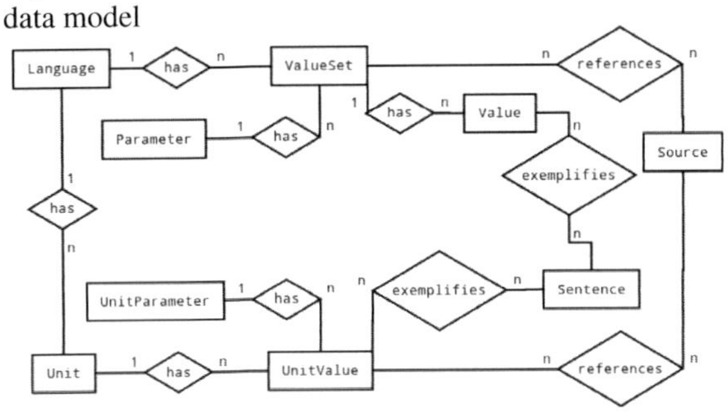

In a concrete incarnation this core data model can be interpreted as shown in Figure 2. Note the additional relation between *Word* and *Counterpart* which is not present in the core model. The `clld` framework uses the *joined table inheritance* feature of the `SQLAlchemy` package to transparently add attributes to entities of the core data model. (see section 2.2.2.).[18]

Figure 2: Entity-relationship diagram of the WOLD data model; *SynSet*s are sets of synonyms, a *Counterpart* is an instance of the many-to-many relation between Words and Meanings in the sense of Haspelmath and Tadmor (2009).

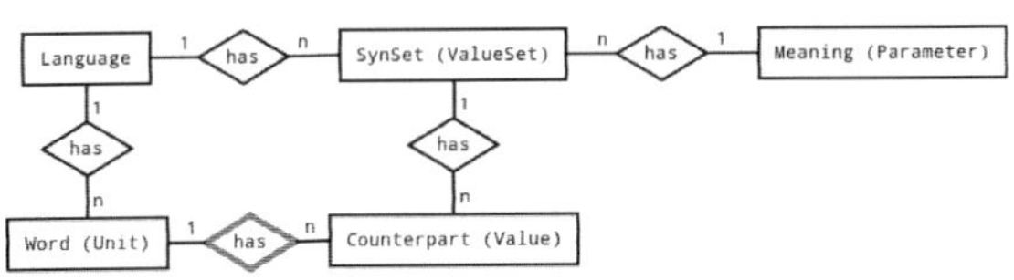

2.2.2. The implementation

CLLD applications are implemented using the `clld` framework.[19] This framework in turn is based on the python packages `pyramid` and `SQLAlchemy` and allows building web applications accessing a relational database. Using an RDF graph database as main storage was out of the question because of its non-standard requirements in terms of deployment, administration and maintenance, which would conflict with the strategy for sustainability described in section 2.3.

These technology choices offer the following two essential mechanisms for extensibility:

1. The joined table inheritance[20] model provided with `SQLAlchemy` allows for transparent extension of core database entities. For each core entity a `clld` application may define an extended entitity, adding attributes and relations. Accessing the database using `SQLAlchemy` makes sure that whenever the core entitity is queried an instance of the extended entity is returned.

2. The Zope component architecture[21] within pyramid[22] provides an implementation of concepts like interface and adapter, which in turn make it possible to provide default behavior for entities which works with extended entities as well and can easily be overridden by registering custom behavior.

Using these mechanisms deviations in terms of data model or user interface are possible, but the default behavior[23] should be good enough most of the time (at least for the data consumed by machines only).

2.3. Sustainability: The idea of graceful degradation of service

Lacking longterm institutional/financial support, a project may employ several methods to gain sustainability:

1. Make fundraising part of the project activities.

2. Make transfer of ownership easy.

With respect to the CLLD databases the latter means that we always have to take into consideration what running such a service entails. From our own experience it seems clear that running interactive web applications without the ability to further develop the software will lead to dysfunctional applications quickly (within a few years).

But since this scenario is not unlikely in the event of a transfer of ownership, we would like to define a more stable, and more easily maintainable level of service for our applications. Thus, we use the Linked Data principles to define a lowest level of service we want to guarantee for CLLD applications. Doing so means that running CLLD applications can be as cheap as hosting static files on a web server (and possibly keeping domain registrations valid).

[15] `http://en.wikipedia.org/wiki/Interlinear_gloss`

[16] `http://www.eva.mpg.de/lingua/resources/glossing-rules.php`

[17] Thus, a CLLD dataset is similar to an edited volume in that it may aggregate data from multiple contributors.

[18] It should be noted that this data model provides sufficient structure to allow conversion to the RDF model for wordlists proposed by Poornima and Good (2010).

[19] `https://github.com/clld/clld`

[20] `http://docs.sqlalchemy.org/en/latest/orm/inheritance.html`

[21] `http://www.muthukadan.net/docs/zca.html`

[22] `http://docs.pylonsproject.org/projects/pyramid/en/latest/narr/zca.html`

[23] By default, each resource class comes with a list view and a detailed view for each instance, which in turn can be serialized in various formats like JSON, RDF+XML, etc.

Essentially we are following the Linked Data principles to provide a REST API for our datasets that is easy to maintain. Notably, this API is already used today by search engines, so this aspect of the service will survive also in the lowest level. This also means that we hope *sustainable operability* as defined by Windhouwer and Dimitriadis (2008) can be provided on top of the Linked Data stack, in particular on top of public sparql endpoints. Thus, we propose Linked Data to serve as the *Integrated Data and Documentation Format* described in Windhouwer and Dimitriadis (2008) with the additional benefit of a well-defined access protocol.

The `clld` framework will provide an "emergency exit" feature, which will create a set of files (corresponding to the list and detailed views in various formats as described above) in an appropriate directory structure to be put on a vanilla webserver. This can be done by enumerating the resource types, instances and available representations.

So while Linked Data is still not the way many researchers interested in our datasets[24] actually do or want to access data (at least if they can get away with csv instead), there is something to be gained for the developer: A stable API across phases of deployment which can be used by any additional services built on top of the data.

2.4. Linked Data

As described above, Linked Data plays an important role in the strategy of the CLLD project. In the following sections I describe our design choices regarding the implementation of Linked Data principles for the publication of CLLD datasets.

2.4.1. URLs and resources

We do not distinguish *things* from *Web documents* as recommended by Sauermann and Cyganiak (2008), because the solutions to achieve this conflict with our requirements for easy hosting of the lowest level of service outlined in section 2.3. These conflicts are also echoed in the list of practical limitations given Tennison (2011). Arguably, using a concept of languages as sets of doculects (following Good and Cysouw (2014)), the *thing* can to some extent be identified with the web document describing it anyway; additionally we rely on the discoverability of context in the sense of Hayes and Halpin (2008), e.g. provided by RDF types or identifiers, to support disambiguation.

While each RDF resource in CLLD datasets links to its originating dataset, and this dataset is described by a VoID description (see below), perhaps the most important bit of provenance information is the domain part of a resource's identifying URL.[25] Each dataset can employ additional schemes of conveying additional provenance information, though, like adding a version history. It is an explicit goal of the project to keep the resource URLs stable and resolvable for as long as possible, thus, we intend our URLs to be "cool" in the old sense, too, and more generally to fulfill the "social contract" between publisher and user outlined in Hyland et al. (2014).

All entities in the clld data model (see section 2.2.1.) map to resource types in the RDF formulation of this model. Since all entities have a local identifier, a name and a description, and each CLLD dataset is served from a distinct domain, we already have all the pieces necessary to fulfill basic requirements for RDF descriptions.[26]

2.4.2. VoID

The `clld` framework provides a VoID dataset description for each dataset. This description is populated from the metadata specified for the dataset, but also using the knowledge the framework has about its entities and capabilities. E.g. the VoID description for Glottolog[28] describes partitions of the dataset into entity-type specific subsets (`void:Dataset`), and points to data dumps for these, because the number of resources would make accessing the data via crawling (while still possible) time consuming.

The VoID description and the backlinks of each resource to the dataset are used to provide provenance and license information for each resource. Following the recommendations for deploying VoID descriptions in Alexander et al. (2011), the description is available at the path `/void.ttl` of `clld` applications as well as via content negotiation at the base URL.

2.4.3. HTTP

The `clld` framework uses content negotiation to make sure that RDF resources can be accessed right now just as they would in the "plain file on webserver" scenario.

HTTP link headers are used to identify canonical URLs and alternative representations. While this feature might not survive in the lowest level of service (unless some custom webserver configuration is added), it shows the capability of the framework to enumerate the URL space of its resource graph.

2.4.4. Linking with other resources and vocabularies

Linking to resources outside the CLLD universe is clearly in need of further investigation. Linking to dbpedia and lexvo based on ISO 639-3 codes of languages is possible. Linking sources to bibliographical records e.g. in WorldCat is hampered by the fact that identification of matching records is error prone and not doable "by hand" for our typical source collections with more than 1000 records.

It should be noted, though, that some of our datasets carry the potential to serve as hubs in the Linked Data cloud themselves, and do so within the CLLD sub-cloud:

- Glottolog as language catalog and comprehensive bibliography. The desirability of alternative language catalogs (in addition to Ethnologue or ISO 639-3) is described in Haspelmath (2013) and can easily be seen looking at a dataset like eWAVE or APiCS, where many of the languages under investigation are not included in either Ethnologue or ISO-639-3.

[24] Most of the datasets under consideration here are more interesting for typologists than for computational linguists.

[25] Since CLLD datasets can be aggregations of multiple contributions, additional – more fine grained – provenance information is typically available, but for purposes of quality assessment the overriding factor will often be the fact that a ValueSet is part of an aggregation compiled under editorial control.

[26] e.g. as specified for bio2rdf in its RDFization-Guide[27]

[28] http://glottolog.org/void.ttl

- IDS and WOLD as providers of semi-standard comparison meanings for the creation of wordlists, i.e. as "concepticons" in the sense of Poornima and Good (2010).[29]

While the comprehensive ambition of the CLLD project might warrant the creation of a CLLD ontology, we have refrained from creating one. This is in large part due to the lack of use cases (evidenced by lack of usage) for the RDF data.

In an environment where the preferred data exchange format is still csv, I did not want to venture on an undertaking that might leave us with a bunch of vocabulary URLs to maintain which no one uses. Thus, CLLD's current RDF model reuses fairly generic terms from the most common vocabularies: `dcterms`, `skos`, `foaf`, `wgs84`. Due to the extensible architecture provided by the `clld` framework described in section 2.2.2. each CLLD application is in complete control of the RDF graphs of its entities, though.[30]

3. Where does this get us?

With WALS, APiCS, WOLD, Glottolog and some more datasets[31] already published as CLLD applications – i.e. with their data available as Linked Data described via VoID – I will try to gauge the impact of the CLLD project looking at some use cases:

- At the most basic level, fulfilling the request "give me all you have on language x" (where x is chosen from one of the supported language catalogs) should be possible – using a local triplestore filled by harvesting the CLLD apps individually or at a later stage using the CLLD portal.[32]
- Testing the conjecture mentioned in WALS chapter "Hand and Arm" (Brown, 2013)

  > The presence of tailored clothing covering the arms greatly increases the distinctiveness of arm parts and renders more likely their labeling by separate terms [...]. Another potentially fruitful investigatory strategy would be to cross-tabulate values against the tailoring technologies of peoples who speak each of the 620 languages of the sample - an enormous research effort this author must leave to future investigators.

  can still not be done fully automatically, but it should be possible to connect languages to descriptions about their speakers via dbpedia and start from there.[33]
- Seeding/expanding datasets like "Tea" (Dahl, 2013)[34] with data from lexical databases like WOLD[35] is already possible.

Arguably, in particular for the case of typological datasets, completely automated use is still far off.[36] The typical process for analysis of typological datasets will remain a sequence of data download, manual inspection, massaging the data, then running analysis software; for this workflow, the uniform access aspect of Linked Data is the most important.

Thus, the future plans for the project focus on

- aggregators or portals:

  Lexicalia the portal to lexical data in CLLD datasets[37] and

  CrossGram the portal to typological data in CLLD datasets[38]

  are already under way. In general we would like to follow the example of bio2rdf in providing a standard, versioned, curated aggregation of linguistic data around which a community can grow and share analyses, methods and data.
- "curated triplestores" and "on-demand triplestores" in the sense of Tennison (2010).[39] On-demand triplestores also look like a good way to go forward with reproducible research[40] without putting the burden of versioning on each database: one will not be able to simply publish a sparql query and the URL of the endpoint, but would have to deposit the triples as well.

[29] It would probably make sense to link these meanings to wordnet wordsenses but it seems difficult to determine authoritative URLs for these.

[30] E.g. in WALS chapters carry information on the corresponding linguistic field which often can be linked to dbpedia; WALS languages can be linked via `dcterms:spatial` relations to geonames.org countries.

[31] `http://clld.org/datasets.html`

[32] Cf. `http://portal.clld.org/?q=english`

[33] If a large, curated database like eHRAF were part of Linked Open Data this could be possible, though. It should also be noted that cultures, thus anthropological data, are often identified/distinguished by their language, so that this kind of data would also fit into the CLLD framework.

[34] This dataset lists for many languages whether the corresponding word for "tea" is derived from Sinitic "cha" or Min Nan Chinese "te".

[35] `http://wold.livingsources.org/meaning/23-9` lists counterparts for "tea" in various languages including their loanword status.

[36] Judging by our experience with making APiCS and WALS structure sets comparable (where APiCS was created with comparability to WALS as an explicit goal), and evidence provided by Round (2013) at ALT 10 for the difficulty of designing comparable datasets, it seems clear that "know your data" will remain an obligation of the researcher that cannot be shifted to the machine.

[37] `http://portal.clld.org/lexicalia`

[38] `http://portal.clld.org/crossgram`

[39] Imagine a service that would allow one to: 1. collect a custom dataset from selected features from WALS, APiCS and eWAVE; 2. post-process it with software from CLLD's community repository; 3. dump it in virtuoso and package the appliance as Amazon EC2 AMI ...

[40] `http://languagelog.ldc.upenn.edu/nll/?p=830`

For these objectives of the project integration with the CLARIN[41] infrastructure could be useful. While the basic data collection and publishing aims more at integration with the web at large, providing computationally intensive expert services like custom triplestores would profit from an environment that allows restricted and limited access by a well defined user community.

4. References

Keith Alexander, Richard Cyganiak, Michael Hausenblas, and Jun Zhao. 2011. Describing linked datasets with the void vocabulary. `http://www.w3.org/TR/void/`.

Peter Austin. 2011. They're out to get you (or your data at least). `http://www.paradisec.org.au/blog/2011/04/theyre-out-to-get-you-or-your-data-at-least/`.

Cecil H. Brown. 2013. Hand and arm. In Matthew S. Dryer and Martin Haspelmath, editors, *The World Atlas of Language Structures Online*. Max Planck Institute for Evolutionary Anthropology, Leipzig.

Östen Dahl. 2013. Tea. In Matthew S. Dryer and Martin Haspelmath, editors, *The World Atlas of Language Structures Online*. Max Planck Institute for Evolutionary Anthropology, Leipzig.

Alexis Dimitriadis. 2006. An extensible database design for cross-linguistic research. `http://languagelink.let.uu.nl/burs/docs/burs-design.pdf`.

Jeff Good and Michael Cysouw. 2014. Languoid, doculect and glossonym: Formalizing the notion 'language'. *Language Documentation & Conservation*, 07.

Martin Haspelmath and Uri Tadmor, 2009. *The Loanword Typology Project and the World Loanword Database*, page 1–33. De Gruyter.

Martin Haspelmath. 2013. Can language identity be standardized? on morey et al.'s critique of iso 639-3. `http://dlc.hypotheses.org/610`.

Martin Haspelmath. 2014. A proposal for radical publication reform in linguistics: Language science press, and the next steps. `http://dlc.hypotheses.org/631`.

Patrick J. Hayes and Harry Halpin. 2008. In defense of ambiguity. *Int. J. Semantic Web Inf. Syst.*, 4(2):1–18.

Bernadette Hyland, Ghislain Atemezing, and Boris Villazón-Terrazas. 2014. Best Practices for Publishing Linked Data. `http://www.w3.org/TR/ld-bp`.

Paola Monachesi, Alexis Dimitriadis, Rob Goedemans, Anne-Marie Mineur, and Manuela Pinto. 2002. A unified system for accessing typological databases. In *Proceedings of the Third International Conference on Language Resources and Evaluation (LREC 3)*.

Sebastian Nordhoff. 2012. Linked data for linguistic diversity research: Glottolog/langdoc and asjp online. In Christian Chiarcos, Sebastian Nordhoff, and Sebastian Hellmann, editors, *Linked Data in Linguistics. Representing and Connecting Language Data and Language Metadata*. Springer, Heidelberg.

Shakthi Poornima and Jeff Good. 2010. Modeling and encoding traditional wordlists for machine applications. In *Proceedings of the 2010 Workshop on NLP and Linguistics: Finding the Common Ground*, NLPLING '10, pages 1–9, Stroudsburg, PA, USA. Association for Computational Linguistics.

Erich Round. 2013. How to design a dataset which doesn't undermine automated analysis. Talk given at ALT 10.

Leo Sauermann and Richard Cyganiak. 2008. Cool URIs for the Semantic Web. `http://www.w3.org/TR/cooluris/`.

Jeni Tennison. 2010. Distributed publication and querying. `http://www.jenitennison.com/blog/node/143`.

Jeni Tennison. 2011. What do uris mean anyway? `http://www.jenitennison.com/blog/node/159`.

Menzo Windhouwer and Alexis Dimitriadis. 2008. Sustainable operability: Keeping complex resources alive. In *Proceedings of the LREC Workshop on the Sustainability of Language Resources and Tools for Natural Language Processing*.

[41] `http://clarin.eu`

Section 4:
Data challenge

Dbnary: Wiktionary as Linked Data for 12 Language Editions with Enhanced Translation Relations

Gilles Sérasset, Andon Tchechmedjiev

Univ. Grenoble Alpes, LIG, F-38000 Grenoble, France
CNRS, LIG, F-38000 Grenoble, France
`firstname.lastname@imag.fr`

Abstract

This paper presents the current state of development of the DBnary dataset. DBnary is a RDF dataset, structured using the LEMON vocabulary, that is extracted from twelve different Wiktionary language editions. DBnary also contains additional relations from translation pairs to their source word senses. The extracted data is registered at `http://thedatahub.org/dataset/dbnary`.

Keywords: Wiktionary, Multilingual Lexical Resource, Lexical Networks, LEMON, RDF

1. Introduction

The GETALP (Study group for speech and language translation/processing) team of the LIG (Laboratoire d'Informatique de Grenoble) is in need for multilingual lexical resources that should include language correspondences (translations) and word sense definitions. In this regard, the set data included in the different Wiktionary language edition is a precious mine.

Alas, many inconsistencies, errors, difference in usage do exist in the various Wiktionary language edition. Hence, we decided to provide an effort to extract precious data from this source and provide it to the community a Linked Data. This dataset won the Monnet Challenge in 2012, when it consisted of 6 language editions. The structure of this dataset, which is intensively based on the LEMON model (Mccrae et al., 2012) is presented in (Sérasset, 2012). This short paper purpose is to present the current state of our dataset.

2. Extracting Data from Wiktionary

2.1. No Common Approach

Errors and incoherences are inherent to a contributive resource like Wiktionary. This has been heavily emphasized in related works by (Hellmann et al., 2013) and (Meyer and Gurevych, 2012b). Still, we suceeded not only in extracting data from 12 different language editions, but we are maintaining these extractor on a regular basis. Indeed, our dataset evolves along with the original Wiktionary data. Each time a new Wiktionary dump is available (about once every 10/15 days for each language edition), the DBnary dataset is updated. This leads to a different dataset almost every day.

Some language editions (like French and English) have many moderators that do limit the number of incoherence among entries of the same language. Moreover, those languages that contain the most data, use many *templates* that simplify the extraction process. For instance, the translation section of the French dictionary usually uses a template to identify each individual translation.

This is not true however, with less developed Wiktionary language editions. For instance, in the Finnish edition, some translations are introduced by a template giving the language (e.g. {fr} precedes French translation) and others are introduced by the string "ranska" which is the Finnish translation for "French". In this case the translator needs to know the Finnish translation of all language names to cope with the second case and avoid losing almost half of the available translation data.

Moreover, since 2012, we have added new languages that exhibits a different use of the Wikimedia syntax. For instance, translations in the Russian Wiktionary are entirely contained in one unique template, where target languages are a parameter. Moreover, in the Bulgarian Wiktionary, the full lexical entry is contained in one single template where sections are the parameters. In such language editions, templates can not be parsed using regular expressions, as they are inherently recursive (template calls are included in parameter values of other templates). This invalidates our initial approach which was based on regular expressions. In order to cope with these languages, we had to use an advanced parser of the Wikimedia syntax (called Bliki engine[1]) to deal with such data.

Our extractors are written in Java and are open-source (LGPL licensed, available at `http://dbnary.forge.imag.fr`).

2.2. Tools to Help Maintenance

In this effort, we also had to develop tools to evaluate the extarctor's performance and to maintain it. Our first tool[2] compares extracted translations with interwiki links. Many of the translations in a Wiktionary language edition do point to entries in the Wiktionary edition of the target language. Such inter-wiki links are available through the Wiktionary API. By randomly sampling the extracted data, we are able to compare the extracted data with such links. This gives us an idea of the extractor performance. However, this relies on the availability of inter-wiki links, which is not the case in some language edition.

When we maintain the extractor, we need to carefully check that the patches we added do not introduce regressions in the extractor. For this, we developped our own `RDFdiff` command line tool which computes the differences be-

[1] `https://code.google.com/p/gwtwiki/`

[2] this heuristic was initially suggested by Sebastian Hellman

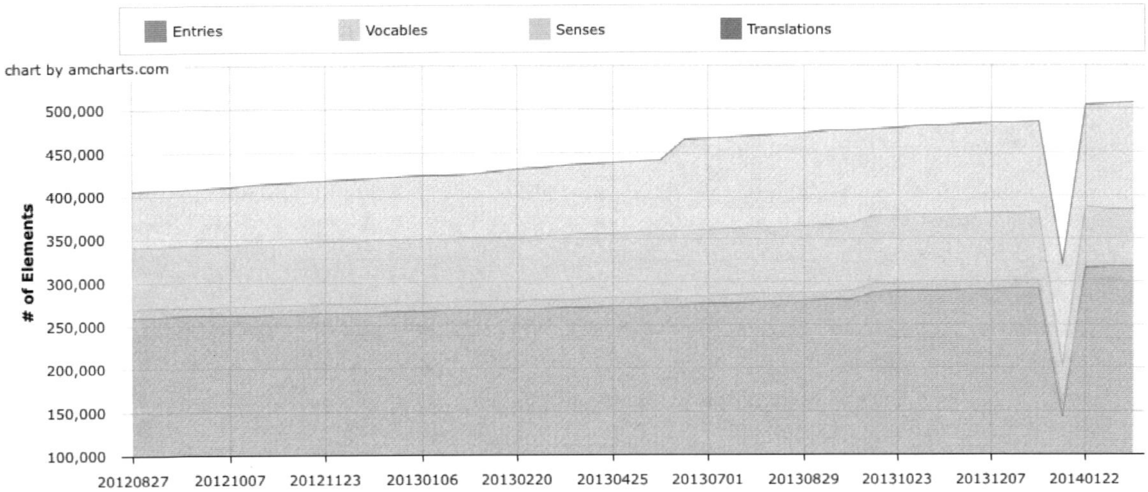

Figure 1: Some of the statistics available about the French extracted data.

Language	Entries	Vocables	Senses	Translations	Total
Bulgarian	18,831	27,071	18,798	13,888	**78,588**
English	553,499	528,341	447,073	1,332,332	**2,861,245**
Finnish	50,813	50,488	59,612	122,724	**283,637**
French	318,101	304,465	383,242	507,359	**1,513,167**
German	211,564	282,902	102,468	390,938	**987,872**
Italian	34,363	101,525	45,022	62,305	**243,215**
Japanese	25,492	25,637	29,679	87,906	**168,714**
Modern Greek (1453-)	246,211	241,845	137,072	57,615	**682,743**
Portuguese	45,788	45,968	81,807	267,801	**441,364**
Russian	130,879	143,653	116,925	365,389	**756,846**
Spanish	58,679	65,854	85,852	114,951	**325,336**
Turkish	64,899	69,383	91,418	66,928	**292,628**
Total	**1,759,119**	**1,887,132**	**1,598,968**	**3,390,136**	**8,635,355**

Table 1: Number of lexical elements in the graphs.

tween 2 RDF dumps. Such a command is already provided in the JENA toolbox, however, the JENA implementation does not correctly deal with anonymous nodes. Indeed, anonymous nodes are always considered as different by the JENA implementation when the RDF specification states that 2 anonymous nodes that share the same properties should be considered equal. Our version of RDFDiff correctly handles such anonymous node (that are heavily used in the LEMON model). With this implementation, it is now easy to compute the difference between the original extraction and the new one and to decide, based on these differences, if the new version is good enough for production.

From time to time, a Wiktionary language edition drastically changes the way it encodes some data. Actively following the discussions on each Wiktionary edition to anticipate such changes is not an option with so many languages. Hence, with each language extraction update, we compute a set of statistics that gives detailed figures on the size of the data . These statistics are available live on the DBnary web site[3]. Overall, the most useful statistics are the ones that capture the evolution of the extracted data over time. For instance Figure 1 shows the evolution of the size of the extracted French datasets since its original extraction. This plot allowed us to detect that a major refactoring was happening on the French language edition. This allowed us to patch the extractor for this new organisation right away.

3. Extracted Data as a LEMON Lexical Resource

3.1. Extracted Entries

The main goal of our efforts is not to extensively reflect the specific structures and constructs of Wiktionary data, but to create a lexical resource that is structured as a set of monolingual dictionaries + bilingual translation information. Such data is already useful for several application, but most importantly it is a sound starting point for a future multilingual lexical database.

[3]http://kaiko.getalp.org/about-dbnary

Language	*syn*	*qsyn*	*ant*	*hyper*	*hypo*	*mero*	*holo*	Total
Bulgarian	17632	0	34	0	0	0	0	**17666**
English	31762	0	6980	1252	1212	112	0	**41318**
Finnish	2478	0	0	0	0	0	0	**2478**
French	31655	2133	6879	9402	3739	970	1898	**56676**
German	29288	0	15079	33251	10413	0	0	**88031**
Italian	9662	0	3425	0	0	0	0	**13087**
Japanese	3828	0	1578	9	14	0	0	**5429**
Greek	4990	0	1428	0	0	0	0	**6418**
Portuguese	3350	0	556	6	4	0	0	**3916**
Russian	24941	0	9888	22832	5140	0	0	**62801**
Spanish	15087	0	1525	741	560	0	0	**17913**
Turkish	3260	0	220	483	164	0	0	**4127**
Total	**177933**	**2133**	**47592**	**67976**	**21246**	**1082**	**1898**	**319860**

Table 2: Number of lexico-semantic relations in the graphs.

Monolingual data is always extracted from its dedicated Wiktionary language edition. For instance, the French lexical data is extracted from the French language edition (the data is available on http://fr.wiktionary.org). However, we do not capture as of yet, any of the French data that may be found in other language editions.

We also filtered out some parts of speech in order to produce a result that is closer to existing monolingual dictionaries. For instance, in French, we disregard abstract entries corresponding to prefixes, suffixes or flexions (e.g.: we do not extract data concerning *in-* or *-al* that are prefixes/suffixes and that have a dedicated page in the French language Edition).

Given that the scope and main focus of our work is the production of lexical data, we do not provide any reference or alignment to any ontology (toward top-level concepts for example).

3.2. LEMON and non-LEMON modelled Extracted Data

All of the extracted data could not be structured using solely the LEMON model. For instance, LEMON does not contain any mechanisms that allow to represent translations between languages, as the underlying assumption is that such translation will be handled by the ontology description. Moreover, LEMON further assumes that all data is well-formed and fully specified. As an example, the synonymy relation is a property linking a *Lexical Sense* to another *Lexical Sense*. While this is a correct assumption in *principle*, it does not account for the huge amount of legacy data that is available in dictionaries and lexical databases and that isn't disambiguated.

In order to cope with such legacy data, we introduced several classes and properties that are not LEMON entities. However, we make sure that whenever a piece of data can be represented as a LEMON entity, it is indeed represented as such. Most of these points have already been covered in (Sérasset, 2012).

3.3. Links to other datasets

The DBnary dataset makes use of other datasets. Firstly, while all extracted lexical entries are associated with a language-specific part of speech that is given by its original Wiktionary language edition, we also add, when available a `lexinfo:partOfSpeech` relation to a standard value defined in the *LexInfo* ontology[4] (Buitelaar et al., 2009). Secondly, while the LEMON model uses a string value to represent languages, we additionally use the property `dcterms:lang` to point to a language entity defined in the *Lexvo* ontology (de Melo and Weikum, 2008).

3.4. Disambiguation of translation sources

Many of the translations present in Wiktionary are associated with a hint used by human users to identify the sense of the source of the translation. Depending on the language, this hint may take the form of a sense number (e.g. in German and Turkish), of a textual gloss (e.g. English) or of both a sense number and a textual gloss (e.g. French, Finnish).

By using an adaptation of various textual and semantic similarity techniques based on partial or fuzzy gloss overlaps, we were able to disambiguate the translation relations. We obtained F-measures of the order of 80% (on par with similar work on English only, such as (Meyer and Gurevych, 2012a)), across the three languages where we could generate a gold standard (French, Portuguese, Finnish). We have shown that most of the disambiguation errors are due to inconsistencies in Wiktionary itself that cannot be detected at the generation of DBnary (shifted sense numbers, inconsistent glosses, etc.).

The relations between translations and lexical senses has also been made part of this dataset.

3.5. Size of the involved data

Table 1 gives an overview of the number of main elements (Entries, Vocables, Senses and Translation), as extracted from the most up-to-date dumps at the time of writing. Table 2 details the number of lexico-semantic relations contained in each extracted languages.

4. Conclusion and Perspectives

The present article exhibits some preliminary results on what is essentially an open source tool to extract a LEMON

[4] `http://www.lexinfo.net/ontology/2.0/lexinfo`

based lexical network from various Wiktionary language editions. Such a work is interesting for many users that will be able to use the extracted data in their own NLP systems. Moreover, as the extracted resource uses the Resource Description Framework (RDF) standard and the LEMON model, the extracted data is also directly usable for researchers in the field of the Semantic Web, where it could be used to ease the construction of ontology alignment systems when terms in different languages are used to describe the ontologies of a domain.

Current work consists in extending the set of extracted languages, generalizing the extraction engine so that maitenance and definition of extractors will be easier, and adding more semantics to the dataset by providing internal and external links to *LexicalSenses* (as we started with translations). We are currently working on cross-lingual string similarity measures that will be used to establish such links.

Also, we believe that the different initiatives aiming the extraction of Lexical Data from Wiktionary (e.g. UBY (Meyer and Gurevych, 2012b) or (Hellmann et al., 2013)), should meet and work conjointely to produce even better and larger Lexical Linked Data.

5. Acknowledgements

This work was conducted as a part of the CHIST-ERA CAMOMILE project, which was funded by the ANR (Agence Nationale de la Recherche, France).

6. References

Paul Buitelaar, Philipp Cimiano, Peter Haase, and Michael Sintek. 2009. Towards linguistically grounded ontologies. In Lora Aroyo, Paolo Traverso, Fabio Ciravegna, Philipp Cimiano, Tom Heath, Eero Hyvönen, Riichiro Mizoguchi, Eyal Oren, Marta Sabou, and Elena Simperl, editors, *The Semantic Web: Research and Applications*, volume 5554 of *Lecture Notes in Computer Science*, pages 111–125. Springer Berlin Heidelberg.

Gerard de Melo and Gerhard Weikum. 2008. Language as a Foundation of the {Semantic Web}. In Christian Bizer and Anupam Joshi, editors, *Proceedings of the Poster and Demonstration Session at the 7th International Semantic Web Conference (ISWC)*, volume 401 of *CEUR WS*, Karlsruhe, Germany. CEUR.

Sebastian Hellmann, Jonas Brekle, and Sören Auer. 2013. Leveraging the Crowdsourcing of Lexical Resources for Bootstrapping a Linguistic Data Cloud. *Semantic Technology*, pages 191—-206.

John Mccrae, Guadalupe Aguado-De-Cea, Paul Buitelaar, Philipp Cimiano, Thierry Declerck, Asunción Gómez-Pérez, Jorge Gracia, Laura Hollink, Elena Montiel-Ponsoda, Dennis Spohr, and Tobias Wunner. 2012. Interchanging lexical resources on the semantic web. *Lang. Resour. Eval.*, 46(4):701–719, December.

Christian M Meyer and Iryna Gurevych. 2012a. To Exhibit is not to Loiter: A Multilingual, Sense-Disambiguated Wiktionary for Measuring Verb Similarity. In *Proceedings of COLING 2012*, pages 1763–1780, Mumbai, India. The COLING 2012 Organizing Committee.

Christian M. Meyer and Iryna Gurevych. 2012b. Wiktionary: a new rival for expert-built lexicons? exploring the possibilities of collaborative lexicography. In Sylviane Granger and Magali Paquot, editors, *Electronic Lexicography*, page (to appear). Oxford: Oxford University Press. (pre-publication draft at the date of LREC).

Gilles Sérasset. 2012. DBnary: Wiktionary as a Lemon-Based Multilingual Lexical Resource in RDF. *Semantic Web Journal - Special issue on Multilingual Linked Open Data*.

A Multilingual Semantic Network as Linked Data: *lemon*-BabelNet

Maud Ehrmann[1], Francesco Cecconi[1], Daniele Vannella[1], John P. McCrae[2], Philipp Cimiano[2], Roberto Navigli[1]

[1] Department of Computer Science, Sapienza University of Rome, Italy
[2] Semantic Computing Group, CITEC, University of Bielefeld, Germany
{ehrmann|vannella|navigli}@di.uniroma1.it, francesco.cecconi@gmail.com, {jmccrae|cimiano}@cit-ec.uni-bielefeld.de

Abstract

Empowered by Semantic Web technologies and the recent Linked Data uptake, the publication of linguistic data collections on the Web is, apace with the Web of Data, encouragingly progressing. Indeed, with its long-standing tradition of linguistic resource creation and handling, the Natural Language Processing community can, in many respects, benefit greatly from the Linked Data paradigm. As part of our participation to the Data Challenge associated to the Linked Data in Linguistics Workshop, this paper describes the *lemon*-BabelNet dataset, a multilingual semantic network published as Linked Data.

1. Introduction

Empowered by Semantic Web technologies and the recent Linked Data uptake, the continuously growing Web of Data offers new opportunities for a wide spectrum of domains, including Linguistics and Natural Language Processing. A grassroots effort by members of the Natural Language Processing (NLP) and Semantic Web (SW) communities, in particular the Open Linguistics subgroup[1] of the Open Knowledge Foundation[2], has initiated the development of a Linked Open Data sub-cloud: the *Linguistic* Linked Open Data (LLOD) cloud. Indeed, stimulated by initiatives such as the W3C Ontology-Lexica community group[3], the publication of linguistic data collections on the Web is progressing encouragingly. As defined by Chiarcos et al. (2013), the challenge is to "store, to connect and to exploit the wealth of language data", with the key issues of (linguistic) resource interoperability, i.e. the ability to syntactically process and semantically interpret resources in a seamless way (Ide and Pustejovsky, 2010), and information integration, i.e. the ability to combine information across resources. All types of linguistic resources are eligible for the LLOD cloud, ranging across lexical-semantic resources (such as machine-readable dictionaries, semantic knowledge bases, ontologies) to annotated linguistic corpora, repositories of linguistic terminologies and meta-data repositories (Chiarcos et al., 2011).

The benefits of such a 'Web of Linguistic Data' are diverse and lie on both Semantic Web and NLP sides. On the one hand, ontologies and linked data sets can be augmented with rich linguistic information, thereby enhancing web-based information processing. On the other hand, NLP algorithms can take advantage of the availability of a vast, interoperable and federated set of linguistic resources and benefit from a rich ecosystem of formalisms and technologies. In the medium term, a web-based integration of NLP tools and applications is inevitable; a few steps have already been taken in this direction with the recent definition of the NLP Interchange Format (NIF) (Hellmann et al., 2013). De facto, common initiatives between SW and NLP are multiplying[4].

This paper gives an overview of the *lemon*-BabelNet linked data set, as submitted to the Data Challenge associated to the Linguistics in Linked Data Workshop. BabelNet (Navigli and Ponzetto, 2012) is a very large multilingual encyclopedic dictionary and ontology whose version 2.0 covers 50 languages. Based on the integration of lexicographic and encyclopedic knowledge, BabelNet 2.0 offers a large network of concepts and named entities along with an extensive multilingual lexical coverage. Its conversion to linked data was carried out using the *lemon* model (**Le**xicon **M**odel for **On**tology) (McCrae et al., 2012a), a lexicon model for representing and sharing ontology lexica on the Semantic Web. Our hope is that the publication of BabelNet as linked data will increase its accessibility, enhance lexical-semantic resource integration and support the development of linked data-based NLP applications.

The remainder of the paper is organized as follows. After introducing the BabelNet resource in Section 2, we detail its conversion to linked data in Section 3. Next, in Section 4, we present its interconnections with other resources on the Web and provide an account for statistics and aspects related to publication. Finally, after a brief overview of the potential applications of the dataset (Section 5), we conclude in Section 6.

2. BabelNet 2.0

BabelNet[5] is a lexico-semantic resource whose aim is to provide wide-coverage encyclopedic and lexicographic knowledge in many languages. More precisely, BabelNet is both a multilingual encyclopedic dictionary, with lexicographic and encyclopedic coverage of terms, and an ontology which connects concepts and named entities in a very

[1] http://linguistics.okfn.org/2011/05/20/the-open-linguistics-working-group/

[2] http://okfn.org/

[3] http://www.w3.org/community/ontolex/

[4] See for example the Multilingual Web Linked Open Data and DBpedia&NLP workshops (http://www.multilingualweb.eu/en/documents/dublin-workshop and http://iswc2013.semanticweb.org/content/dbpedia-nlp-2013) respectively).

[5] http://www.babelnet.org

large network of semantic relations, made up of more than 9 million entries, called *Babel synsets*. Adopting a structure similar to that of a WordNet (Fellbaum, 1998), each Babel synset represents a given meaning and contains all the synonyms, called *Babel senses*, which, in different languages, express that meaning. The resource provides, for example, lexical knowledge about the concept *apple* as a fruit, with its part of speech, its definitions and its set of synonyms in multiple languages, as well as encyclopedic knowledge about, among other entities, the *Apple Inc.* company, anew along with definitions in multiple languages. Thanks to the semantic relations, it is furthermore possible to learn that *apple* is an *edible fruit* (or a *fruit comestible*, a *frutta* an *essbare Früchte*) and that *Apple Inc.* is related to *server* and *Mountain View California*. While 6 languages were covered in the prime version 1.0, BabelNet 2.0 makes giant strides in this respect and covers 50 languages. This new version is obtained from the automatic integration of:

- *WordNet*, a popular computational lexicon of English (version 3.0),
- *Open Multilingual WordNet* (OMWN), a collection of wordnets available in different languages,
- *Wikipedia*, the largest collaborative multilingual Web encyclopedia, and
- *OmegaWiki*, a large collaborative multilingual dictionary.

BabelNet 2.0 covers, in addition to English, 50 languages belonging to diverse language families such as, among others, Indo-European, Indo-Iranian, Uralic and Semitic. Overall, the resource contains about 9.3 million concepts. These concepts gather around 50 million senses, are interconnected through more than 260 million lexico-semantic relations and are described by almost 18 million glosses. Further statistics about coverage per language, composition of BabelSynsets and polysemy are available on BabelNet's website[6].

The characteristics of BabelNet, as both a dictionary and an ontology, naturally led to the choice of the *lemon* model for achieving its conversion as linked data.

3. Rendering BabelNet as Linked Data with Lemon

3.1. The *lemon* Model

lemon (McCrae et al., 2011) is a model developed for the representation of lexica relative to ontologies in RDF format. In line with the principle of semantics by reference (Buitelaar, 2010), the model maintains a clean separation of the lexical and semantic layers, enabling lexica to be easily reused to describe different ontologies. As outlined in Figure 1, the core of the lemon model consists of the following elements:

- *Lexical entry*, which comprises all syntactic forms of an entry,

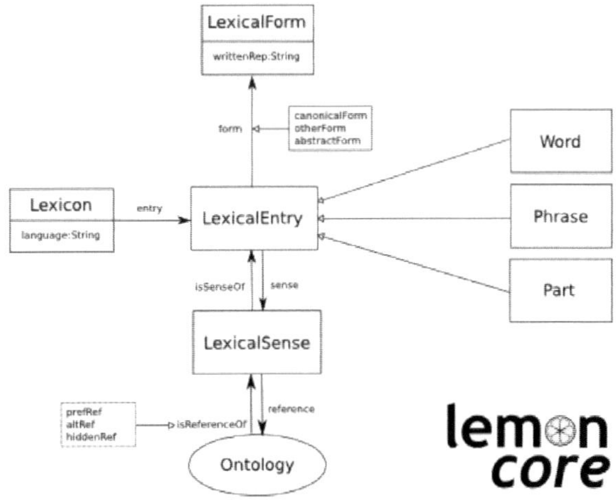

Figure 1: The core of the *lemon* model.

- *Lexical form*, which represents a single inflection of a word, with its *representation*(s), *i.e.*, the actual string(s) used for the word, and
- *Lexical sense*, which represents the usage of a word as a *reference* to a concept in the ontology.

As such the model has already been used for the representation of a number of lexica (Villegas and Bel, 2013; Eckle-Kohler et al., 2014) and proposals have been made to extend the model in new ways (Khan et al., 2013). Specifically designed as an interface between lexical and ontological knowledge and allowing the expression of linguistic information, *lemon* perfectly meets the needs of Babelnet as a candidate for the Linked Data Cloud.

3.2. BabelNet as Linked Data

BabelNet contains a lot of information; yet, its conversion into RDF mainly involves the consideration of its two core elements, namely Babel senses and Babel synsets. As advocated above, ontological and lexical layers should be kept separated. Therefore, while *lemon* provided us with the means of representing lexical information, i.e., Babel senses, we chose to represent collections of equivalent senses, i.e., Babel synsets, using the class *Concept* of the SKOS (Simple Knowledge Organization System) model[7]. We additionally reused the existing vocabulary of *LexInfo 2* (Buitelaar et al., 2009; McCrae et al., 2012b) to encode some of the semantic relations between Babel synsets. Finally, when no existing vocabulary element was available, we defined our own classes and properties. At the lexical level, Babel sense lemmas are encoded as *lemon* lexical entries. Each lexical entry receives a language tag via the *rdfs:label* property, the indication of its part of speech (*lexinfo:partOfSpeech*) and is further described by means of a lexical form encoding the Babel sense lemma as written representation of the entry. According to their language, these entries are assembled into different *lemon* lexicons (51 in total). In accordance with the principle of semantics by reference applied in *lemon*,

[6]http://babelnet.org/stats.jsp

[7]http://www.w3.org/TR/skos-reference

possible meanings of lexical entries are expressed by way of lexical senses pointing to adequate Babel synsets encoded as SKOS concepts. Besides pointing to a referent, lexical senses[8] encode meta-data information with, first, the source of the sense (WordNet, OMWN, Wikipedia or OmegaWiki) and, when relevant, the way it was obtained: *via* automatic translation or thanks to a Wikipedia redirection page (boolean properties). Additionally, these *lemon* senses support the expression of translation variants between Babel senses; indeed, translations pertain to lexical sense relations as they should be stated between disambiguated words (i.e., the lexical senses of lexical entries), which do not necessarily refer to the same concept. As an illustration of the encoding of these lexical elements, Figure 2 depicts the *lemon* representation of the Italian Babel sense 'Web semantico' in Turtle format[9] (prefixes are defined in the Figure). Encoded as a *lemon:LexicalEntry* (bn:Web_semantico_n_IT) this entry is part of the Italian *lemon:Lexicon* (bn:lexicon_IT), it shows a *lemon:Form* (bn:Web_semantico_n_IT/canonicalForm), as well as a *lemon:LexicalSense* (bn:Web_semantico_IT/s02276858n).

From the ontological perspective, we used *skos:Concept(s)* to represent our 'units of thought', i.e., Babel synsets. These Babel SKOS concepts encode two types of information: regarding the concept itself, and regarding its semantic relations with other concepts. As a base, Babel SKOS concepts are linked back to the entries of the *lemon* lexica thanks to the property *isReferenceOf.* Next, a BabelNet property (*bn-lemon:synsetType*) indicates whether the Babel synset is a concept or a named entity (NE). Most importantly, multilingual glosses which provide a description of the concept in up to 50 languages, are specified through a *bn-lemon:definition* property referring to a *bn-lemon:BabelGloss*. Although the *skos:definition* would have been the ideal candidate to represent this piece of information, it nevertheless does not enable the expression of additional (meta-data) information about the definition. We therefore defined a class, namely *BabelGloss*, so as to be able to specify the source of the definition (WordNet, OMWN, Wikipedia or OmegaWiki), as well as its license. This is the only BabelNet component for which we could not reuse an element of an existing vocabulary. As regards the semantic relations between Babel synsets, these are encoded as *skos:narrower* and *skos:broader* for hyponyms and hypernyms, respectively, as *lexinfo* relations when adequate (member meronym, member holonym, participle, *etc.*), and as *skos:related* when less specified. Finally, Wikipedia categories (in dozens of languages) and their DBpedia twin (in English) are reported for each concept *via* a dedicated property. Following up with the 'Web semantico' example, Figure 2 shows the concept to which this entry refers, i.e. the *skos:Concept* bn:s02276858n. It holds the above mentioned properties, and links to a *BabelGloss* (here the German one, bn:s02276858n_Gloss1_DE).

[8]Lexical senses URIs are based on the 'full' lemma of Babel senses; when originating from Wikipedia, they are thus made up from the sense-tagged lemmas as in 'Apple_(Fruit)' and Apple_(Computer).

[9]http://www.w3.org/TeamSubmission/turtle/

```
@prefix bn: <http://babelnet.org/2.0/> .
@prefix bn-lemon: <http://babelnet.org/model/babelnet#>
@prefix lemon: <http://www.lemon-model.net/lemon#> .
@prefix skos: <http://www.w3.org/2004/02/skos/core#> .
@prefix wikipedia-da: <http://da.wikipedia.org/wiki/Kategori/> .
@prefix wikipedia-it: <http://it.wikipedia.org/wiki/Categorie/> .
@prefix dcterms: <http://purl.org/dc/terms/> .
 ...

bn:lexicon_IT
      a   lemon:Lexicon;
      dc:source   <http://babelnet.org/>;
      lemon:entry   bn:Web_semantico_n_IT, ... ;
      lemon:language   "IT".

bn:Web_semantico_n_IT
      a   lemon:LexicalEntry;
      rdfs:label   "Web_semantico"@IT;
      lemon:canonicalForm   bn:Web_semantico_n_IT/canonicalForm;
      lemon:language   "IT";
      lemon:sense   bn:Web_semantico_IT/s02276858n ;
      lexinfo:partOfSpeech   lexinfo:noun.

bn:Web_semantico_n_IT/canonicalForm
      a   lemon:Form ;
      lemon:writtenRep   "Web_semantico"@IT.

bn:Web_semantico_IT/s02276858n
      a   lemon:LexicalSense ;
      dc:source   <http://wikipedia.org/>;
      dcterms:license  <http://creativecommons.org/licenses/by-sa/3.0/>;
      bn-lemon:wikipediaPage   wikipedia-it:Web_semantico;
      lemon:reference   bn:s02276858n .

bn:s02276858n
      a   skos:Concept;
      bn-lemon:synsetType   "NE";
      bn-lemon:synsetID   "bn:02276858n";
      bn-lemon:wikipediaCategory   wikipedia-da:Kategori:Internet;
      lemon:isReferenceOf   bn:Web_semantico_IT/s02276858n ...;
      skos:exactMatch   dbpedia:Semantic_Web;
      bn-lemon:definition   bn:s02276858n_Gloss1_DE ... ;
      dcterms:license  <http://creativecommons.org/licenses/by-nc-sa/3.0/>;
      skos:related   bn:s00076736n , bn:s03586460n ... .

bn:s02276858n_Gloss1_DE
      a   bn-lemon:BabelGloss;
      bn-lemon:gloss   "Das Semantische Web ist... "@DE ;
      lemon:language   "DE" ;
      dc:source   <http://wikipedia.org/>;
      dcterms:license  <http://creativecommons.org/licenses/by-sa/3.0/> .
```

Figure 2: An excerpt of BabelNet as RDF in Turtle format.

Based on a *lemon*-SKOS model, the RDF edition of BabelNet is able to render most of the information contained in the stand-alone version, offering a large multi-domain and linguistic linked dataset, associated with an extensive multilingual lexical coverage. Yet, beyond its content, one of the key features of a linked dataset is to set connections to other datasets and to be accessible over the Web.

4. Interlinking and Publishing on the Web

4.1. Interlinking *lemon*-Babelnet

Generated from the integration of various existing resources, the most natural way of linking *lemon*-BabelNet is to consider the RDF versions, if available, of these resources. *lemon*-BabelNet includes in the first place links to encyclopedic resources: links to Wikipedia pages are established at the sense level (when originating from Wikipedia), and links to Wikipedia *category* pages at the SKOS concept level. These links are set up from the Wikipedia dump from which the resource is derived. Regarding DBpedia, links are set at the SKOS level only, with pointers to DBpedia English pages and English category pages. The URIs of these links are set up by swapping Wikipedia names-

Resource	
# SKOS concepts	9,348,287
# babel glosses	17,961,157
# semantic relations	262,663,251
# lemon senses	50,282,542
# lemon lexical entries	44,486,335
# lemon lexicons	51
Outgoing links	
# Wikipedia page	35,784,593
# Wikipedia category	45,520,563
# DBpedia category	15,381,861
# DBpedia page	3,829,053
# lemon WordNet 3.0	117657
# lemon OmegaWiki (En)	15140
Total number of outgoing links	100,648,867
Total number of triples	1,138,337,378

Table 1: Statistics concerning the *lemon*-BabelNet 2.0 RDF dataset.

pace for the DBpedia one[10]; no links are provided towards localized versions of DBpedia for now. Additionally, we provide links to lexical resources by setting connections to the *lemon* versions of WordNet 3.0[11] and OmegaWiki[12] (English version), both at the SKOS concept level. In both cases, URIs are taken from the RDF dumps of these datasets, using the synsets IDs to match the resources.

4.2. Statistics

The RDF version of BabelNet 2.0 features an overall number of 1.1 billion triples. Table 1 gives further details about the nature of these triples, which naturally reflect the standalone version, especially for SKOS concepts and lemon lexical senses. Most importantly, the resource contains a significant number of outgoing links, with around 80 million connections to either Wikipedia pages or categories, 19 million similar relations to DBpedia and, at the level of genuine lexical knowledge, a complete linkage to the *lemon* edition of Princeton WordNet 3.0 and 15k links to the English OmegaWiki edition of *lemon*-UBY. These connections to other *lemon* resources are of particular interest as they lay the foundations for further linked data-based integration of ontology lexica.

4.3. Publication on the web

BabelNet 2.0 and its Linked Data edition is published under the Creative Commons Attribution-NonCommercial-ShareAlike 3.0 License. Additionally, as it is based on a collection of independent resources, special attention must be paid to the licensing policies of these grounding works. *lemon*-BabelNet respects the copyrights of the original resources, and reproduces the different licenses under which they were issued, in two different ways: by releasing different RDF dump files according to groups of compatible licenses in the first place, by specifying a license property (dcterms:license) on triples in the second. As advocated by Rodríguez-Doncel et al. (2013), our aim is to achieve maximum transparency, which such explicit rights declarations should guarantee.

On a more concrete standpoint, BabelNet is served on the Web in three ways, *via*:

- a set of RDF dump files (URIs and IRIs) in n-triples format downloadable at the following URL: `http://babelnet.org/download.jsp`,
- a public SPARQL endpoint set up using the Virtuoso Universal Server[13] and accessible from the following URL: `http://babelnet.org:8084/sparql/`, and
- dereferenceable URIs, supported by the Pubby Web application, a Linked Data frontend for SPARQL endpoints[14] (`http://babelnet.org/2.0/`).

Since BabelNet is released on a periodiocal basis, it is important to enable the tracking of different versions. To this end, the version number is explicitely mentioned in the URL; URIs are therefore fixed for each version, and the previous can easily be mapped to the next.

5. Possible applications of the dataset

We anticipate several uses of the *lemon*-BabelNet linked dataset. The resource can, in the first place, be used for multilingual ontology lexicalization. In this regard, a recent work by Unger et al. (2013) proposes a *lemon* lexicon for the DBpedia ontology; it covers the most frequent classes and properties of the DBpedia schema, and provides manually created lexical entries for English. The continuation of such a work for other languages could benefit greatly from the availability of a resource such as *lemon*-BabelNet. Besides enriching the lexical layer of ontologies, *lemon*-BabelNet can help in manipulating this information, e.g. for cross-lingual ontology mapping. Another application is, naturally, Word Sense Disambiguation. In this respect, we can mention the work of Elbedweihy et al. (2013), which uses BabelNet to bridge the gap (by performing query disambiguation) between natural language queries and linked data concepts. Furthermore, because it focuses both on word senses and named entities (what is more cross-lingually interconnected in many languages), BabelNet opens up the possibility to perform jointly the tasks of Word Sense Disambiguation and Entity Linking, as demonstrated by (Moro et al., 2014). With the additional knowledge that can be discovered and gathered on the (L)LODs, *lemon*-BabelNet can potentially increase the performance of such disambiguation process. Finally, one could also consider to take advantage of the LLOD to improve some of its components: in the frame of lexical-semantic resources for example, one could consider the possibility of cross-resource validation of sense alignments over linked data.

[10] http://dbpedia.org/resource/
[11] http://lemon-model.net/lexica/pwn/
[12] http://lemon-model.net/lexica/uby/ow_eng/
[13] http://virtuoso.openlinksw.com/
[14] http://wifo5-03.informatik.uni-mannheim.de/pubby/

6. Conclusion

In this paper we presented *lemon*-BabelNet, such as submitted to the Data Challenge. Based on the *lemon* model, the dataset features about 1 billion triples which describe 9 million concepts with encyclopedic and lexical information in 50 languages. The resource is interlinked with several other datasets of encyclopedic (DBpedia) and lexicographic (WordNet, Uby) nature. We believe that this wide, multilingual and interconnected lexical-semantic dataset, together with other linguistic resources in the LLOD, represent a major opportunity for Natural Language Processing. Indeed, if carefully published and interlinked, those resources could, potentially, turn into a huge body of machine-readable knowledge. Future work naturally includes the upgrading of *lemon*-BabelNet to take account of any expansion of BabelNet itself, e.g., its full taxonomization (Flati et al., 2014) and validation (Vannella et al., 2014), as well as the diversification and integration of links to other resources (Pilehvar and Navigli, 2014).

Acknowledgments

Sapienza affiliated authors gratefully acknowledge the support of the ERC Starting Grant MultiJEDI No. 259234.

The authors also acknowledge support from the LIDER project (No. 610782), a support action funded by the European Commission under FP7. Warm thanks go to Victor Rodríguez-Doncel for the helpful discussion on (linked data) copyrights.

7. References

P. Buitelaar, P. Cimiano, P. Haase, and M. Sintek. 2009. Towards linguistically grounded ontologies. In *Proc. of the 6th Annual European Semantic Web Conference*, pages 111–125.

P. Buitelaar. 2010. Ontology-based semantic lexicons: Mapping between terms and object descriptions. *Ontology and the Lexicon*, pages 212–223.

C. Chiarcos, S. Hellmann, and S. Nordhoff. 2011. Towards a linguistic linked open data cloud: The open linguistics working group. *TAL (Traitement automatique des langues)*, 52(3):245–275.

C. Chiarcos, J. McCrae, P. Cimiano, and C. Fellbaum. 2013. Towards open data for linguistics: Linguistic linked data. In A. Oltramari, P. Vossen, L. Qin, and E. Hovy, editors, *New Trends of Research in Ontologies and Lexical Resources*, pages 7–25. Springer.

J. Eckle-Kohler, J. McCrae, and C. Chiarcos. 2014. *lemon*Uby-a large, interlinked, syntactically-rich resource for ontologies. *Semantic Web Journal, Special issue on Multilingual Linked Open Data.*

K. Elbedweihy, S. Wrigley, Fabio F. Ciravegna, and Z. Zhang. 2013. Using BabelNet in bridging the gap between natural language queries and linked data concepts. In *Proc. of the 1st International Workshop on NLP and DBpedia*, pages 21–25.

C. Fellbaum, editor. 1998. *WordNet: An Electronic Database.* MIT Press, Cambridge, MA.

T. Flati, D. Vannella, T. Pasini, and R. Navigli. 2014. Two Is Bigger (and Better) Than One: the Wikipedia Bitaxonomy Project. In *Proc. of the 52nd Annual Meeting of the Association for Computational Linguistics*.

S. Hellmann, J. Lehmann, S. Auer, and M. Brümmer. 2013. Integrating NLP using linked data. In *Proceedings of the 12th International Semantic Web Conference*, pages 97–112.

N. Ide and J. Pustejovsky. 2010. What does interoperability mean, anyway? Towards an operational definition of interoperability for language technology. In *Proc. of the 2nd Conference on Global Interoperability for Language Resources.*

F. Khan, F. Frontini, R. Del Gratta, M. Monachini, and V. Quochi. 2013. Generative lexicon theory and linguistic linked open data. In *Proceedings of the 6th International Conference on Generative Approaches to the Lexicon*, pages 62–69.

J. McCrae, D. Spohr, and P. Cimiano. 2011. Linking lexical resources and ontologies on the semantic web with lemon. In *The Semantic Web: Research and Applications*, pages 245–259. Springer.

J. McCrae, G. Aguado de Cea, P. Buitelaar, P. Cimiano, T. Declerck, A. Gómez-Pérez, J. Gracia, L. Hollink, E. Montiel-Ponsoda, D. Spohr, et al. 2012a. Interchanging lexical resources on the semantic web. *Language Resources and Evaluation*, 46(4):701–719.

J. McCrae, E. Montiel-Ponsoda, and P. Cimiano. 2012b. Collaborative semantic editing of linked data lexica. In *Proceedings of the 8th International Conference on Language Resource and Evaluation*, pages 2619–2625, Istanbul, Turkey.

A. Moro, A. Raganato, and R. Navigli. 2014. Entity Linking meets Word Sense Disambiguation: A Unified Approach. *Transactions of the Association for Computational Linguistics*, 2.

R. Navigli and S. P. Ponzetto. 2012. BabelNet: The automatic construction, evaluation and application of a wide-coverage multilingual semantic network. *Artificial Intelligence*, 193:217–250.

M. T. Pilehvar and R. Navigli. 2014. A Robust Approach to Aligning Heterogeneous Lexical Resources. In *Proceedings of the 52nd Annual Meeting of the Association for Computational Linguistics.*

V. Rodríguez-Doncel, A. Gómez-Pérez, and N. Mihindukulasooriya. 2013. Rights declaration in linked data. In *Proc. of the 3rd International Workshop on Consuming Linked Data.*

C. Unger, J. McCrae, S. Walter, S. Winter, and P. Cimiano. 2013. A *lemon* lexicon for DBpedia. In S. Hellmann, A. Filipowska, C. Barriere, P. Mendes, and D. Kontokostas, editors, *Proc. of 1st Int'l Workshop on NLP and DBpedia*, Sydney, Australia.

D. Vannella, D. Jurgens, D. Scarfini, D. Toscani, and R. Navigli. 2014. Validating and Extending Semantic Knowledge Bases using Video Games with a Purpose. In *Proc. of the 52nd Annual Meeting of the Association for Computational Linguistics.*

M. Villegas and N. Bel. 2013. PAROLE/SIMPLE 'lemon' ontology and lexicons. *Semantic Web Journal.*

Linked-Data based Domain-Specific Sentiment Lexicons

Gabriela Vulcu, Raul Lario Monje, Mario Munoz, Paul Buitelaar, Carlos A. Iglesias

Insight, Centre for Data Analytics, National University of Ireland, Galway, Ireland
gabriela.vulcu@insight-centre.org, paul.buitelaar@insight-centre.org,
Paradigma Tecnologico, Madrid, Spain
rlario@paradigmatecnologico.com, mmunoz@paradigmatecnologico.com,
Universidad Politecnica de Madrid, Spain
cif@dit.upm.es

Abstract

In this paper we present a dataset composed of domain-specific sentiment lexicons in six languages for two domains. We used existing collections of reviews from TripAdvisor, Amazon, the Stanford Network Analysis Project and the OpinRank Review Dataset. We use an RDF model based on the lemon and Marl formats to represent the lexicons. We describe the methodology that we applied to generate the domain-specific lexicons and we provide access information to our datasets.

Keywords: domain specific lexicon, sentiment analysis

1. Introduction

Nowadays we are facing a high increase in the use of commercial websites, social networks and blogs which permit users to create a lot of content that can be reused for the sentiment analysis task. However there is no common way to representing this content that can be easily exploited by tools. There are many formats for representing the reviews content and different annotations. The EUROSENTIMENT project[1] aims to developing a large shared data pool that bundles together scattered resources meant to be used by sentiment analysis systems in an uniform way.

In this paper we present domain-specific lexicons organized around domain entities described with lexical information represented using the lemon[2] format (McCrae et al., 2012) and sentiment words described in the context of these entities whose polarity scores are represented using the Marl[3] format (Westerski et al., 2011). Our language resources dataset consists of fourteen lexicons covering six languages: Catalan, English, Spanish, French, Italian and Portuguese and two domains: Hotel and Electronics. Part of the lexicons are built directly from the available review corpora using our language resource adaptation pipeline and part using an intermediary result of sentiment dictionaries built semi-automatically by Paradigma Tecnologico. In section 2. we list the data sources that we used to build the lexicons. In section 3. we describe the methods, tools and algorithms used to build the lexicons. In section 4. we provide details about the RDF structure of our lexicons conversion.

2. Datasources

We used 10000 aspect-based annotated reviews from the TripAdvisor[4] reviews dataset and 600 reviews from the Electronics dataset from Amazon[5]. The TripAdvisor data contains rated reviews at aspect level. Listing 1 shows the TripAdvisor data format:

Listing 1: TripAdvisor data format.

```
<Author>everywhereman2
<Content>THIS is the place to stay at
    when visiting the historical area
    of Seattle. ...
<Date>Jan 6, 2009
<img src="http://cdn.tripadvisor.com/
    img2/new.gif" alt="New"/>
<No. Reader>-1
<No. Helpful>-1
<Overall>5
<Value>5
<Rooms>5
<Location>5
<Cleanliness>5
<Check in / front desk>5
<Service>5
<Business service>5
```

The Amazon electronics corpus consists of plain text reviews with custom ratings annotations. Listing 2 shows the Amazon electronics data format. The annotation [t] stands for the title of the review whereas the numbers in brackets stand for the rating of a certain aspect in the review.

Listing 2: Amazon electronics data format.

```
[t]the best 4mp compact digital
    available camera[+2]##this camera
    is perfect for an enthusiastic
    amateur photographer. picture[+3],
    macro[+3]##the pictures are razor-
    sharp, even in macro...
```

[1] http://eurosentiment.eu/
[2] http://lemon-model.net/lexica/pwn/
[3] http://www.gi2mo.org/marl/0.1/ns.html
[4] http://sifaka.cs.uiuc.edu/wang296/Data/index.html
[5] http://www.cs.uic.edu/ liub/FBS/Reviews-9-products.rar

Paradigma used the Stanford Network Analysis Project (SNAP)[6] and the OpinRank Review Dataset[7] (Ganesan and Zhai, 2011). The Stanford Network Analysis Project dataset consists of reviews from Amazon. The data spans a period of 18 years, including 35 million reviews up to March 2013. Reviews include product and user information, review-level ratings, and a plain text review as shown bellow in Listing 3

Listing 3: SNAP data format.

```
product/productId: B00006HAXW
review/userId: A1RSDE90N6RSZF
review/profileName: Joseph M. Kotow
review/helpfulness: 9/9
review/score: 5.0
review/time: 1042502400
review/summary: Pittsburgh
review/text: I have all of the doo wop
    DVD's and this one is as good ...
```

The OpinRank dataset provides reviews using teh XML format and contains no ratings. The data format is described in Listing 4

Listing 4: OpinRank data format.

```
<DOC>
 <DATE>06/15/2009</DATE>
 <AUTHOR>The author</AUTHOR>
 <TEXT>The review goes here..</TEXT>
 <FAVORITE>User favorites things about
     this hotel.</FAVORITE>
</DOC>
```

The annotated reviews are in English and they cover two domains: 'Hotels' and 'Electronics'. It is important to remark that we do not publish these reviews; we publish the derive lexicons by processing such reviews (i.e.: domain, context words, sentiment words). Addressing the language resources heterogeneity was one of the motivation for the EUROSENTIMENT project.

3. Method and Tools

One of the tasks of the EUROSENTIMENT[8] project is to develop a methodology that generates domain-specific sentiment lexicons from legacy language resources and enriching them with semantics and additional linguistic information from resources like DBpedia and BabelNet. The language resources adaptation pipeline consists of four main steps highlighted by dashed rectangles in Figure 1: (i) the Corpus Conversion step normalizes the different review corpora formats to a common schema based on Marl and NIF[9]; (ii) the Semantic Analysis step extracts the domain-specific entity classes and named entities and identifies links between these entities and concepts from the LLOD Cloud. It uses pattern-based term extraction algorithm with a generic domain model (Bordea, 2013) on each document, aggregates the lemmatized terms and computes their ranking in the corpus(Bordea et al., 2013) to extract entity classes that define the domain. We use the AELA framework for Entity Linking that uses DBpedia as reference for entity mentioning identification, extraction and disambiguation (Pereira et al., 2013). For linking the entities to WordNet we extend each candidate synset with their direct hyponym and hypernym synsets. Synset words are then checked for occurrence within all the extracted entity classes that define the language resource domain. (iii)The Sentiment Analysis step extracts contextual sentiments and identifies SentiWordNet synsets corresponding to these contextual sentiment words. We base our approach for sentiment word detection on earlier research on sentiment analysis for identifying adjectives or adjective phrases (Hu and Liu, 2004), adverbs (Benamara et al., 2007), two-word phrases (Turney and Littman, 2005) and verbs (Subrahmanian and Reforgiato, 2008). Particular attention is given to the sentiment phrases which can represent an opposite sentiment than what they represent if separated into individual words (e.g. 'ridiculous bargain'). For determining the SentiWordNet link to the sentiment words we identify the nearest SentiWordNet sense for a sentiment candidate using Concept-Based Disambiguation (Raviv and Markovitch, 2012) which utilizes the semantic similarity measure 'Explicit Semantic Analysis' (Gabrilovich and Markovitch, 2006) to represent senses in a high-dimensional space of natural concepts. Concepts are obtained from large knowledge resources such as Wikipedia, which also covers domain specific knowledge. We compare the semantic similarity scores obtained by computing semantic similarity of a bag of words containing domain name, entity and sentiment word with bags of words which contain members of the synset and the gloss for each synset of that SentiWordNet entry. We consider the synset with the highest similarity score above a threshold. (iv) the Lexicon Generator step uses the results of the previous steps, enhances them with multilingual and morphosyntactic (i.e. using the CELEX[10] dataset for inflections) information and converts the results into a lexicon based on the lemon and Marl formats. Different language resources are processed with variations of the given adaptation pipeline. For example the domain-specific English review corpora are processed using the pipeline described in Figure 1 while the sentiment annotated dictionaries like the ones created by Paradigma are converted to the lemon/Marl format using a workflow that consists only of the Lexicon Generator component.

3.1. Paradigma Tecnologico sentiment dictionaries

At Paradigma Tecnologico we used the SNAP and OpiRank review corpora to build the intermediary sentiment dictionaries linked to WordNet synset id following a semi-automatic approach that involved linguists. We used term frequency analysis on the reviews and we ranked the extracted terms based on their occurrences after filtering out the stop words. These sorted lists were reviewed by linguists to filter only the domain-specific entities. The relevant entities are context entities (e.g. 'room', 'food' etc.) and sentiment words (e.g. 'clean', 'small' etc.).

[6]http://snap.stanford.edu/data/web-Amazon-links.html

[7]http://archive.ics.uci.edu/ml/datasets/OpinRank+Review+Dataset

[8]http://eurosentiment.eu/

[9]http://persistence.uni-leipzig.org/nlp2rdf/

[10]http://celex.mpi.nl/

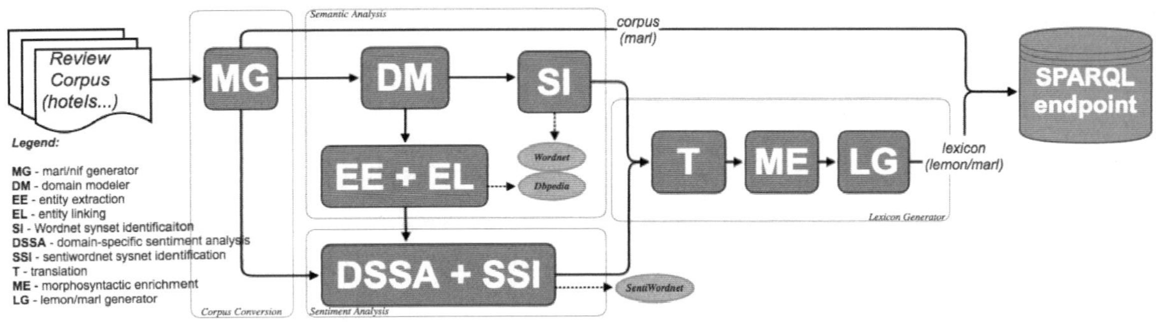

Figure 1: Methodology for Legacy Language Resources Adaptation for Sentiment Analysis.

Then we used a searching-chunking process to achieve the most relevant collocations of the corpora. This task consisted of identification of collocated context entities and sentiment words using a 3-word sliding window. The calculated collocations were reviewed again by linguists.
A simple web application helped the linguists to:

- Accept or reject the collocations. Do they make sense? Are they useful in this domain?
- When accepted, disambiguate the context entity and the sentiment word included in the collocation using WordNet 3.0[11]. The linguists read the gloss and synonyms included in the corresponding synset and we chose the most agreed upon appropriate meaning (synset ID).
- Scoring the collocation from a sentiment perspective, in a [0..1] range [10]. Figure 2 shows a snapshot of the web application where linguists could provide their inputs for the sentiment scores.

A trade-off decision, between domain coverage and effort, was taken to include as many important domain entities as possible.
At the end of this process the resulted sentiment dictionaries are provided as CSV files, one file per language and domain, with the following fields:
$entity$, $entityWNid$, $entityPOS$, $sentiment$, $sentiWNid$, $sentiPOS$, $score$ where $entity$ is the context entity; $entityWNid$ is the WordNet synset id agreed for the $entity$; $entityPOS$ is the part-of-speech of the context entity; $sentiment$ is the sentiment word that occurs in the context of the $entity$; $sentiWNid$ is the SentiWordNet id agreed for the sentiment word; $sentiPOS$ is the sentiment word's part-of speech and finally $score$ is the polarity score assigned to the sentiment words by the linguists.
As an example consider the following result from the 'Hotel' domain in English:
04105893, n, $room$, 01676517, a, $fantastic$, 0.75. Here we see that the sentiment word fantastic is an adjective with the sysnet id 01676517 and has a polarity score of 0.75 in the context of the entity room which is a noun with the synset id 04105893.
Paradigma provided also sentiment dictionaries in the following languages: Catalan, French, Spanish, Italian and Portuguese. The non-english dictionaries were built using MultiWordNet[12] translation based on the WordNet synset ids from the English dictionaries.

4. Lexicon

The results from the language resource adaptation pipeline and the sentiment dictionaries from Paradigma were converted to RDF using the RDF extension of the GoogleRefine[13] tool to create the RDF lexicons. We used the following namespaces listed in Listing 5 : $lemon$ - the core lemon lexicon model, $marl$ - vocabulary to describe sentiment polarities, w - WordNet 3.0 synsets, $lexinfo$ - for part-of-speech properties, ed - domain categories, el - lexicon prefix, ele - lexical entries prefix.
The URIs for the lexical entries are built from the lee namespace and the name of the lexical entry. For each lexical entry we add their written form and their language within a $lemon : CanonicalForm$ object and their part-of-speech information using a $lexinfo$ object. For each different synset id of the same context entity we build a $lemon : sense$ For each sense we add the connections to other datasets using the $lemon : reference$ property to refer to the Dbpedia and WordNet links. The sentiment words are represented similarly: for each sentiment word we create a lexical entry and for each of its distinct polarity values and synset pairs we create a different sense of the lexical entry. Differently from the lexical entries generated for entity classes and named entities, the senses of the sentiment word lexical entries contain also the sentiment polarity values and polarity using Marl sentiment properties $marl : polarityValue$ and $marl : hasPolarity$ respectively.
Figure 3 shows an example of a generated lexicon for the domain 'hotel' in English. It shows 3 *lemon:LexicalEntries*: 'room ' (entity class), 'Paris' (named entity) and 'small' (sentiment word) which in the context of the lexical entry 'room' has negative polarity.

[11] http://wordnet.princeton.edu/

[12] http://multiwordnet.fbk.eu/english/home.php

[13] http://refine.deri.ie/

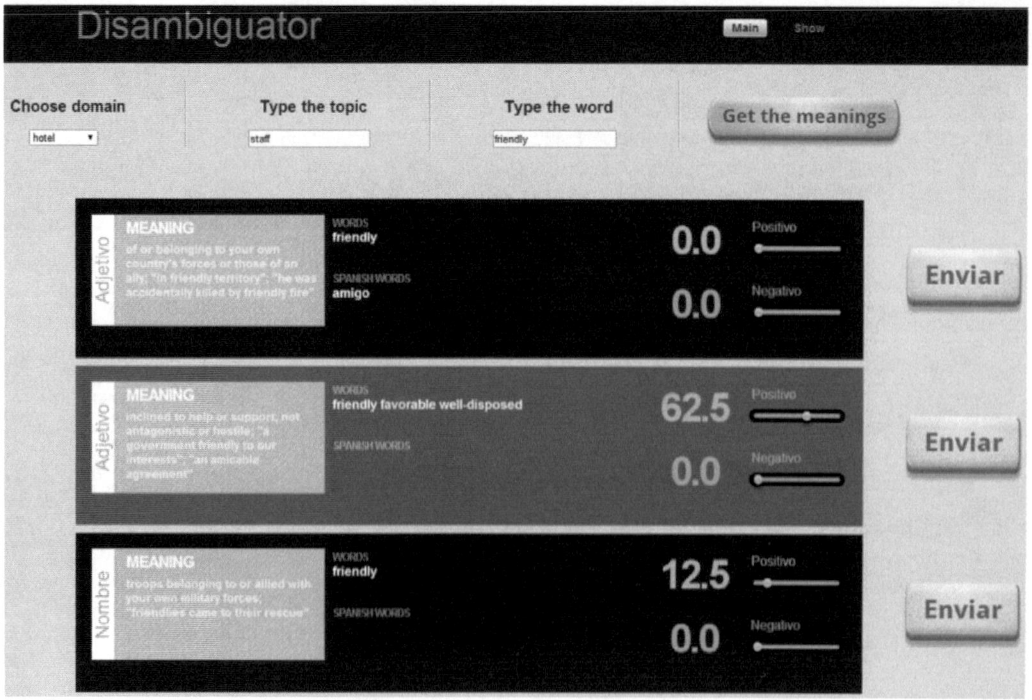

Figure 2: Snapshot of the Web application that allows linguists to specify the sentiment scores.

Listing 5: Namespaces used in the RDF lexicons..

```
lemon: http://www.monnet-project.eu/lemon
marl:  http://purl.org/marl/ns
wn:    http://semanticweb.cs.vu.nl/europeana/lod/purl/vocabularies/princeton/wn30
lexinfo: http://www.lexinfo.net/ontology/2.0/lexinfo
ed:    http://www.eurosentiment/domains
le:      http://wwww.eurosentiment.com/lexicon/<language>/
lee:   http://www.eurosentiment.com/lexicalentry/<language>/
```

Each of them consists of senses, which are linked to DBpedia and/or WordNet concepts.

We use named graphs to group the data from each lexicon. The URIs that we use for the named graphs are the lexicon URIs and they are built after the following pattern: `http://eurosentiment.eu/dataset/<domain>/<language>/lexicon/paradigma` for the lexicons obtained from the sentiment dictionaries from Paradigma and `http://eurosentiment.eu/dataset/<domain>/<language>/lexicon/ta` and `http://eurosentiment.eu/dataset/<domain>/<language>/lexicon/amz` for the lexicons obtained from the TripAdvisor and Amazon corpora.

5. Availability

The domain-specific lexicons are are available as and RDF dump that can be accessed from: `http://eurosentiment.eu/datasets/domain-specific-sentiment-lexicons.tar` and are also loaded in a Virtuoso[14] SPARQL endoint which can be accessed from: `http://eurosentiment.eu/sparql`. We also installed the linked data frontend pubby[15] on top of this SPARQL endpoint to allow for easier browsing of the provided lexicons. For example one can start at the following link `http://eurosentiment.eu/dataset` to see the available lexicons. Then he/she can click on the uri of any of the lexicons to explore its lexical entries.

6. Acknowledgements

This work has been funded by the European project EUROSENTIMENT under grant no. 296277.

7. References

Farah Benamara, Carmine Cesarano, Antonio Picariello, Diego Reforgiato, and V. S. Subrahmanian. 2007. Sentiment analysis: Adjectives and adverbs are better than adjectives alone. In *Proceedings of the International Conference on Weblogs and Social Media*, ICWSM'07.

[14]http://virtuoso.openlinksw.com/

[15]http://wifo5-03.informatik.uni-mannheim.de/pubby/

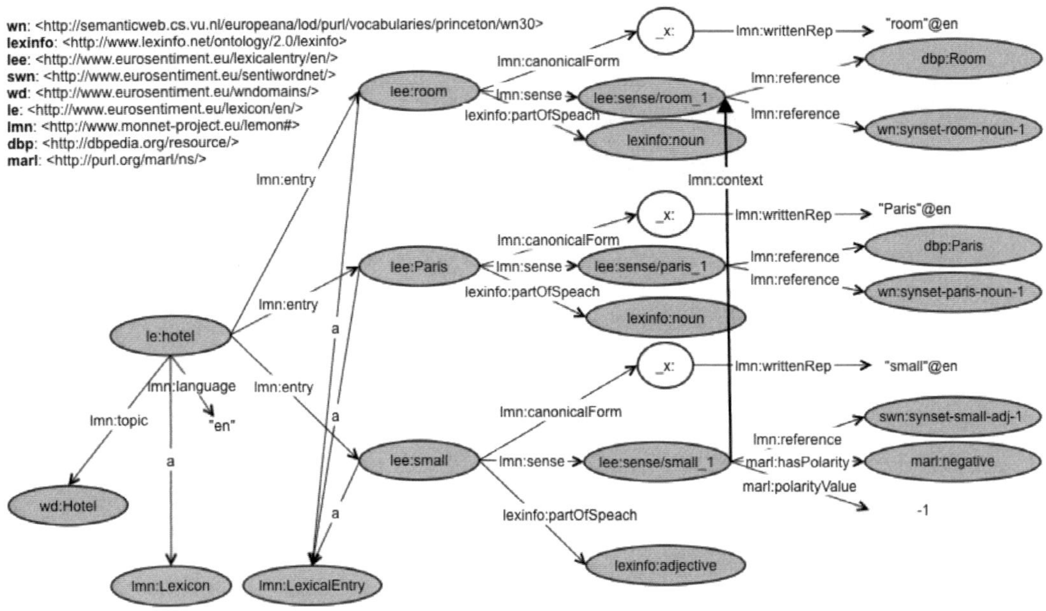

Figure 3: Example lexicon for the domain 'hotel' in English.

Georgeta Bordea, Paul Buitelaar, and Tamara Polajnar. 2013. Domain-independent term extraction through domain modelling. In *Proceedings of the 10th International Conference on Terminology and Artificial Intelligence*, TIA'13, Paris, France.

Georgeta Bordea. 2013. *Domain Adaptive Extraction of Topical Hierarchies for Expertise Mining*. Ph.D. thesis, National University of Ireland, Galway.

Evgeniy Gabrilovich and Shaul Markovitch. 2006. Overcoming the brittleness bottleneck using wikipedia: Enhancing text categorization with encyclopedic knowledge. In *Proceedings of the 21st National Conference on Artificial Intelligence*, AAAI'06. AAAI Press.

Kavita Ganesan and ChengXiang Zhai. 2011. Opinion-based entity ranking. *Information Retrieval*.

Minqing Hu and Bing Liu. 2004. Mining and summarizing customer reviews. In *Proceedings of the Tenth ACM SIGKDD International Conference on Knowledge Discovery and Data Mining*, KDD '04, New York, NY, USA. ACM.

John McCrae, Guadalupe Aguado de Cea, Paul Buitelaar, Philipp Cimiano, Thierry Declerck, Asuncin Gmez-Prez, Jorge Gracia, Laura Hollink, Elena Montiel-Ponsoda, Dennis Spohr, and Tobias Wunner. 2012. Interchanging lexical resources on the semantic web. *Language Resources and Evaluation*.

Bianca Pereira, Nitish Aggarwal, and Paul Buitelaar. 2013. Aela: An adaptive entity linking approach. In *Proceedings of the 22nd International Conference on World Wide Web Companion*, WWW'13, Republic and Canton of Geneva, Switzerland.

Ariel Raviv and Shaul Markovitch. 2012. Concept-based approach to word-sense disambiguation. In *Proceedings of the 26th AAAI Conference on Artificial Intelligence*.

V.S. Subrahmanian and Diego Reforgiato. 2008. Ava: Adjective-verb-adverb combinations for sentiment analysis. *Intelligent Systems*.

Peter D. Turney and Michael L. Littman. 2005. Corpus-based learning of analogies and semantic relations. *Machine Learning*.

Adam Westerski, Carlos A. Iglesias, and Fernando Tapia. 2011. Linked Opinions: Describing Sentiments on the Structured Web of Data. In *Proceedings of the 4th International Workshop Social Data on the Web*.

Linked Hypernyms Dataset - Generation Framework and Use Cases

Tomáš Kliegr[1], Václav Zeman[1], and Milan Dojchinovski[1,2]

[1] Department of Information and Knowledge Engineering
Faculty of Informatics and Statistics
University of Economics, Prague, Czech Republic
first.last@vse.cz
[2] Web Engineering Group
Faculty of Information Technology
Czech Technical University in Prague
milan.dojchinovski@fit.cvut.cz

Abstract. The Linked Hypernyms Dataset (LHD) provides entities described by Dutch, English and German Wikipedia articles with types taken from the DBpedia namespace. LHD contains 2.8 million entity-type assignments. Accuracy evaluation is provided for all languages. These types are generated based on one-word hypernym extracted from the free text of Wikipedia articles, the dataset is thus to a large extent complementary to DBpedia 3.8 and YAGO 2s ontologies. LHD is available at `http://ner.vse.cz/datasets/linkedhypernyms`.

1 Introduction

The Linked Hypernyms Dataset provides a source of types for entities described by Wikipedia articles. The dataset follows the same data modelling approach as the well-known DBpedia [6] and YAGO [1] knowledge bases. The types are extracted with hand-crafted lexico-syntactic patterns from the free text of the articles. The dataset can thus be used as enrichment to DBpedia and YAGO, which are populated from the structured and semistructured information in Wikipedia. The dataset consist of two subdatasets:

Hypernyms dataset contains only the raw plain text hypernyms extracted from the articles. An example entry is: `DiegoMaradona;manager`. This dataset can be used as gazetteer.

Linked Hypernyms Dataset identifies both the entity and the hypernym by a DBpedia URI, either a DBpedia resource or a DBpedia ontology class (preferred). Example entries (n-triples format) are:

```
<http://dbpedia.org/resource/Diego_Maradona> <http://www.w3.org/1999/02/22
-rdf-syntax-ns#type> <http://dbpedia.org/resource/Manager> .

<http://dbpedia.org/resource/Diego_Maradona> <http://www.w3.org/1999
/02/22-rdf-syntax-ns#type> <http://dbpedia.org/ontology/SoccerManager> .
```

The work presented here complements papers [7,8], the former describes LHD 1.0 in detail and the latter, a statistical type inference algorithm, which was used to extend the coverage of DBpedia Ontology classes in LHD 2.0 Draft. This paper has the following focus areas:

- **Section 2:** updated LHD generation framework,
- **Section 3:** LHD 1.0/2.0 comparison – size and accuracy,
- **Section 4:** use cases,
- **Section 5:** future work – extending LHD to other languages, and
- **Section 6:** dataset license and availability.

2 Dataset Generation

The dataset generation is a process in which the textual content of each Wikipedia page is processed, the word corresponding to the type is identified, and finally this word is disambiguated to a DBpedia concept. In this paper, we describe the updated LHD generation framework, which is available at `http://ner.vse.cz/datasets/linkedhypernyms`.

The first step in the process is the extraction of the hypernym from first sentences of Wikipedia articles. To avoid parsing of Wikipedia pages from the XML dump, the updated framework performs hypernym extraction from the DBpedia RDF n-triples dump. The hypernym is extracted from the textual contents of the DBpedia property `dbo:abstract`[3], which contains the introductory text of Wikipedia articles.[4]

The hypernym extraction step was implemented as a pipeline in the GATE text engineering framework.[5] The pipeline consists of the following processing resources:

1. ANNIE English Tokenizer
2. ANNIE Regex Sentence Splitter
3. ANNIE Part-of-Speech Tagger (English), TreeTagger (other languages)
4. JAPE Transducer

The hypernym extraction is performed with hand-crafted lexico-syntactic patterns written as a JAPE grammar [2]. The JAPE grammars are designed to recognize several variations of Hearst patterns [5]:

"[to be] [article] [modifiers] [hypernym]".

[3] `dbo` refers to the `http://dbpedia/ontology/` namespace, and `dbpedia` to the `http://dbpedia/resource/` namespace

[4] The statistics reported in Section 3 relate to the original version of the dataset, where Wikipedia dump is used as input.

[5] `https://gate.ac.uk/`

Only the first sentence in the `dbo:abstract` content is processed and only the first matched hypernym is considered. The manually tagged corpora used for the grammar development were made available on the dataset website. The three corpora (English, German and Dutch) contain more than 1,500 articles, which were used to develop the grammars.

> *Example.*
> The first sentence in the `dbo:abstract` for the DBpedia instance `dbpedia:Diego_Maradona` is as follows: *Diego Armando Maradona Franco is an Argentine football manager.*
> The English JAPE grammar applied on this POS-tagged sentence will result in marking the word *manager* as a hypernym. The word *is* is matched with the `[to be]` part of the grammar, word *the* with the `[article]` and *Argentine football* is captured by the `[modifiers]` group.

Next, the hypernym is mapped to a DBpedia Ontology class. The process of mapping is two stage.

- Hypernym is mapped to a DBpedia instance using Wikipedia Search API. This naive approach provided average performance in a recent entity linking contest [4].
- In order to improve interconnectedness, mapping to a DBpedia Ontology class is attempted.
  - In LHD 1.0 the mapping is performed based on a total textual match in order to maximize precision. A set of approximate matches (based on a substring match) is also generated.
  - In LHD 2.0 the mapping is performed using a statistical type inference algorithm.

At this point, the hypernym is represented with a Linked Open Data (LOD) identifier in the `http://dbpedia/resource/` namespace. The result from the processing is an RDF triple:

> *Example.* The output of the first stage is `dbpedia:Diego_Maradona rdf:type dbpedia:Manager`
> Since the type is in the less desirable `dbpedia` namespace, the system tries to find a fitting DBpedia Ontology class. The total textual match fails in DBpedia 3.8. However, the statistical type inference algorithm is more successful, yielding additional triple `dbpedia:Diego_Maradona rdf:type dbo:SoccerManager`

3 Dataset Metrics

The size of the LHD dataset for individual languages is captured on Table 1.

Table 1. Hypernyms and Linked Hypernyms datasets - size statistics.

dataset	Dutch	English	German
Hypernyms dataset	866,122	1,507,887	913,705
Linked Hypernyms Dataset	664,045	1,305,111	825,111
- type is a DBpedia Ontology class (LHD 1.0)	78,778	513,538	171,847
- type is a DBpedia Ontology class (LHD 2.0)	283,626	1,268,857	615,801

Table 2. Hypernyms and Linked Hypernyms datasets - accuracy .

dataset	Dutch	English	German
Hypernyms dataset	0.93	0.95	0.95
LHD 1.0	0.88	0.86	0.77
LHD 2.0 inferred types	NA	0.65	NA

Human evaluation of the correctness of both dataset was performed separately for the entire English, German and Dutch datasets, each represented by a randomly drawn 1,000 articles. The evaluation for English were done by three annotators. The evaluation for German and Dutch were done by the best performing annotator from the English evaluation. The results are depicted on Table 2. The average accuracy for English, which is the largest dataset, is 0.95 for the plain text types and 0.86 for types disambiguated to DBpedia concepts (DBpedia ontology class or a DBpedia resource).

LHD 2.0 [8] increases the number of entities aligned to the DBpedia Ontology to more than 95% for English and to more than 50% for other languages. Since a statistical type inference algorithm is used, the increase in coverage comes at a cost of reduced accuracy. The new triples added in LHD 2.0 have estimated accuracy of 0.65 (one annotator). LHD 2.0 Draft is thus an extension, rather than a replacement for LHD 1.0. The reason is not a decrease in reliability of the types, but also the fact that the types are complementary. For Diego Maradona, the LHD 1.0 type is `dbpedia:Manager`, while the LHD 2.0 type is `dbo:SoccerManager`.

More information about the evaluation setup and additional results can be found at [7] and at `http://ner.vse.cz/datasets/linkedhypernyms/`.

4 Uses Cases

The purpose of LHD to provide enrichment to type statements in DBpedia and YAGO ontologies. We have identified the following types of complementarity:

- LHD allows to choose the *most common* type for an entity. According to our observation, the type in the first sentence (the hypernym) is the main type that people typically associate with the entity. Therefore, the LHD dataset can be also used as a dataset which provides "primary", or "most common" types. Note that the content in Wikipedia is constantly updated and the type can thus be also considered as temporally valid.

- LHD provides a more *specific* type than DBpedia or YAGO. This is typically the case for less prolific entities, for which the semistructured information in Wikipedia is limited.
- LHD provides a more *precise* type, giving an alternative to an erroneousness type in DBpedia or YAGO.
- LHD is the only knowledge base providing *any type information*.

As a complementary resource to other knowledgebases, LHD can be used in common entity classification systems (wikifiers). `Entityclassifier.eu` is an example of a wikifier, which uses LHD alongside DBpedia and YAGO [3].

5 Future work - LHD for Other Languages

Creating LHD for another language requires the availability of a POS tagger and a manually devised JAPE grammar. Currently we are investigating a new workflow, which could lead to a fully automated LHD generation: generating a labeled set of articles by annotating as hypernyms noun phrases that match any of the types assigned in DBpedia, and subsequently using this set to train a hypernym tagger, e.g. as proposed in [9]. The hypernyms output by the tagger could be used in the same way as hypernyms identified by the hand-crafted JAPE grammars, leaving the rest of the LHD generation framework unaffected.

6 Conclusions

LHD is downloadable from `http://ner.vse.cz/datasets/linkedhypernyms/`. The dataset is released under a Creative Commons License. In order to stipulate the generation of the dataset for other languages, we are providing also the source code for the LHD extraction framework at `http://ner.vse.cz/datasets/linkedhypernyms` in a form of a Maven project.

Acknowledgements

This research was supported by the European Union's 7th Framework Programme via the LinkedTV project (FP7-287911).

References

1. C. Bizer, *et al.* DBpedia - a crystallization point for the web of data. *Web Semant.*, 7(3):154–165, Sep. 2009.
2. H. Cunningham, D. Maynard, and V. Tablan. JAPE - a Java Annotation Patterns Engine (Second edition), Department of Computer Science, University of Sheffield, 2000. Tech. rep., 2000. Technical Report.
3. M. Dojchinovski and T. Kliegr. Entityclassifier.eu: real-time classification of entities in text with Wikipedia. In *ECML'13*, pp. 654–658. Springer, 2013.

4. M. Dojchinovski, T. Kliegr, I. Lašek, and O. Zamazal. Wikipedia search as effective entity linking algorithm. In *Text Analysis Conference (TAC) 2013 Proceedings*. NIST, 2013. To appear.
5. M. A. Hearst. Automatic acquisition of hyponyms from large text corpora. In *Proceedings of the 14th conference on Computational linguistics - Volume 2*, COLING '92, pp. 539–545. ACL, Stroudsburg, PA, USA, 1992.
6. J. Hoffart, F. M. Suchanek, K. Berberich, and G. Weikum. YAGO2: A spatially and temporally enhanced knowledge base from Wikipedia. *Artificial Intelligence*, 194:28–61, 2013.
7. T. Kliegr. Linked hypernyms: Enriching DBpedia with Targeted Hypernym Discovery. 2013. Under review.
8. T. Kliegr and O. Zamazal. Towards Linked Hypernyms Dataset 2.0: complementing DBpedia with hypernym discovery and statistical type inferrence. In *Proceedings of The Ninth International Conference on Language Resources and Evaluation, LREC 2014*. To appear.
9. B. Litz, H. Langer, and R. Malaka. Sequential supervised learning for hypernym discovery from Wikipedia. In A. Fred, J. L. G. Dietz, K. Liu, and J. Filipe, (eds.) *Knowledge Discovery, Knowlege Engineering and Knowledge Management*, vol. 128 of *Communications in Computer and Information Science*, pp. 68–80. Springer-Verlag, Berlin Heidelberg, 2011.

PDEV-lemon: a Linked Data implementation of the Pattern Dictionary of English Verbs based on the Lemon model

Ismaïl El Maarouf, Jane Bradbury, Patrick Hanks

University of Wolverhampton
i.el-maarouf@wlv.ac.uk, J.Bradbury3@wlv.ac.uk, patrick.w.hanks@gmail.com

Abstract

PDEV-Lemon is the Linguistic Linked Data resource built from PDEV (Pattern Dictionary of English Verbs), using the Lemon lexicon model (Mccrae et al., 2012). PDEV is a dictionary which provides insight into how verbs collocate with nouns and words using an empirically well-founded apparatus of syntactic and semantic categories. It is a valuable resource for Natural Language Processing because it specifies in detail the contextual conditions that determine the meaning of a word. Over 1000 verbs have been analysed to date. PDEV-Lemon is built using the Lemon model, the LExicon Model for ONtologies.

Keywords: Semantic Web, Linguistic Linked Data, PDEV, CPA, lemon model, Lexicography, Lexicon, Ontology

Introduction

This paper introduces the first Semantic Web adaptation of PDEV (Pattern Dictionary of English Verbs; `http://pdev.org.uk`), using the Lemon lexicon model (Mccrae et al., 2012). PDEV is a dictionary which provides insight into how verbs collocate with nouns and other words using an empirically well-founded apparatus of syntactic and semantic categories. PDEV is a valuable resource for NLP because it specifies in detail the contextual conditions that determine meaning of a word. Thus the main motivation for building a Semantic-Web-compliant resource is to provide the Semantic Web and the NLP communities with an easier access to PDEV.

Section 1 provides an overview of PDEV, and of its specific characteristics. Section 2 describes PDEV-lemon. Section 3 reviews applications of PDEV-Lemon.

1. Background for the Pattern Dictionary of English Verbs

PDEV is an electronic resource (work in progress) consisting of an inventory of English verbs that identifies all the *normal patterns of use* of each verb and associates each pattern with a meaning, implicature, and/or entailment. Patterns are the conventional collocational structures that people use, and are identified from large corpora using a technique named CPA (Corpus Pattern Analysis (Hanks, 2013)).

This technique provides means for identifying patterns and for mapping meaning onto words in text. It is based on the Theory of Norms and Exploitations (TNE) (Hanks, 2004; Hanks, 2013; Hanks and Pustejovsky, 2005). TNE proposes to classify word uses in two main categories: *norms*, which are conventional uses of a word, frequently observed, and *exploitations*, which consist in deviations from those norms. This double helix theory of language use transcends, and sheds a new light on, traditional phenomena such as idioms, metaphors, or coercions.

TNE is a theory of language which emerged from extensive corpus analysis in corpus linguistics, but it is also influenced by the theory of the Generative Lexicon (Pustejovsky, 1995), Wilks's theory of Preference Semantics (Wilks, 1975), and Frame Semantics (Fillmore, 1985; Baker et al., 1998). Its roots in corpus linguistics are set in Sinclair's ground-breaking work on corpus analysis and collocations (Sinclair, 2010; Sinclair, 1991; Sinclair, 2004), the COBUILD project (Sinclair, 1987), and the Hector project (Atkins, 1993; Hanks, 1994). TNE therefore bridges the gap between corpus linguistics and semantic theories of the lexicon by combining insights from both perspectives to provide a model for empirically well-founded lexical resources.

PDEV, which draws on TNE, offers the analysis of over 1,000 verbs, over 4,000 patterns, and more than 100,000 annotated lines tagged as evidence, out of the list of 5793 verbs retained in this lexicon. PDEV lexicographers identify patterns using large corpora such as the British National Corpus[1] (BNC) and the Oxford English Corpus[2] (OEC). The analysis is corpus-driven and is therefore empirically well-founded. Noun collocates are organized into lexical sets in relation to the verbs with which they habitually co-occur. The lexical sets are organized according to semantic type, in a shallow ontology. The shallow ontology consists of fewer than 250 semantic types, which, it turns out, are sufficient to disambiguate the senses of the verbs analysed so far. The ontology is hierarchically organized, with *Entity* and *Eventuality* being the two top types.

2. PDEV-Lemon

2.1. Specifications

PDEV is being developed over a dedicated system which includes Javascript user interfaces, an SQL database, the DEB platform[3], and the SketchEngine corpus query system (Kilgarriff and Rychly, 2010). PDEV-Lemon is a derived resource in RDF based on the Lemon lexicon model. The development of a Semantic Web compliant resource was based on the following specifications:

[1] `http://www.natcorp.ox.ac.uk/`
[2] `http://www.oxforddictionaries.com/words/the-oxford-english-corpus`
[3] `http://deb.fi.muni.cz/index.php`

- Simplicity and usability of the lexicon.
- Faithfulness to the principles of PDEV.
- Identification of unstructured data in the lexicon.
- Adaptability allowing future automatic generation of dumps.
- Availability to the NLP community at large.

To create the resource, the following main tasks were carried out:

1. Study of the Lemon model and adaptation to the PDEV lexicon.
2. Creation of an ontology framework to provide external vocabulary for PDEV specific descriptive categories.
3. Creation of a system to process the data and generate RDF dumps of the database on demand.

2.2. Lemon: the backbone

One of the standard models for building Semantic Web machine-readable dictionaries is Lemon (The Lexicon Model for Ontologies (Mccrae et al., 2012; Buitelaar et al., 2011))[4]. This RDF-native model provides the general structure and features to enable an easy instantiation of a lexicon using an ontology framework such as OWL[5]. In Lemon, it is possible to create word entries, provide lexical variants, specify word morphology parts, syntactic frames, lexical meaning, and much more.
The primary issue when using Lemon to model syntactic resources is how to map a syntactic frame, selected by a lexical entry, to a meaning. Lemon does not provide direct links between a frame and a lexical sense: a lexical sense combines a lexical entry with a reference to a meaning (defined in an external ontology), and the contextual environment in which this meaning occurs is underspecified. The only way to map frames to a lexical meaning in Lemon is by the mediation of the frame's arguments, provided correlated units exist in external ontologies: the lexical sense is in this case indirectly induced [6].
This is not satisfactory from the point of view of understanding and processing the meaning of texts. One of PDEV's contribution is to show the ways in which syntax and semantics do not map neatly onto each other, because of phraseology. As an example, an idiom cannot be mapped because its parts are not interpreted as concepts: the whole meaning of an idiom is different from the sum of the meaning of its parts. Since a large part of language is phraseological, it seems safer to alter the Lemon model to allow for a direct mapping of frame with lexical sense.
We therefore provide two new Object properties to link one *Frame* to one *Lexical Sense*. Following *lemon:senseOf* and *lemon:sense*, which are used to map lexical senses with lexical entries, PDEV-Lemon adds *:frameSense* and *:isFrameSenseOf* to map lexical senses with frames (Fig. 1).

[4]`http://lemon-model.net`

[5]`http://www.w3.org/TR/owl-features/`

[6]for examples of implementation see `http://lemon-model.net/lexica/lexica.php`

```
:frameSense
  rdf:type rdf:Property,owl:ObjectProperty ;
  rdfs:label "Frame Sense"@en ;
  rdfs:comment "Links to the lexical sense of a
frame"@en ;
  rdfs:domain :Frame ;
  rdfs:range :LexicalSense .

:isFrameSenseOf
  rdf:type rdf:Property,owl:ObjectProperty ;
  rdfs:label "Frame Sense of"@en ;
  rdfs:comment "Indicate that a sense is realised
by the given frame"@en ;
  rdfs:domain :LexicalSense ;
  rdfs:range :Frame ;
  owl:inverseOf :frameSense .
```

Figure 1: *frameSense* and *isFrameSenseOf* properties

2.3. The PDEV-Lemon entry

PDEV-Lemon makes use of the Lemon core to create the lexicon and its individuals. As an example, Fig. 2 shows the PDEV-Lemon entry, in TURTLE syntax, for *organize*.

```
pdevl:PDEV_LexicalEntry_organize
  rdf:type lemon:LexicalEntry, owl:NamedIndividual;
  lexinfo:partOfSpeech lexinfo:verb ;
  rdfs:label "PDEV Lexical Entry organize"@eng ;
  lemon:canonicalForm
    pdevl:PDEV_LexicalEntry_organize_CanonicalForm ;
  ps:lexicalFrequencyOf
    pdevl:PDEV_LexicalEntry_organize_sampleSize ;
  ps:lexicalFrequencyOf
    pdevl:PDEV_LexicalEntry_organize_bncFreq ;
  ps:lexicalFrequencyOf
    pdevl:PDEV_LexicalEntry_organize_bnc50Freq ;
  ps:lexicalFrequencyOf
    pdevl:PDEV_LexicalEntry_organize_oecFreq ;
  lemon:sense pdevl:PDEV_Implicature_organize_1;
  lemon:sense pdevl:PDEV_Implicature_organize_2;
  lemon:sense pdevl:PDEV_Implicature_organize_3;
  lemon:sense pdevl:PDEV_Implicature_organize_4;
  lemon:sense pdevl:PDEV_Implicature_organize_5;
  lemon:sense pdevl:PDEV_Implicature_organize_6;
  lemon:synBehavior pdevl:PDEV_Pattern_organize_1;
  lemon:synBehavior pdevl:PDEV_Pattern_organize_2;
  lemon:synBehavior pdevl:PDEV_Pattern_organize_3;
  lemon:synBehavior pdevl:PDEV_Pattern_organize_4;
  lemon:synBehavior pdevl:PDEV_Pattern_organize_5;
  lemon:synBehavior pdevl:PDEV_Pattern_organize_6;
  lemon:language "eng".
```

Figure 2: Example of lexical entry: the example of *organize* *(ps stands for pdevl-structure ontology.)*

As can be seen, an entry contains information regarding part of speech, language, canonical form, lexical frequency in a given corpus, links to lexical senses and to syntactic frames. Most properties link the lexical entry to URIs which describe lexical information, such as the form (Fig. 3), which itself may contain a link to a variant form.

2.4. The PDEV-Lemon pattern

A PDEV entry contains at least one pattern, from the *lemon:Frame* class. A PDEV pattern is an abstract syntactic and semantic representation of a word's context, and is rephrased as an implicature. More specifically, what PDEV offers through the pattern structure is a set of collocational preferences mapped onto syntactic arguments which are interconnected through the pattern. The structure of a pattern, as well as the properties and categories of its arguments,

```
pdevl:PDEV_LexicalEntry_organize_CanonicalForm
  rdf:type lemon:Form, owl:NamedIndividual;
  lemon:writtenRep "organize"@eng ;
  lemon:formVariant
    pdevl:PDEV_LexicalEntry_organise_VariantForm;
  rdfs:label "Canonical Form of organize"@eng .
pdevl:PDEV_LexicalEntry_organise_VariantForm
  rdf:type lemon:Form, owl:NamedIndividual;
  lemon:writtenRep "organise"@eng ;
  rdfs:label "Variant Form of organize"@eng;
  ps:formVariantof
    pdevl:PDEV_LexicalEntry_organize_CanonicalForm.
```

Figure 3: Instance of the *Form* class: *organize*
(ps stands for pdevl-structure ontology)

have been developed on the basis of observation of empirical data to meet the needs of lexicographers for modeling a pattern's contextual features appropriately.

The structure of a verb pattern is based on the SPOCA model from Systemic Functional Grammar (Halliday, 1994). A verb pattern may consist of arguments from any of the following clause roles: a Subject, a Predicator, an Object, a Complement, and an Adverbial (as well as Indirect objects).

Each argument may be structured into components such as an introductory word (like a preposition), a specifier (like a determiner) and a head. Each component can in turn be represented according to several layers:

- a Grammatical Category (noun, *-ing* forms or quotes),
- a Semantic Type (ST; Human, Animal),
- a Contextual Role (CR; Judge, Plaintiff),
- a Lexical Set (LS; instances of lexical words).

Some of the grammatical categories have been based on the LexInfo ontology (Cimiano et al., 2011), where relevant. In some cases (mainly for adverbials), there can be more than one obligatory argument for the same clause role; ST, CR and LS can also express alternative realizations.

All PDEV patterns are connected to a set of tagged concordances taken from a random sample of the BNC (usually 250 lines) and accessible online on the PDEV public access (`http://pdev.org.uk`). There are two types of links: normal uses of the pattern and exploitations. These links between the dictionary and the BNC have been preserved in PDEV-Lemon. In addition, frequency information for each pattern's normal use and exploitation have been added to PDEV-Lemon. For each entry, it is therefore possible to produce percentages for each pattern.

Fig. 4 gives the full representation in TURTLE syntax of pattern 2 of the verb *zap*.

2.5. The PDEV-Lemon Linked Data suite

An instance of a pattern is always linked to an instance of the *lemon:LexicalSense* class, the reference of which is a unique concept in an external ontology, named *pdev-lemon-PatSenses*. This ontology describes the senses referred to by Frames using their implicatures. Senses have also been

```
pdevl:PDEV_Arg_S_M_zap_2
  rdf:type lemon:Argument, owl:NamedIndividual ;
  ps:syntacticCategory ps:NounPhrase ;
  ps:SemanticType po:PdevSemanticType_36 ;
  ps:argStatus ps:Prototypical .
pdevl:PDEV_Arg_A_M-1_zap_2
  rdf:type lemon:Argument, owl:NamedIndividual ;
  ps:preposition pdevl:PDEP_LexicalEntry_10 ;
  ps:syntacticCategory ps:PrepositionalPhrase ;
  ps:SemanticType po:PdevSemanticType_11 ;
  ps:ContextualRole pt:PdevContextualRole_623 ;
  ps:argStatus ps:Prototypical .
pdevl:PDEV_Arg_A_M-2_zap_2
  rdf:type lemon:Argument, owl:NamedIndividual ;
  ps:preposition pdevl:PDEP_LexicalEntry_27 ;
  ps:syntacticCategory ps:PrepositionalPhrase ;
  ps:SemanticType po:PdevSemanticType_11 ;
  ps:ContextualRole pt:PdevContextualRole_624 ;
  ps:argStatus ps:Prototypical .
pdevl:PDEV_Pattern_zap_2
  rdf:type lemon:Frame, owl:NamedIndividual ;
  ps:isNoObj "true" ;
  ps:senseFrequencyOf pdevl:Freq_norm_zap_2 ;
  ps:senseFrequencyOf pdevl:Freq_exploitation_zap_2 ;
  ps:subject pdevl:PDEV_Arg_S_M_zap_2;
  ps:Predicator "zap" ;
  ps:adverbial pdevl:PDEV_Arg_A_M-1_zap_2;
  ps:adverbial pdevl:PDEV_Arg_A_M-2_zap_2;
  pdevl:frameSense pdevl:PDEV_LexicalSense_zap_2 .
pdevl:Freq_norm_zap_2
  rdf:type ps:Frequency, owl:NamedIndividual ;
  ps:ofCorpus "BNC50" ;
  ps:frequencyValue 2 .
pdevl:Freq_exploitation_zap_2
  rdf:type ps:Frequency, owl:NamedIndividual ;
  ps:ofCorpus "BNC50" ;
  ps:frequencyValue 0 .
```

Figure 4: Example of a PDEV-Lemon pattern: *zap*
(ps, po, pt are prefixes which stand for pdevl-structure, pdevl-CPASO, pdevl-CoRoTaxo ontologies, respectively.)

grouped into semantic classes (530 patterns have been classified), and linked to external resources such as FrameNet[7] (1492 links manually identified by lexicographers). In addition, the PDEV-Lemon resource includes four ontologies which list the descriptive categories used to characterize patterns and entries.

- *pdev-lemon-domain*: describes the domains used to characterize PDEV patterns;
- *pdev-lemon-register*: describes the registers used to characterize PDEV patterns;
- *pdev-lemon-CPASO*: describes the Semantic Types used to characterize PDEV patterns;
- *pdev-lemon-CoRoTaxo*: describes the taxonomy of Contextual Roles used to characterize PDEV patterns.

Finally, *pdev-lemon-structure* specifies the OWL classes and properties needed to alter the Lemon model (23 classes, 22 Object properties, and 8 Datatype properties). The resource *pdev-lemon* contains the dictionary information. All seven developed resources are also available as linked data from `http://pdev.org.uk/PDEVLEMON.html`. Table 1 lists the most frequently used properties in the whole resource.

PDEV-Lemon consists of 217,634 triples, 3702 patterns and 10799 arguments. It contains lexical entries for 984

[7] `http://framenet.icsi.berkeley.edu/`

Frequency	Property
80956	<http://www.w3.org/1999/02/22-rdf-syntax-ns#type>
11309	<http://pdev.org.uk/pdevlemon/pdevlemon-structure/argStatus>
11298	<http://pdev.org.uk/pdevlemon/pdevlemon-structure/frequencyValue>
11298	<http://pdev.org.uk/pdevlemon/pdevlemon-structure/ofCorpus>
11234	<http://pdev.org.uk/pdevlemon/pdevlemon-structure/syntacticCategory>
9388	<http://pdev.org.uk/pdevlemon/pdevlemon-structure/SemanticType>
7403	<http://www.monnet-project.eu/lemon#value>
7402	<http://pdev.org.uk/pdevlemon/pdevlemon-structure/senseFrequencyOf>
7402	<http://www.monnet-project.eu/lemon#example>
6959	<http://www.w3.org/2000/01/rdf-schema#label>
5301	<http://pdev.org.uk/pdevlemon/pdevlemon-structure/subject>
3896	<http://pdev.org.uk/pdevlemon/pdevlemon-structure/lexicalFrequencyOf>
3702	<http://www.monnet-project.eu/lemon#sense>
3702	<http://www.monnet-project.eu/lemon#synBehavior>
3701	<http://pdev.org.uk/pdevlemon/pdevlemon-structure/frameSense>
3701	<http://pdev.org.uk/pdevlemon/pdevlemon-structure/isFrameSenseOf>
3701	<http://pdev.org.uk/pdevlemon/pdevlemon-structure/Predicator>
3701	<http://www.monnet-project.eu/lemon#reference>
3363	<http://pdev.org.uk/pdevlemon/pdevlemon-structure/directObject>
2606	<http://pdev.org.uk/pdevlemon/pdevlemon-structure/adverbial>
2317	<http://pdev.org.uk/pdevlemon/pdevlemon-structure/preposition>
2077	<http://lexinfo.net/ontology/2.0/lexinfo#partOfSpeech>
2077	<http://www.monnet-project.eu/lemon#entry>
1676	<http://pdev.org.uk/pdevlemon/pdevlemon-structure/ContextualRole>
1176	<http://pdev.org.uk/pdevlemon/pdevlemon-structure/isNoObj>
1106	<http://www.monnet-project.eu/lemon#language>
986	<http://www.monnet-project.eu/lemon#writtenRep>
974	<http://www.monnet-project.eu/lemon#canonicalForm>
973	<http://pdev.org.uk/pdevlemon/pdevlemon-structure/LexicalSet>
908	<http://www.monnet-project.eu/lemon#optional>

Table 1: Most frequent properties used in PDEV-Lemon

verbs, 1030 nouns, and 93 prepositions. It contains 94 domains, 34 registers, 248 semantic types, 662 contextual roles, and 3702 pattern senses.

3. Applications of PDEV-Lemon

As a Linguistic Linked Data resource, PDEV-Lemon will enable the NLP community as well as the Semantic Web community to extract pattern information and integrate it in various applications and resources.

3.1. Leveraging resources

PDEV patterns include nouns and prepositions in argument slots, which have been turned into lexical entries in PDEV-Lemon. This is a first step on which to bootstrap further analyses of noun and preposition pattern dictionaries (Litkowski, 2012).

PDEV is not the only project based on TNE. Italian (Jezek and Frontini, 2010) and Spanish (Renau and Battaner, 2012) versions have been developed with identical resources and tools. The Italian pattern dictionary contains about 3000 patterns for more than 800 verbs and a Spanish version has been developed on more than 150 verbs. PDEV-Lemon has therefore a potential to connect these languages, given that they use the same descriptive apparatus. Such a multiligual resource could be an important asset for research in Machine Translation.

From a more general perspective, PDEV-Lemon allows to connect more easily other lexical resources such as those developed in the UBY framework[8], particularly FrameNet and VerbNet. Immediate plans include the use of FrameNet links (from the *pdev-lemon-PatSenses* ontology) manually defined by lexicographers to leverage information from the Framenet resource and FrameNet annotated corpora. Since FrameNet frames are matched with PDEV patterns, FrameNet can also benefit from an accurate description of the context where lexical units trigger frames. Beyond that, it is also possible to imagine to connect PDEV-Lemon to the resources to which FrameNet is connected, e.g. Wordnet, Verbnet.

3.2. Applications

Pattern discovery and disambiguation.

PDEV patterns involve both an analysis of a word's context and its correlation with meaning. The main goal of the

[8] `http://www.ukp.tu-darmstadt.de/data/lexical-resources/uby/`

DVC project[9] (Disambiguating Verbs by Collocation) is to build a pattern dictionary of 3,000 verbs following the principles of TNE. Since PDEV-Lemon can be automatically generated, the results of the DVC project will be made regularly available through its future releases.

One of the motivations for building patterns is the observation that while words in isolation are highly ambiguous, corpus analysis shows that patterns are mostly unambiguous. PDEV therefore tackles the Word Sense Disambiguation (WSD) (Navigli, 2009) problem by sidestepping it: instead of asking about the meaning of words, it asks about the meaning of the patterns in which words are used. This resource therefore provides the opportunity to develop new semantic parsers, which can identify patterns in texts as well as their arugments. Preliminary research performed on automatic pattern disambiguation provides promising results (El Maarouf et al., 2014).

Making PDEV-Lemon widely available will be a means to allow researchers to test these patterns at a large scale.

Modeling links between corpus and lexical resources.

PDEV-Lemon includes links to examples of norms and exploitations for each pattern (more than 100,000 concordance lines). In PDEV-Lemon, these links refer to whole concordances available on the PDEV public access. Future plans include specifying the structure of these concordances and map PDEV pattern arguments onto tokens. This will be achieved by taking avantage of standards for Linked annotated resources (such as based on the NLP Interchange Format model[10]) and PDEV-Lemon.

Language Learning.

Beyond NLP applications, PDEV can also be used in pedagogical applications such as tools and interfaces to improve learners' command of idiomaticity, to design a syllabus, and for error correction. For example, the detailed mapping of how certain Semantic Types and adverbial patterns are preferred in certain patterns of certain verbs can help L2 (non-native speakers) students to achieve a high level of naturalness in their speech and writing. A resource such as PDEV-Lemon will facilitate the development of tools for this community.

4. Conclusion

This paper has presented PDEV-Lemon, a new Linguistic Linked Data resource based on PDEV. PDEV is a dictionary of English verbs that identifies all the normal patterns of use of each verb. Patterns are conventional collocational structures linked to a unique meaning, as identified from large corpora.

PDEV-Lemon comes with a suite of OWL ontologies which characterize descriptive categories used in PDEV patterns: domains, registers, semantic types, contextual roles, and pattern senses.

PDEV-Lemon was developed to disseminate PDEV largely in the NLP and Semantic Web communities. It is distributed in an *Attribution-ShareAlike Creative Commons licence* and is available at `http://pdev.org.uk/PDEVLEMON.html`.

[9] `http://clg.wlv.ac.uk/projects/DVC/`

[10] `http://nlp2rdf.org/nif-1-0`

Acknowledgements

This work was supported by an AHRC grant [Disambiguating Verbs by Collocation project, AH/J005940/1, 2012-2015].

5. References

Beryl T. S. Atkins. 1993. Tools for computer-aided corpus lexicography: the hector project. *Acta Linguistica Hungarica*, 41.

Collin F Baker, Charles J Fillmore, and John B Lowe. 1998. The berkeley framenet project. In *Proceedings of the 17th international conference on Computational linguistics-Volume 1*, pages 86–90. Association for Computational Linguistics.

Paul Buitelaar, Philip Cimiano, John McCrae, Elena Montiel-Ponsada, and Thierry Declerck. 2011. Ontology lexicalisation: The lemon perspective. In Monique Slodzian, Mathieu Valette, Nathalie Aussenac-Gilles, Anne Condamines, Nathalie Hernandez, and Bernard Rothenburger, editors, *Workshop Proceedings of the 9th International Conference on Terminology and Artificial Intelligence*, pages 33–36, Paris, France, November. INALCO.

Philipp Cimiano, Paul Buitelaar, John McCrae, and Michael Sintek. 2011. Lexinfo: A declarative model for the lexicon-ontology interface. *Web Semantics journal*, 9(1):29–51.

Ismaïl El Maarouf, Vít Baisa, Jane Bradbury, and Patrick Hanks. 2014. isambiguating verbs by collocation: Corpus lexicography meets natural language processing. In *Proceedings of LREC*.

Charles J. Fillmore. 1985. Frames and the semantics of understanding. *Quaderni di Semantica*, 6(2):222–254.

Michael A. K. Halliday. 1994. *An introduction to Functional Grammar*. Edward Arnold.

Patrick Hanks and James Pustejovsky. 2005. A pattern dictionary for natural language processing. *Revue Franaise de Linguistique Appliquee*.

Patrick Hanks. 1994. Linguistic norms and pragmatic exploitations, or why lexicographers need prototype theory and vice versa. In F. Kiefer, G. Kiss, and J. Pajzs, editors, *Papers in Computational Lexicography: Complex '94*. Hungarian Academy of Sciences.

Patrick Hanks. 2004. Corpus pattern analysis. In *Euralex Proceedings*, volume 1, pages 87–98.

Patrick Hanks. 2013. *Lexical Analysis: Norms and Exploitations*. MIT Press.

Elisabetta Jezek and Francesca Frontini. 2010. From pattern dictionary to patternbank. In Gilles-Maurice de Schryver, editor, *A Way with Words: Recent Advances in Lexical Theory and Analysis*. Menha Publichers, Kampala.

Adam Kilgarriff and Pavel Rychly. 2010. Semi-automatic dictionary drafting. In Gilles-Maurice de Schryver, editor, *A Way with Words: Recent Advances in Lexical Theory and Analysis*. Menha Publichers, Kampala.

Ken Litkowski. 2012. Corpus pattern analysis of prepositions. Technical report, Damascus, MD: CL Research.

John Mccrae, Guadalupe Aguado-De-Cea, Paul Buitelaar, Philipp Cimiano, Thierry Declerck, Asunción Gómez-Pérez, Jorge Gracia, Laura Hollink, Elena Montiel-Ponsoda, Dennis Spohr, and Tobias Wunner. 2012. Interchanging lexical resources on the semantic web. *Language Resources Evaluation journal*, 46(4):701–719.

Roberto Navigli. 2009. Word sense disambiguation: A survey. *ACM Comput. Surv.*, 41(2):10:1–10:69.

James Pustejovsky. 1995. *The Generative Lexicon*. MIT Press.

Irene Renau and Paz Battaner. 2012. Using cpa to represent spanish pronominal verbs in a learner's dictionary. In *Proceedings of Euralex*, Oslo, Norway.

John Sinclair. 1987. Grammar in the dictionary. In John Sinclair, editor, *Looking up : an account of the COBUILD Project in lexical computing and the development of the Collins COBUILD English language dictionary*, pages 104–115. Collins ELT, London.

John Sinclair. 1991. *Corpus, concordance, collocation*. Oxford University Press.

John Sinclair. 2004. *Trust The Text : Language, Corpus and Discourse*. Routledge.

John Sinclair. 2010. Beginning the study of lexis. In C. E. Bazell, J. C. Catford, M. A. K. Halliday, and R. H. Robins, editors, *In Memory of J.R. Firth*, pages 410–431. Longman, London.

Yorick Wilks. 1975. A preferential, pattern-seeking, semantics for natural language inference. *Artif. Intell.*, 6(1):53–74.